ECHOES OF SUICIDE

Edited by Siobhán Foster-Ryan
and Luke Monahan

VERITAS

First published 2001 by
Veritas Publications
7/8 Lower Abbey Street
Dublin 1
Ireland

Email publications@veritas.ie
Website www.veritas.ie

ISBN 1 85390 504 6

Acknowledgements
'Stuck in a Moment You Can't Get Out Of' by U2. Reprinted with permission. Extract from 'Acquainted with the night' by Robert Frost, from 'The Poetry of Robert Frost', edited by Edward Connery-Lathem. Published by Jonathan Cape. Reprinted here by permission of Random House Group Ltd. 'A Blessing in Bereavement' by Marjorie Dobson, from *A World of Blessings: Benedictions from Every Continent and Many Cultures* edited by G. Duncan. Copyright © Canterbury Press (Norwich, 2000). Extract from *Night* by Elie Wiesel. Copyright © Bantam Books (1982). 'Oh My Lovely Young One' by Christy Moore – Bal Music. Reprinted with permission.

A catalogue record for this book is available from the British Library

Cover design by Bill Bolger
Printed in the Republic of Ireland by Betaprint Ltd, Dublin

Veritas books are printed on paper made from the wood pulp of managed forests. For every tree felled, at least one tree is planted, thereby renewing natural resources.

ACKNOWLEDGEMENTS

The contributors to this publication are the centre-piece of our list of thanks. We owe a tremendous debt of gratitude to them for taking the time and effort to be part of this project. We thank Patricia Conway and all those involved in organising the special conference on Youth and Suicide in Dublin in October 2000 that proved the spark for this book. Bishop Eamonn Walsh was the initiator of the idea to publish and we thank him for his encouragement. Tony Byrne was another supporter from the early days of this undertaking and his advice and direction have been invaluable. We want to very especially thank Br Stephen O'Gorman for his wonderful collection of reflections, which add so much to the publication.

As the book took shape, others became a great source of help – Geraldine Carberry in particular was invaluable and ever-patient with the typing and re-typing required. We acknowledge

Noel Canavan, Donald Moxham and Ned Prendergast, who offered astute comment and guidance at key stages. We thank Veritas, especially Maura Hyland and Toner Quinn, for their support at all stages of this work.

We wish to acknowledge the financial contribution that the Irish Association of Pastoral Care in Education (IAPCE) has given to this publication. We also thank the Marino Institute of Education and the SPHE National Support Service for their help throughout this project.

Finally, to family and friends who had to put up with the inevitable inconvenience and distraction that editing a book entails – we thank you for your patience.

Siobhán Foster-Ryan
Luke Monahan

CONTENTS

INTRODUCTION:
A STARTING POINT

*E*choes *of Suicide* began its journey to publication with a gathering of contributions from speakers at a conference on youth and suicide, organised by the archdiocese and held in Dublin in October 2000. From this small beginning the publication has grown into this present wide-ranging resource and catalogue of personal testimonies. This journey to publication has been characterised by courage, generosity, honesty, sensitivity and insight on the part of the contributors – it has indeed been a once in a lifetime privilege to edit this book. Our first duty is to recognise our contributors – we do so gladly.

The major task we had as editors was to discern how best to organise the wealth of material, so as to truly celebrate and make accessible the variety of perspectives being offered to you, the reader. Arranging the order of contributions has been guided by the aims we had for the book – these can be summarised as follows:

- giving a voice to the suicide bereaved
- offering a range of 'connection points' for those touched by suicide in any way
- providing a range of perspectives to facilitate some understanding of the nature of suicide
- exploring the impact of suicide in different contexts – family, school, local community
- examining some of the relevant research in the area
- reflecting on the spiritual and theological dimension
- supporting those in a caring role
- informing the reader about the range of practical supports, resources and organisations available

The book opens with a number of Personal Stories recounted by those who have lost a loved one through suicide. They trace the journey of pain and struggle, of guilt and despair, of forgiveness and acceptance in the hope that something of their stories may echo in the hearts of those readers whose lives have been touched by suicide. A number of reflections are also included in this section, providing readers with an opportunity for prayer or reflection.

The second section, 'Towards an Understanding', explores a range of perspectives on the nature of suicide. The section begins with two investigations of the particular nature of bereavement following suicide. These are followed by an examination of a suicide prevention strategy that has been put in place in Northern Ireland. The area of government policy development in respect of suicide is then outlined in two contributions. In particular, the challenges for future provision are discussed and the role of the media is explored. This section ends with a provocative reflection on the nature of Irish society in the context of suicide.

The publication then moves to consider 'The Response of the School Community'. The section begins by offering a comprehensive framework to guide the school in its multi-dimensional response at the levels of prevention, intervention and postvention, the term used to outline a school's response after a suicide has occurred. The following contributions examine the role of counsellor, chaplain and principal, and indeed, that of the whole staff in the school setting. An outline of a programme for schools dealing with issues of bereavement, loss and suicide concludes this section.

'Faith Perspectives' provides a range of contributions that explore the questions of faith that exist for many when confronted by suicide. Following a reflective piece on hope and suicide, the moral questions are examined. Feelings of anger and hope towards God are then investigated. A resource for developing a retreat day and some guidelines for homilies and pastoral ministers are also offered. The section finishes with a reflection on suffering.

'Supports for the Suicide Bereaved' is the final section, offering an insight into the various agencies and programmes that are available to anyone in need of advice and support. In particular, the work of the Samaritans, Dochas, Sólás/Barnardos and Rainbows is highlighted. Information is also given on a number of courses offered to those bereaved by suicide. The section ends with the provision of a resource list of useful reading material and supportive organisations.

It is hoped that, while not attempting to answer every question, *Echoes of Suicide* will inform, support and challenge those in a caring role in our society. For those striving to make sense of the tragedy of suicide, may this book be a source of strength and a guide on your own very personal journey of loss.

The Editors

1
PERSONAL STORIES

On Hearing of a Young Mother's Suicide

When I was told this morning
That they had found your body
Grazing on the lack of air
On top of a lake
I, like others, wondered
At what had taken you to that end.

Was it because you had taken enough
Of all that rubbish with the bills?
The children crying for things
Too far beyond your means?
Or had too many bullets been shot
From the happiness of others
Who had never known
What it was like
To have dug a hole
To descend a ladder
To the bottom of the soul?

But when you did have time
Did you try to re-ascend your dark
By use of memory?
Young, clean skirt, your hair combed
and guarded in place by slides,
Going out with a best friend
On a rare visit to Ecstasy's store
When you were perhaps returned a desired gaze
From across a crowded dance floor?
But in recalling such pictures

Too many times
Did the colour fade, wrinkle and die?
Could your sapless spirit
No longer be softened,
The dream resin you wanted
No longer supplied?
Was it taking too much effort
To spring clean that unmarvellous inner mess?
Little grows in a tundra of thanklessness.

What made you realise
That death wore the normality of choice
As you walked down to the water
Slapping on the quay with the birds' dawn voice ?
The fish, your audience,
Wanted you so much
They came in close to take a look
And plucked souvenirs of skin from your face.

Such sadness I feel
From deaths like yours
Increasingly makes me speculate
On what, if anything,
Makes me more fortunate.
Was it all just a sudden impatience,
a tattering of tolerance ?
Or was it because
You could not find
Or were not shown
That one great important light
That can warm the blood
And keep the darkness out?

Mel McMahon

LOSING MY FATHER – BARRY'S STORY

Barry Kilgannon

My father took his own life on the 24 June 1988. The country had basked in hot weather for the previous two weeks and the Irish football team had recently beaten England in the European football championships. I remember that the general mood of the country was one of euphoria at the time. I was nineteen years of age and things were going well for me. I had just finished my second year in college and was reasonably satisfied that my exams had been negotiated without too much anguish. I had returned home to work for the summer in the local petrol station, where I had been a fixture for the previous six summers.

I remember my father as a very impressive, proud man. Always well presented, he stood six feet tall and walked with an air of quiet confidence. This confidence was undoubtedly bolstered by his position as a garda detective in the town. Everyone knew him and he knew everyone. I always felt that his physical stature and the way he carried himself helped to single him out for respect. He was fair with people and did not abuse the power entrusted in him. He was also an alcoholic.

I saw my father drunk twice. The first time was on Christmas Eve, and I was no more than eight years of age. My mother was laughing at him and we thought it was very funny too, to see this man giggling like a young boy. My mother indulged my father's drinking. He was never violent and never seemed to drink too much. But he would go for a pint every night of the week. Looking back, it was obvious that he was dependent upon alcohol. This dependency deepened in the year after he retired from the Garda Síochána. He had been unsettled in the job for some time, unable to come to terms with the new bureaucracy and officialdom that he saw overtaking the old, common sense ways of policing a small country town. He retired soon after his fiftieth birthday with no real plan of action for what he was going to do next. Within a year he was dead. He had become very depressed since retiring and this depression was exacerbated by his drinking, which had seemed to spiral out of control.

On arriving home from college after my exams, I was shocked to see what had become of the proud man I once knew. He had lost the sparkle from his eyes and seemed to have lost interest in his appearance. I knew that my mother was very worried about him and had pleaded with him to go to a local counsellor to talk about his depression. But Daddy was too proud. Going to see a counsellor would have been an admission of failure and weakness, and he was still adhering to the principles of the macho culture in which he had spent all of his working life.

The second time I saw my father drunk was on the night before he took his life. It was an absolutely exquisite midsummer night, and I was watching a football match on television when he came in. My mother was also in the room. She chastised him mildly when he arrived, eyes bleary and unsteady on his feet. He sat down and he cried and cried. He told us that he loved us dearly. It was the first time that he had ever said anything like that. He never needed to say it. He never let his family want for anything, and each one of us had a very secure and happy upbringing. He also said that he had contemplated taking his life that very day, and it was not until he went down to the petrol station for a paper that he changed his mind. He said that he saw me and realised that he was very proud of me and my brothers and sister and that he couldn't leave us behind.

At two o'clock the next day he was dead. He swallowed some weed killer in the garage and went upstairs to lie down. He asked my mother to ring an ambulance. The nurse on duty in the casualty department later told my mother that he whispered to her to keep him alive as they wheeled him in to be pumped out. My father was fifty-one years of age and he left behind a forty-two year old wife and four children ranging in age from twenty-one to twelve.

My feelings afterwards are very difficult to describe. My helplessness at the sight of this big man crying like a child on the night before his death had now been consumed by a numbness. I cried, but I did not cry too much. Older men shook my hand at the morgue or in the church and told me to be strong for my mother's sake. I put my arm around my twelve-year-old sister as uniformed gardaí lowered my father's body into the grave – but I did not cry. I felt guilty that I couldn't cry. Did I love my father at all or was I just a cold-hearted bastard who could bury a family member and then just get on with life? I played a football match later that week and was the star of the show. I went out for pints with my friends, returned to my summer job and got on with the business of living.

Returning to college in late September was more difficult for my friends than for me. I knew that they were uncomfortable at first and I tried my best to lessen their discomfort by showing a cheerful exterior. I remember feeling that it was difficult to concentrate on my course work that year, but I somehow muddled through to Christmas and returned home for the holidays. My mother cried as we ate our Christmas dinner, and again I felt guilty that I couldn't shed a tear.

The premier colleges' soccer competition, the Collingwood Cup, was held in Galway in January and I was one of the mainstays of a very good college team that had been narrowly defeated in the final the previous year. After a gruelling week of playing football every day in inclement weather and on cabbage patch pitches, we had reached the semi-final. Our coach, an expert motivator, had gathered us together in our hotel on the morning of the match and reminded us of the importance of the match for ourselves, our college and even our families. It was then that I had my first real feeling of terrible, painful loneliness. I put my head down in that crowded room, filled with friends and teammates and cried quietly. I cried for about two hours, long after the meeting had adjourned and the others had left. The coach put his arm around me and all I could do was cry like a baby. I went upstairs and said a little prayer to my father to give me the strength to go on and support my team mates, got ready for the game and left. I played excellently that day and scored one of the goals that helped us into the final. It may sound stupid now, but that incident gave me the belief that my father, even though he was not with me, was still looking out for me.

That belief was strengthened further in June of that year when I was debating whether or not to go in for an exam. I had studied well, but I felt that I was not prepared enough. Five minutes before the exam I was outside by the river bank, feeling miserable and lonely and I asked my father for help. I got the strength to go in and I came first in my class.

Mourners are always told that time is a great healer. With suicide, however, I think that there is a hurt that will never go away. I often think about my father. I would love to be able to go for a round of golf with him and have a few pints afterwards. I feel envious of my friends who can do these things. I would love to think that he is proud of me, that his son has turned into a man in his own image. People say that we are quite alike in our appearance and in our personalities. In some strange way, however, I don't want to be like him. I resent the fact that his memory will always be tarnished by the manner in which he died. I often wonder what those people in our town think when they think about him now. Do they remember the proud and affable big man, or do they simply remember him as the guard who committed suicide?

I feel that, although there is a much greater acceptance of the reality of suicide in Ireland nowadays, there is still a stigma attached to the act. My father was fifty-one years of age and therefore fell outside the classic danger ages of the eighteen to thirty-five-year-olds. When people ask me how my father died, I generally tell them that he had a heart attack. I suppose I do this to lessen their discomfort. There is also a little bit of embarrassment involved from my side. I have heard some people say that suicide is a cowardly and selfish act, yet my father was one of the bravest and most selfless people I have known.

Suicide is not a comfortable subject for people to talk about. Even amongst my friends, I detect an air of discomfort whenever I mention my father. Families, such as my own, are left with a lot of unanswered questions and much guilt. I felt really guilty that I did not do more to help my father when I saw him so depressed. That guilt remains with me to this day. I also feel guilty that I have only visited his grave three times in the thirteen years since he died. I didn't cry on any of those occasions. And yet I cry at what some people might think would be stupid events. Mayo reached the All-Ireland final in 1996 and I remember sitting in the Cusack stand, looking around at the green and red flags swaying deliriously in the air as the teams arrived out on the pitch, and feeling very lonely. I thought of him and how, even though he was from Sligo, he would have loved it all and I shed a tear in his memory. I also feel a little bit cheated. By doing what he did, he turned his back, however unintentionally, on his family. He has missed out on girlfriends and boyfriends, on birthdays and graduations, successes and failures. My brother is getting married next month, the first wedding in our family, and I know that it is going to be a day filled with some poignancy, because Daddy won't be there. While time is a healer, a death like my father's is something that is very difficult to understand and to cope with, and it has left a huge hole in my life and the lives of my family. I miss him terribly.

Hope

Where are you hope?
I cry in my despair,
What purpose life?
With my life's purpose dead.

Where are you God?
'My God,
Have you deserted me?'
I pray with Christ.

In the mayhem, devastation,
And the horror of this moment,
In the absence of conviction,
when all certainty has vanished from my life,
Only faith still keeps You there,
My God.

Then You give me Holy Week –
The betrayal, the desertion,
And the utter desolation –
To remind me
Christ is present here;
He knows the way I feel.

And You send Easter to revive
Again my hope,
That the final word is not with death
But with the Lord of Life.

Stephen O'Gorman

LOSING MY HUSBAND

This is the anonymous account of a conversation about the impact of the loss of a husband.
The interview was with the editors.

Q: *How would you describe your husband?*
A: He was all full of life, he was very keen to do all kind of things. He was continually at machinery, he was go, go, go all the time. He had a great interest in everything until about two years before he died. He went into a depression then. He was a real people person; every one knew him, he was always on the go.

Q: *What change did you notice in him?*
A: He just got depressed, he wouldn't get treatment for it and he couldn't pull himself out of it. He went downhill, I could see him nearly dying. He lost weight, he had no interest in eating. He used to go on terrible sessions of drink, and he'd be real hyper when he would be drinking. He could spend maybe two days drinking, then he would grow very depressed afterwards and he would not speak to anyone in the family. Yet when anyone from outside came in – then he could change.

Q: *You are saying it was quite sudden?*
A: He was diagnosed with epilepsy just two years before he died, and he never could accept that. He had the old fashioned understanding about epilepsy that people would treat it as you know...

Q: Not fully right or something?
A: Yes, a bit possessed or something. He never would accept that. He knew that drinking didn't help. The medication he was on was not working, he would still drink and then he used to get fits and he would be in agony with pain, you know it was a vicious circle. He wouldn't get help.

Q: To go to get help would be admitting something about it that he couldn't accept.
A: He wouldn't admit it, no. He had a serious problem with drink, but he wouldn't admit he had. He thought he was just having craic, even though he would be literally falling down on the floor, he would be that bad with it. He wouldn't admit he had a problem at all.

Q: It must have been hard looking on?
A: I think only for I started going to Al-Anon meetings. That helped me cope with the suicide better than if I hadn't. He decided to drink, that was his decision, he was a free person to do what he wanted. I think when he committed suicide as well, it helped me to realise that it was not anyone's fault. It was his decision to do it, even though I don't mean that in a cold-hearted way. He was an adult. He was supposed to be able to deal with his own life. If that was the way he decided to deal with it.... At the same time, it didn't make it any easier. But it made me understand, and take the blame away from myself and the kids. I mean, when he was drinking, everybody was wrong. I suppose he was a typical alcoholic, you know; he was right, and everybody else was wrong.

Q: Can you describe the time around his death?
A: The day before he died he was breathalised. I think that brought it home to him – that drink was a problem for him. He thought he was going to get away with it, because he had a brother a guard. He went to see the brother, but didn't get to

speak to him. I think when he realised that it was not going to be quashed it brought home to him the consequences of what he did.

Q: *That was the last event, did he communicate at all with you that day?*
A: Yes. I was talking to him, he was working for this fella that was doing contract work and he came home to put on boots. He did a delivery round as well, he asked me would I be able to do that, I said, 'Of course I would, I'm very flexible at work, you know. Why wouldn't I?' I said to him, 'You know, if you broke a leg wouldn't you be off the road anyway, so it's only going to be a year and a half or two years anyway.' He said 'Grand', and went off to work. That was it, he never said a word to the kids, there was only one of them there that day.

Q: *It must have been very hard for them.*
A: It was very hard for them. I didn't tell them he was missing, I thought he was actually gone on a 'session' and that he would be back.

Q: *How was the news communicated to you, how did you find out?*
A: The priest.

Q: *When it came to the time of the funeral, do you remember how that was for you?*
A: To be honest, I don't remember very much of it at all. The day he was found, they came to me about half past one, the rest of that day is sort of blank.

Q: *A real time of shock. During this time was there anything that was helpful, did you want to be on your own, did you want people calling in?*
A: I wanted to be on by own, yes, even though the house was full of neighbours in those early days. Nothing seemed real, it

was just so hard to take in. I just wished they would go. There are two people that work with me, they used to call every single day, at lunch time, they tried to get me to go back to work. I said to myself, 'Just leave me alone'. In hindsight, I'm glad that they did keep coming back, because I didn't have an interest to get out of bed even, and then they would ring and say they were coming, so that gave me support.

Q: *So it was good that they were persistent in a way?*
A: Yes, even though at the time I was cursing them.

Q: *What about your kids, how did they do?*
A: They couldn't take it in. My daughter was going to school, all her mates rallied around her and were great really. She could relate to two friends in particular; one girl went through a terrible traumatic time when her family separated, and they kind of knew then what one another were going through. If it was my father that had committed suicide, at that time, there would not have been anybody to talk to. It would not even have been admitted.

Q: *When you went back to work, what was helpful in the way people dealt with you, and what was unhelpful?*
A: People just treated me as normal, you know what I mean. I was dreading going back to work because I thought people were going to be whispering. Maybe they were, but I didn't notice it. People just carried on as normal.

Q: *It was a relief, I'd say.*
A: It was, yes, because the first day – it was such a nightmare to go back that first day, but everybody was so good – the manager said 'Come and go as you please, you are not to work nine to five', which was great, I am very lucky to be working where I am.

Q: The people just treated you normally?
A: Nobody talked about it, I was glad, to be honest with you. I would not have been able to cope with talking about it.

Q: Later on, as time went by, did you want to talk about it or did you remain wanting to be left by yourself with it?
A: I could talk to certain people, those that we would have socialised with together. But to casual friends, no, I didn't want to.

Q: In terms of your two daughters, then, over time did you talk about the death much?
A: Yes, I did not know how to react, whether or not to bring it up with them. If they brought it up I'd talk about it. I didn't know whether I should or shouldn't. The youngest girl, at the time, was difficult to handle and I couldn't say anything to her. So naturally I backed off.

Q: Did you get over that after a couple of months?
A: I think she is more adjusted now. She is easier to get on with, she is getting more adult. I'm not recommending this approach - just that's what happened to me.

Q: She is getting easier to talk to. She is more a friend now. Now coming to the third anniversary of your husband's death, how do you look back on that time now?
A: Well, at the time I could never look three years ahead. I think, in the meantime, the time has gone so quick, you wouldn't think you could survive that long. Still, every day when I wake up, it's there, it never goes away. It's the first thing that hits every morning. It never eases. I remember when my father died, I'd say after two years you would think about it, but you wouldn't think about it all the time. It just hits and is always in the background. I'd say that is probably the difference between a natural death and a suicide.

Q: Do you still have questions, or do feel you have a good understanding of the frame of mind he was in, or as you said it was his choice?

A: To be honest with you, I feel suicide is a very selfish thing, very, very selfish. I mean, it's often harder to go on living than it is to choose suicide. If I had decided to do the same thing the same day, I mean, the two girls were going to be left on their own. For all he knew, I could have. So I think it was very, very foolish. It's a cop-out to me. I suppose people can get that down. It's still a bit hard to take in. I mean, Sunday he was in the pub all day, having the crack with everyone, and then to go off and do that. It seems very dramatic.

Q: In yourself, what got you three years down the line? What has kept you going?

A: I would say probably the girls, really. I would say being there for them. My youngest daughter was going to school at the time, now she is going to college. I have to go out and make a living, I will always have to have money for her. I couldn't spoil her chances. No matter what happened, I would say that giving her a chance was what gave me the kick to keep going.

Q: If you were to offer support to someone else who was bereaved by suicide, what do you think would be the most helpful thing you could say or do?

A: First of all, I'd tell them not to blame themselves. I mean, there are a lot of people out there with a notion that someone could have done something, but what do you do? You can't put someone on a chair and sit with them day and night. If they want to do it, if they are an adult and they have their minds made up.

Q: So really, not to blame themselves.

A: There is a woman that was here with me the night before he committed suicide. She saw that he was down over being breathalised. She was here the other day and she was on about it, saying she should have done something, and we should have done something, but I cannot see how anyone can stop someone from committing suicide if that person has their mind made up to do it.

Q: *Is your faith in this at all, or is that a difficult area for you?*
A: I go to Mass very regularly, sometimes during the week. I'm not this Sunday Catholic – OK, go into Mass and come out and do what you like and go back again next Sunday and you are grand. I would talk to God rather than praying.

Q: *You mentioned that here in the west, in particular, it's very hard to come out and talk to each other. Do you think some kind of opportunity for people to come together who have been bereaved by suicide could help?*
A: I would imagine it would help. I would imagine it would, because if you are talking about this neighbourhood, this particular village has, we'll say, maybe ten houses. You can't relate to the bereaved family next door, because if someone died belonging to them of a natural death, it's very different to what I have experienced.

Q: *You say they don't talk about these issues because they know each other, or because of shame. Is that why?*
A: I would say a certain amount of people, yes, they just wouldn't like to be seen to talk. It's like going into Al-Anon or AA or anything like that. There is an awful lot of people who wouldn't go into them because of who would be there, they might see neighbours, that kind of thing.

Q: *But you say that Al-Anon is helpful to you, just to understand what is going on?*
A: I did find great support at the time from Al-Anon members, whereas people who don't know what those meetings are about, they have a different view on people. I could pretend all along

that every thing was hunky-dory and there was nothing wrong, but when I went to an Al-Anon meeting it was admitting that there was something wrong. I know families where there is a lot of drinking going on, but they wouldn't admit it. They pretend.

Q: You have to go somewhere where at least you can be honest and truthful and you don't have to put up this sort of mask.
A: Yes, and you knew that the people there were not going to say to anyone else what you said, it was totally anonymous, everybody was there for the same reason.

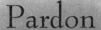

Pardon

The human heart is mystery land;
A region of our being
So beyond our power to know
Or understand.

Now, the host to joy
So glorious
We can scarce contain within it,
Lest it soar into the heavens
In delight.

Then, the home of grief
So painful
That we feel the ache will crush it
'Till it burst.

The gift of having someone really special
To share life with,
Had me floating free
Through time
And I thought it could not end.

When you cut the cord
That held me there,
You sent me crashing to the depths
Beyond despair.

My heart took me through cold numbness and desertion,
On to anger;
Through depression, disbelief,
And shattered dreams.

A faith in Someone bigger
Than the both of us together,
And our love,
Brought a level of acceptance –
Fragile peace.

'Though the heart that's pierced
By death and separation all too sudden
Slowly heals.

Still the words of Christ in death,
Brought a calmness and a peace
I could not have hoped
Were there
Till I too prayed:
'I forgive…'

In that moment
I could understand
The heart of God.

The one who's always ready,
Always waits with open arms
To receive us and embrace us
With a pardon so expansive
Not a single soul is missed.

In this life or beyond death
The heart can only rest secure
That finds its home in him.

Stephen O'Gorman

THE LAST EIGHT WEEKS

Elma Molloy

Elma's story is one of loss and of a journey towards understanding.

I remember precisely the Sunday afternoon I got the call. I lifted the telephone and, as I looked out into the garden, the stray black and white kitten ran up the garden wall. 'Mum,' said Christopher, my middle child, 'I was taken in last night for being over the limit. Nothing serious happened. It will be okay. I have to go now. Bye'. He hung up abruptly. Christopher did not live with me at this time and I was unable to comfort him until the following evening.

I did get a hurried account from him about being taken to a Garda Station for a few hours. The necessary procedures were followed and he mentioned that he was treated kindly there. His girlfriend collected him and drove him home. He had his car for a year and, like any twenty-one-year-old, was thrilled the day he became a car owner for the first time. Yet this car was to prove catastrophic in his life. I did not fully comprehend it at the time, but he was sinking into a dark pit after the arrest. As a mother, my sympathy and support was indisputable. I wanted to take away his pain, but he had inflicted a situation upon himself that was beyond a mother's aid.

He was twenty-one, tall, good-looking. He had a girlfriend who loved him, a good job and family support, but right now he was up against a wall. As far as he was concerned, and here I quote his exact words, 'There is no hope'. Of course, there was no hope of having his charge made void. That had to be faced. But he could see no life beyond the humiliation of a court case. He was now 'at risk' and felt he was sinking, but would not admit or face this reality.

I appealed to him and said 'Christopher, don't you think that you should be in hospital?'

He jumped up when I said this and said 'Mum, I'd kill myself first before I would go into hospital.'

He was still the same vibrant, young Christopher to me, but now with a massive battle to face. His fatal weakness was that he just could not deal with this situation. It really was 'The Agony in the Garden' for him. He felt frightened and alone. He really felt that there was no way through this ordeal for him. He would say to me – when he realised the implications of his charge – 'Mum, can you imagine me, standing in the pissing rain – waiting for a bus'. The luxury of driving would no longer exist – for a while anyway. Yes, it was tough and bleak for a twenty-one year old boy.

Yet he had a lot going for him. His girlfriend loved him – his parents supported him. Why did he feel so desperate? An interesting episode in the Gospel comes to mind where Jesus, although with his disciples in the Garden of Gethsemane, feels totally alone (Luke 22:39-46). Two thousand years later, nothing has changed. A lot of young men, especially when troubled, feel totally alone. In this age of mass communication, never has there been such loneliness.

I witnessed Christopher phoning friends who were not able to help him. On account of his impending difficulties, he did feel socially isolated. He wanted to succeed in life, which is natural, and he could not face failure. In the early stage of his desperation he asked me 'Mum, is Prozac good?' Prozac he was given, and Prozac was not to be his particular cure.

As a child, I was taught to always pray for a 'happy death'.

This was one of faith's gifts – a happy death. My mother prayed this with me every night when she switched off my bedroom light. I related a happy death to lying in one's bed, surrounded by family and – very importantly – comforted by receiving the Last Rites. Did I ever imagine that my dear son would die so alone and so violently? No priest or doctor to comfort him on a stormy, dark November night.

He did write a final note. It is consoling to read, because it sets out clearly what was on his mind. In it, he says how sorry he is for having to take the route he did. He speaks of heaven three times in the note. It is such a loving, gentle letter. If he speaks of heaven – there must be hope for us (his family) on earth? But there are so many 'if only's' in his note.

I appeal to anyone in this situation never to be too proud to seek help and advice. Christopher has found the answers now, but at what cost to his family and friends?

Don't ignore the warning signals. Death is final, and suicide is final. But with suicide, there are no answers and never will be, in this life at least.

From my experience the warning signs would be:

- an inability to cope with a major set-back in life
- low self-esteem and a sudden lack of confidence
- mood changes
- a sense of hopelessness
- a lack of personal hygiene and not being careful about one's personal appearance etc

There was a Memorial Service for Christopher in the Chapel of Trinity College, Dublin in December, 1998 – a month after his death.

A few lines from the Gaelic Hymn 'Be thou my Vision' struck me

> Be thou my best thought
> in the day and the night

because Christopher was tormented both day and night by fears, and nobody, it seems, could help him. Now is the time to help those with problems and anxieties. I feel the Samaritans offer tremendous support. I know Christopher rang the Samaritans in Dublin in the days before his death. I feel they are most helpful as they are a 24-hour service, and so deserve our support, both financial and otherwise. They become the friends that perhaps we are too proud to phone.

Life after suicide is difficult. Apart from the loss, one has to cope with the awkwardness and embarrassment of others, who really don't know what to say to you. One is left feeling isolated, but it's nobody's fault. The living are left to carry on regardless. I know there are lists of support groups for the despairing – but sometimes an individual just needs a friend who has time and an ear – a rare thing in this age of prosperity.

I firmly believe that Christopher is at peace now. I feel he is supporting the family. We visit his grave near Bray often. The mountains surround the cemetery and I am glad to go to his final resting place and pray for him. I often read his final note which indicates so much about him. He was very loving. He says he is sorry to hurt all the people he loved. He tells us he loves us all, and hopes to see us in heaven some day. He also refers to his deep remorse for drinking and driving. What a fatal consequence that had upon his young life. The stark reality is that with suicide – there are no answers.

We miss you Christopher and you are always in our thoughts and prayers.

May you rest in peace.

Mother of Sorrow –
Mother of Hope

I stood all alone on Calvary hill
'Mother of Sorrows', they call me, 'the sorrowing one'.
I silently prayed for the men who would kill
My innocent, beautiful Son.

I know of your anguish, your pain and your grief,
In the loss of your beautiful boy.
I have witnessed your pain; I have seen your tears.
Know that I am with you in your letting go.

I am present in all your Good Fridays.
I was there by your side when your baby was born.
I will be there again with your son and Mine.
When we celebrate your Easter morn'.

Stephen O'Gorman

A Husband's Suicide

*This anonymous account gives a glimpse into the journey
being travelled through the very particular bereavement
that accompanies suicide.
The interview was with the editors*

Q: *How would you describe your husband?*
A: He had a very outgoing personality. He was very chatty and
witty – a gregarious character. But looking back over time, I now
realise that there was an underlying depression that he would
have been covering up. This pain would have been an ongoing
struggle for him and I tried to reach that pain on many
occasions. It was clear also that our marriage was in difficulties.
We went to counsellors together to pinpoint what was wrong in
our marriage. You cannot just suss out in one day in a
counselling session that someone has depression. It became
clear that he wanted out of the marriage and I decided that I
didn't, so I went for marriage guidance counselling, which he
did for a while with me. He also had problems with gambling
and drinking. I knew that the family were being affected. It
wasn't just an overnight problem, it was over three or four years
– we were doing basically everything that we could do and that
is why I am not overwhelmed with guilt.

Q: *How did you live with his depression?*
A: I tried to reach that pain by saying I am here for you, talk to
me, you can trust me. I really did try to do that, but I couldn't fix
it. I feel that I really did suffer. I feel from my own personal point
of view that if you don't speak out about how you feel when you

start getting depressed, it goes to another level where you are in denial about it or that you don't want to know it's there. Pride is a very big issue too, and perhaps especially for men.

Q: *What was it like for you around the death?*
A: I was in shock. People found it very hard to know what to say to me. I had all sorts of feelings. I would say in those first six weeks I was mostly lost.

Q: *What were the reactions in work and family?*
A: My family were wonderful in every way. My workmates were very good to me, they were on the phone, they visited, they couldn't have been more helpful. For my child it was the hardest, he was seven, so that was so difficult. He has done Rainbows, the support group for children of bereaved and separated families – he has done that on a one to one basis. Also, family therapy was a great catalyst, helping us to grieve together.

Q: *With regards to yourself, in what ways do you think you helped your own recovery around this issue or survival or moving through it the way you describe it?*
A: I would say I am coping because I know it is a hard one to deal with, therefore I am reaching out to other people. For me, identifying what has happened to me with other people was more important for my help, talking to other people who have been through the same. To be able to identify with someone else who has been through the same has been essential in my recovery. I think that the bottom line is you need to talk about it. This is so important because your children can talk about it when they know you are able to. I have met so many special friends who I would hit off ideas with, especially about children, how to talk to children about suicide, to bring it out in the open. If you hide it away, I think it is carried on, that is my own opinion. I have encouraged my son to speak about how he feels. How are you feeling today? It is OK to be sad, it is OK to be

happy, it is OK to be angry, it is OK to be all of those things. It is what you do about them that it is important. I suppose the more information and support that you have, the better the chance. If I am honest, my greatest fear would be that my son would take the easy way out like his father.

Q: *Anything else that helped?*
A: Initially, we had so many week-ends away – that was a great way for us to get together. That helped a lot. To put everything on hold. Also, my parents have been fantastic. They have been constantly there for me, I know they have open ears for me, no matter what is going on in their lives. Once you know you have a listening ear, especially if there is something going on for you, even depression, if you know that somebody is listening and that they love you and support you, then that is half of your problem gone. I think if you can walk into your family home, if you know that you are accepted and loved … that is what I have to show to my child every day. Friends from my past contacted me, and this was so supportive. Recreation has also been a great help – I love to swim, it is so refreshing.

Q: *What did you notice in how people reacted after the death?*
A: People want to help, they do genuinely want to help because they know you are in pain. Those early days after the bereavement people call and phone, but six months or a year down the line the reality kicks in. I know, deep down, that that is a normal reaction to grief. I think going back to work, going through that door, was the hardest part for me in my recovery, but looking back it was the best thing I could have done. People were so good and allowed me to focus on work. It was good to have that, because I would have been sitting at home even today. I love my job, I love what I am doing. It's the beginning of saying I am not cracking up and I am going to get through this. I do feel very lucky. I am looking out for a support group and meeting other families who would have dealt with the same

situation. I feel privileged, I am able to get up in the morning and hear the birds singing. I feel that at this stage in my bereavement I want to move on and that there is hope in my life.

Q: *Was faith a support during this time?*
A: I carry rosary beads in my bag. I do pray and I believe in prayer and I take time out everyday to stop everything and listen. I get peace from knowing that I am meant to be where I am and there is a reason on a spiritual level. If there is any way that I can help even one person through my experience, then it is not a waste of an event. I am just happy to be alive and to have my health and I hope to go on living as long as I can. It has given me a different angle, despite being given this trauma of having to deal with this issue in my life. I feel I am a lot more determined in my life and have a sense of peace in the journey that is my life.

Full of Mercy

He cures the sick.
He heals the lame.
He makes the blind to see.
We know He came among us,
To set the troubled free.

He welcomes back the Prodigal.
He pardons Peter too.

He prays, 'Father please forgive them,
They know not what they do'.

He is our faithful shepherd
Our companion on life's road,
He freely lays His own life down
That life may be restored.

Our God is full of mercy.
Of tender love and care.
He watches for the weak and small.
It's 'the least' He came to save.

He judges with compassion
For he sees into the soul.
He won't condemn or cast away.
His compelling love saves all.

Stephen O'Gorman

LOSING A BROTHER

Stella O'Connor

*In this account, Stella tells of her brother's death
and of the life-story that surrounds this event.*

On 8 May 1999, my brother John died by suicide. He was forty-four years old. John was the fourth of six children – the youngest boy. I, Stella, am the youngest of the family. He was a handsome man, with many talents – singer, guitarist, artist and sportsman (being very accomplished at golf, darts, and snooker). His wife, Terry, and he had decided to separate for a while about six months previously.

As children, we came from a dysfunctional family. My parents separated many times when we were young, and we never knew from day-to-day which of our sisters and brothers we'd be living with, or where we would be living. My mum had a tendency to move on the spur of the moment, taking with her some of the children. She always returned to get the rest of us. She loved my Dad. Our father died undergoing bypass surgery in July 1980 at the age of fifty-four. My Mum died in January 1982, she was also fifty-four years old. She died of an aneurysm.

John and I were always close. We understood each other, we could see beneath the surface of each other's life. John was always telling jokes and having fun. He was the life and soul of the party, but I saw right through him, and he knew it.

In 1997, I began to search for my roots. I went to England to spend time with John and my two sisters as they all lived within an hours drive of each other. The day with John was the most interesting. We hadn't seen each other for almost sixteen years, and we were reminded of how much we loved each other. It also became very clear how traumatic our lives had been, we both were suffering from a lack of self-worth and a very poor self-image. We vowed to get to know each other and continue to deepen the bond that was naturally present. In the following year, we spent many weeks together and many hours on the telephone to each other. It was clear that John was unhappy with his life. He was living in council housing and working in a factory job. His marriage of twenty-five years was very strained. John was stubborn and not good at communication, keeping his pain well hidden – even from himself. To the onlooker, he was the happiest man alive, with everything going for him. But he had an inner scream audible only to wounded hearts.

In July 1998 we had a family reunion; my brother Colm came home from Australia for a month with his wife and three children. In hindsight, this proved a difficult time for John. It seemed to him that each of us had made more of a success of our lives. We were all house-owners and had steady careers.

On Holy Thursday, April 1999 I had a phone call at 10.00 p.m. It was John and he was very depressed. He was anxious and nervous and told me he didn't feel that he could go on living. His wife had begun a new relationship and he realised now how much he needed her and what a mistake it had been to split up. We talked for over two hours and after he said goodbye, I rang many friends to pray for him, and kept several candles burning all night. I was very worried about his state of mind. He rang me the next day and thanked me for hearing him. I rang my sister, concerned that he should not be left alone. On Easter Saturday, I had another frantic phone call, this time from my sister. John was gone, he'd left his watch and his car keys and a note on the kitchen table. I prayed all day for him, worrying deeply for his safety. About 9.00 p.m. John rang me, he had tried to drown himself but couldn't go through with it. He had walked for hours, and eventually come home. I told him that I was glad he'd come home, and that I loved him, and how disappointed I would have been if he didn't say goodbye to me. So he promised faithfully that should it happen again he'd say goodbye to me.

About five days later, John took a lot of paracetemol and drink and rang me to say goodbye. 'The deed is done, Sis', he said, 'The grim reaper's coming to get me.' I remained calm (with some difficulty) and told him 'It's not too late, John. You can ring the hospital and they'll pump out your stomach'. My sister's husband was there with him, calling him names, and I suppose trying to make John see sense. But John was cold and callous and quite determined to punish his wife for the rejection that he felt. Again, we talked for a long time and said goodbye. He eventually rang for help and was taken to hospital, where they pumped his stomach. He refused to speak to a psychiatrist and, despite my sister's pleas in the hospital, he signed himself out. He finally agreed to come to Ireland and spend some time with me.

I met him at the airport and for the first time, I saw him cry. He was uncontrollable, physically shaking, apparently as a result of the overdose, and was distraught. He said he had never before been alone, that every time he came to Ireland it was with Terry, or at least he'd go home to share the whole experience with her. He said he'd never felt pain like this before, but he couldn't escape it. Then he said 'I could ignore it again. I always knew I couldn't handle these emotions, that's why I chose to ignore them, but at least this is real – but it still hurts.' I said that if he could stay in the pain that there was light at the end of the tunnel and this could be a great turning point in his life.

John stayed five days with me, and we talked every day. He became a little more relaxed, and I asked him to list his good and bad qualities as he perceived them. He had a very long list on the bad side, but could not come up with one item to list as a good quality. So I asked him to list my qualities and he had no problem. We read the list together and I pointed out that a lot of things on my list also belonged on his. He was kind and generous, warm-hearted and friendly, caring and loving, a good father and husband (he was unsure of this one), a good listener and sensitive. The following day, he could not remember one good thing. I brought him to see a good friend of mine and she listened to his pain and helped him to see his worth.

John had become obsessed with his wife, placing all his hope in her. I tried to help him see that he needed to place his hope in God. He felt unloved by our Dad and, I think, had never mourned the death of our parents. Pain, undealt with, had accumulated in him and now totally overwhelmed him. John returned to England with determination to find his real self. He had a couple of books that I lent him, including John Powell's *Happiness is an Inside Job*. I continued to pray for him, but I decided that I had to let him go. He needed to make his own decisions and either way, God would support both of us.

On 8 May, John was found dead in his car, several miles from his home. He left a tape for his wife, blaming her, although his last words to me on leaving Ireland were 'Let Terry know it's not her fault'. He left letters for his son and daughter and his sisters, though Terry in her distress destroyed them. It was so very sad. Such loss for all the family, indeed, all who knew him. My brothers found it particularly hard, as they were unaware of his depression (John's own choice). His daughter – then 19 – knew nothing of his depression either, as she was living on the Isle of Man.

John was, I believe, almost saved from suicide, but needed medication or counselling to take him out of the danger zone. He was not willing to take that step. I know I tried with all my heart to affirm John, to let him know he was loved, but I know he's at peace now and helping me to grow whole and grow in holiness, out of my brokenness. I don't blame John, because he told me

'It's like an overwhelming darkness surrounds you, and you feel hopeless and out of control.' I believe this is what happened to him. I don't believe he chose to die, because he was in complete darkness, outside of his own control. I know he is forgiven for 'He knows not what he does!'

Sadly, suicide is touching more and more families. This inner scream goes unheard for too long. Only someone who understands and knows their own pain can put voice to that scream. No one is to blame for suicide, but we need to listen more from the heart, set up a deeper form of communication with more love and understanding, so that utter despair never sets in.

I want to thank God for John. He was a good brother and friend. I loved him and I know he loved me, and I'm very glad our hearts met. I ask God to bless all those who have taken their lives and all their families, let them have the strength to let go of blame and shame and to move towards embracing God's love and mercy, which will carry them in their great loss.

Fear not – I have redeemed you

Do not be afraid.
For I have called you by your name.
You are mine.

I have carved you in the palm of my hand.
I will guard you as the apple of my eye.
I have redeemed you.
You are mine.

Do not fear the darkness of the night;
Nor the scorching sun by the day.
I have redeemed you.
You are mine.

I have loved you with an everlasting love.
I have loved you more than life itself.
I have redeemed you.
You are mine.

I have gone to prepare a place for you.
That your joy may be full.
I have redeemed you.
You are mine.

Before the world ever knew you,
I redeemed you.
And for eternity – forever –
You are mine.

Stephen O'Gorman

Offering a Light

Peter Gerard

*The following is an account, in Peter's own words, of reaching out
and trusting in his own wisdom to support someone in distress.*

I attend to the mooring and unmooring of some ships at a
port in the North East. This was a very cold winter's night
and even though it was dry I put my pull-ups on – because I do
not wear long-johns! This time of year, the quays can be so cold
you would think you had no trousers on! The ship was sailing at
2.30 a.m.; I decided to get there at 2.00 a.m., as I like to be early.

As I was going along on my bicycle I thought I would enter
the quays from a different entrance than the usual. When I
arrived there, I got off the bicycle and started walking to a place
I usually leave it. It was then I saw this man standing very close
to the edge of the pier. He asked me for a match to light a
cigarette. I said I didn't smoke and walked on.

As I left the bicycle out of my hand I began to think that this
man had a troubled look about him and I felt more and more
uneasy. I got back as quick as I could to him and began to talk
with him. He told me he wanted to have one last cigarette before
he jumped. I was quite shocked, but told him I would get a
match from one of the sailors who were nearby getting the ship
ready to sail. He promised me he would stay where he was, so I
ran to the ship where one decent man threw a box on to the

quay where I was standing and told me to keep them. I got back as fast as I could. After he lit his cigarette, I tried to think of something to say to him to stop him from jumping. I then told him a lie and said I could not swim, because I had no desire to follow him into the water – I was thinking of the two of us ending up in the freezing waters where our hearts might stop! I told him it was none of my business, but I asked him what his trouble was anyhow. He was wiping the tears from his eyes. I tried to calm him by saying that I often cried. He then told me that the only one that ever loved him was now buried. His mother had died two weeks before. I said to him, 'I bet you did not cry at her funeral', he said that that was true.

To myself I asked God to help us both. Then I said to him that his mother was in heaven and what he was going to do would make this a hell for his mother for all time. He turned and looked at me and said he never thought of it that way. I asked him to come away from the edge of the quay. He did that and, still crying, he threw his arms around me and said thanks – it was 2.20 a.m. I told him to try and get to his bed and in the morning to talk to someone about how he was feeling. I told him that I often pop into a church or talk to a friend if I'm feeling low. He said thanks again and went home. I know this man is still alive, but I have never met him since that night.

ECHOES OF SUICIDE

Reflection on 'Offering a Light'

A Challenge
How does this real life story challenge us? Many feel that the Ireland of this new millennium is suffering from a breakdown in family and community structures, leaving more and more people isolated, disconnected and in despair. Hence, the challenge is to bridge the gap from our self-absorbing concerns to a real and visible commitment to community. We can see from this story that Peter was challenged to overcome his initial response to walk by and not get involved, and instead turn back and offer what support he could in the situation.

Do we have a role to play?
We have a growing tendency not to trust our own ability to offer some measure of support to those in crisis. We fear that we will say or do the wrong thing, and therefore make the situation worse. As a result of these fears we may *too easily* bypass the essential first port of call in any crisis situation, which is our own human contact with the person.

What can we offer?
To answer this let us look again at Peter's story:

- he was alert to the distressed signals given out by the individual
- he responded to the opening given by the distressed man when he asked for a 'light'
- he took the time *and risk* to get involved
- in a non-threatening way, he gave the man an opportunity to talk about his problem

- he listened to and acknowledged the man's pain and despair
- he called on his own resources and personal faith in his response
- he talked about ways he himself coped in times of difficulty
- he offered the man another way of looking at the situation
- he gently encouraged him to take steps back from the edge of the quay
- he offered a way of coping with the next few hours
- he recognised the limit of what he could do and suggested others who might help him

This story prompts us to trust in our own capacity to reach out in some way to those in need. Many of us forget that it is simply the basic human skills that can make a real difference – skills like listening, showing concern and taking the time to be sensitive to the signal of those in pain. While recognising the vital role of professional individuals and agencies, the challenge presented by this story is that there are situations where we can be the first, and vital, link in responding to those in distress.

The Editors

Stuck in a Moment You Can't Get Out Of

U2

Following a request to contribute to this publication, the members of U2 met and discussed which of their compositions would be most appropriate to the themes being explored in 'Echoes of Suicide'. Their choice offers insightful reflections that will resonate with many. We are very grateful for their contribution to and interest in this book.

I'm not afraid of anything in this world
There's nothing you can throw at me that I haven't already heard
I'm just trying to find a decent melody
A song that I can sing in my own company

I never thought you were a fool
But darling, look at you
You gotta stand up straight, carry your own weight
These tears are going nowhere, baby

You've got to get yourself together
You've got stuck in a moment and now you can't get out of it
Don't say that later will be better now you're stuck in a moment
And you can't get out of it

I will not forsake the colours that you bring
But the nights you filled with fireworks
They left you with nothing
I am still enchanted by the light you brought to me
I still listen through your ears, and through your eyes I can see

And you are such a fool
To worry like you do
I know it's tough, and you can never get enough
Of what you don't really need now... my oh my

You've got to get yourself together
You've got stuck in a moment and now you can't get out of it
Oh love look at you now
You've got yourself stuck in a moment and now you can't get out of it

I was unconscious, half asleep
The water is warm till you discover how deep...
I wasn't jumping... for me it was a fall
It's a long way down to nothing at all

You've got to get yourself together
You've got stuck in a moment and now you can't get out of it
Don't say that later will be better now you're stuck in a moment
And you can't get out of it

2

TOWARDS AN
UNDERSTANDING

SUICIDE: ISSUES, CHALLENGES AND RESPONSES

Minister Mary Hanafin

*Mary Hanafin is Minister of State
at the Department of Health and Children*

Suicide is a serious social problem in this country. There were 413 deaths from suicide in 2000. While this figure represents a decrease on both the 1999 figure of 439 and the 1998 figure of 504, we cannot be complacent about the high number of suicides. The high incidence of suicide in the general population is not confined to Ireland, but is a growing global problem. A disturbing feature is the significant rise in the male suicide rate which accounted for 79 per cent of deaths from suicide in 1999 and 82 per cent of deaths from suicide in 2000. Young males and older males aged sixty-five years and over have shown a significant increase in the rate of suicide. These are worrying trends which require further research so that better strategies are developed to help people who are particularly at risk.

Through information from relatives, it has become clear that most people who committed suicide had long-lasting emotional problems such as depression, anxiety, unhappy relationships, alcohol and drug-related problems, unemployment, feelings of loneliness and guilt, problems with relatives and so on. This information confirms that the factors that lead a person to take his or her own life are of a long-lasting nature, and in order to understand why people commit suicide we have to take into consideration the individual's character traits, coping abilities, social support and life events.

We also need to understand the social origins of individual emotional problems. In the early childhood of people who committed suicide, we quite often find broken homes, separation and divorce, loss of one or both parents, rape and sexual abuse, incest, domestic violence, alcohol abuse by parents, exam and peer pressure and other adverse life events. In later life, events such as sexual abuse and violence in the home may also be contributing factors to why a person might take his or her own life. There is evidence that suicide victims have experienced more of these traumatic events than others. Another social factor that needs to be considered is the availability of means to commit suicide. It is clear that stability in social relations and healthy cultural attitudes towards emotional problems are needed in the fight against suicide.

> Young males and older males aged 65 years and over have shown a significant increase in the rate of suicide.

The National Task Force on Suicide

As the suicide figures increased in the early 1990s, my Department became aware of the need for reliable and concrete information on which to build a national strategy to address the growing problem of suicide in Ireland. The National Task Force on Suicide was therefore established in 1995 to address the growing prevalence of suicide in Irish society. The Task Force comprised fifteen individuals from a range of backgrounds including the coroner services, an Garda Síochána, nursing psychiatry, psychology, public health and voluntary organisations. The terms of reference of the Task Force were as follows:

- to define numerically and qualitatively the nature of the suicide problem in Ireland

- to define and to quantify the problems of attempted suicide in Ireland

- to make recommendations on how service providers can most cost effectively address the problems of suicide and parasuicide (attempted suicide)

- to identify the various authorities with jurisdiction in suicide prevention strategies and their respective responsibilities

- to formulate, following consultation with all interested parties, a national suicide prevention/reduction strategy

In September 1996, the Task Force published its Interim Report. It contained a detailed analysis of statistics relating to suicide and attempted suicide in Ireland and a preliminary analysis into the factors that could be associated with suicidal behaviour.

The Final Report was published in January 1998, and marked the completion of detailed examination of the incidence of suicide and attempted suicide and outlined a comprehensive strategy to reduce the incidence of suicide and attempted suicide in Ireland. It identified the various authorities with jurisdiction in suicide prevention strategies and their respective responsibilities. Relevant Government Departments have been contacted with a view to implementing the Task Force recommendations insofar as they are concerned. All other statutory agencies identified in the report with jurisdiction in suicide prevention strategies have also been contacted requesting that the necessary measures are put in place to ensure the implementation of the recommendations that relate to their respective areas.

The Task Force also recommended that steps be taken to make the mental health services more accessible to the public, particularly to young people. Concern was also expressed at the risk of suicide in older people. Additional funding has been made available to further develop consultant-led child and adolescent psychiatry, and old age psychiatry services, to assist in the early identification of suicidal behaviour and provide the necessary support and treatment to individuals at risk.

Data on mortality are routinely published in the Annual and Quarterly Reports on Vital Statistics compiled by the Central Statistics Office. The recording of the incidence of suicide by the CSO is dependent on information set out on Form 104 completed by the Garda Síochána in respect of each inquest and forwarded to the CSO. The Task Force proposed that a new Form 104 that addresses the deficiency of the lack of detailed medical or psychiatric information relating to the deceased be completed by the Garda Síochána. The new Form 104 is now in use.

Suicide Prevention

The key components of the overall strategy aimed at reducing suicide include the implementation of measures aimed at high risk groups, the provision of information and training on suicide prevention to relevant professionals and organisations, and the improvement of services that would benefit those at risk of suicide and those who attempt suicide.

Health boards, in particular, have a major role to play in co-ordinating efforts to help reduce the level of suicide and attempted suicide in this country. The majority of health boards have established working groups to examine the implementation of the recommendations of the Task Force. The working groups are multi-sectoral and multi-disciplinary and engage in the promotion of positive mental health and the de-stigmatisation of suicide, provide information in relation to suicide and parasuicide, liaise with the media and provide training requirements for staff in relation to all aspects of suicide and parasuicide.

Resource Officers have been appointed in all the health boards with specific responsibility for implementing the Task Force's recommendations. Their responsibilities include the recruitment of additional staff, the provision of staff training in risk assessment, production of information literature and events aimed at raising public awareness of suicide and parasuicide.

Each person presenting with a mental health problem to the health boards' mental health services is assessed and an individual care plan is prepared. Support on an outpatient and, if appropriate, an in-patient basis is provided to patients with suicidal ideation. Those who are chronically suicidal are closely monitored by the mental health multi-disciplinary team, in liaison with the person's general practitioner. Active intervention takes place when crises occur.

Health boards... have a major role to play in co-ordinating efforts to help reduce the level of suicide and attempted suicide in this country.

Support is also needed for voluntary organisations dealing with people suffering from depression, mental illness, bereavement, etc. who are more at risk of suicide and attempted suicide.

Suicide Prevention in Schools

Preventing suicide means influencing, in a corrective and constructive way, a person's development and their own resources at different phases of life. Adolescence is traditionally viewed as a time of profound change, when young people make the transition to adult status. This transition is not easy and for many young people is accompanied by levels of self-doubt, fear and stress. An important aspect of suicide prevention in schools will be to promote self-esteem and self-confidence and to ensure that all students develop personal and social skills. Children and young people need support in gaining control over their lives and coping with their problems.

National Suicide Review Group

An important aspect of the strategy has been the establishment, by the chief executive officers of the health boards, of a National Suicide Review Group. Members of this Group include experts in the areas of mental health, public health and research. Its main responsibilities are to review ongoing trends in suicide and parasuicide, to coordinate research into suicide and to make appropriate recommendations to the health boards. A researcher has been appointed to the Group to collate existing research materials, both national and international, to examine the effectiveness of intervention programmes and to liaise with local coordinators in each of the health boards. This Group published its first Annual Report in 1999. This report provides a comprehensive overview of activities in suicide prevention in each health board area.

Irish Association of Suicidology

Since its foundation in 1996, this Association has done much to help promote public awareness of suicide and suicidal behaviour, especially through the organisation of conferences and workshops.

The Association highlights the rising rates of suicide among young people and the importance of suicide prevention, which represents a serious challenge to all interested parties tackling this growing problem. It is important to ensure that the public is informed about the rising rates of youth suicide and ways of preventing it. It is also very encouraging that the Association is developing as an all-Ireland organisation.

National Suicide Research Foundation

The National Suicide Research Foundation was founded in January 1995 by the late Dr Michael J. Kelleher. It consists of a multi-disciplinary research team with contributions from a broad range of disciplines including psychology, psychiatry and sociology.

The primary aims of the Foundation are to define the true extent of the problem of suicidal behaviour in Ireland; to identify and measure the factors which induce and protect against suicidal behaviour; and to develop strategies aimed at preventing suicidal behaviour. To date, the bulk of the Foundation's work has involved the monitoring of parasuicide. Other work includes the carrying out of in-depth interviews with individuals who have engaged in parasuicide so as to be able to identify the social, psychological and psychiatric factors associated with suicidal behaviour. On a yearly basis, data relating to every suicide and undetermined death registered in Ireland is sent to the Foundation by the Central Statistics Office. These data are analysed, so as to produce up-to-date age-specific and age-standardised rates with respect to demographic variables. These statistics are also provided in response to the numerous requests the Foundation receives from professional bodies, students and the public for information relating to suicide.

I am aware that due to the Foundation's reputation for high quality research, it has been invited to participate in several important international studies, among them the WHO/Euro Multicentre Study of parasuicide.

International studies have found parasuicide to be one of the most significant risk factors associated with suicide - those who engage in parasuicide are twenty times more likely to eventually kill themselves. Studies have shown that at least one third of all suicides have a history of parasuicide. To this end, the Association has now launched the National Parasuicide Registry. This important project is being undertaken by the National Suicide Research Foundation, with funding from the Department of Health and Children.

The Registry will provide information on the general characteristics of people who attempt suicide. It will provide a better knowledge of suicidal behaviour, and specify trends in parasuicide over time and in the different regions of the country.

The analysis of this general information will be useful in the development of policies and the implementation of measures aimed at preventing suicide. The Registry will also be very useful in the allocation of resources. It will help identify groups that are particularly vulnerable and will assist health boards to evaluate the impact of the preventative and clinical services being provided.

Promoting Positive Mental Health

Mental illness has traditionally been a hidden illness that people were embarrassed to talk about. We are all aware of the pressures on young people, such as bullying, emotional distress, addictions, peer pressure and exam pressure. We often tend to think that people are weak if they suffer from anxiety, depression, inability to cope, or have suicidal tendencies, but it is widely acknowledged that one in four women and one in ten men will experience depression during their lifetime. Many of these people are successful people, role models, celebrities who we all know.

> Better understanding of mental illness encourages people to access professional help sooner rather than later...

The promotion of positive mental health will contribute significantly to combating the ignorance and stigma that often surround mental illness, and will also be effective in the area of suicide prevention, especially among young people. This enables people to talk about their feelings and emotional problems and to seek help without fear of being labelled a failure.

Better understanding of mental illness encourages people to access professional help sooner rather than later, and this facilitates early recovery. We must also continue to improve the quality of life of people with long-standing, recurrent or acute mental health problems and that of their families and friends.

My Department recognises the importance of early intervention and positive mental health, and also the important work of voluntary agencies who work hand-in-hand with the statutory agencies. The Department of Health and Children has supported and developed many initiatives over the past number of years in the area of young people's health (including mental health), often in co-operation with the voluntary agencies.

The commitment and dedication of the volunteers working with the voluntary organisations is to be commended. Their input is invaluable, not only in providing support for those most vulnerable in our society, but also in heightening awareness of the importance of self-help and empowerment of the individual in attaining positive mental health and in overcoming the crises of life.

Health (Miscellaneous Provisions) Bill 2000
The Health (Miscellaneous Provisions) Bill 2000, which has recently completed Report Stage in the Dáil, was amended to include the following amendment:

> The Minister for Health and Children shall, not later than nine months after the end of each year, beginning with the year 2002, make a report to each House of the Oireachtas on the measures taken by health boards during the preceding year to prevent suicides.

This provides that the Minister for Health and Children will make a report each year to each House of the Oireachtas on the measures taken by health boards in the preceding year to address the problem of suicide

Funding
A sum of £18.64 million is being provided in 2001 for improvements in mental health services. Priority is being given to the further development of community based mental health

services; the further expansion of Child and Adolescent Psychiatry and the Psychiatry of Old Age; and the implementation of the recommendations of the Task Force on Suicide. Provision is also being made for additional funding to voluntary bodies.

Of this, £830,000 will go towards suicide prevention programmes in the health boards and towards research aimed at improving our understanding of this disturbing social problem. This includes an additional £100,000 for the National Suicide Research Foundation in Cork to support its work in the development of a National Parasuicide Register.

The significant increase in the level of capital funding available for the development of mental health facilities in the community will ensure that services become more accessible to people who may be at risk of suicide.

BEREAVED BY SUICIDE

Carmel McAuliffe

Carmel, a research psychologist of the National Suicide Research Foundation, examines the nature of bereavement in the context of suicide. She brings to bear the literature and experience in the field in order to deepen our understanding of the issues involved. The National Suicide Research Foundation is a unit of the Health Research Board in Ireland.

Although it is not widely acknowledged, bereavement following suicide has been described as 'the largest mental health casualty area' associated with suicide[1] for two reasons: firstly, because of the actual number of people directly and indirectly affected; and secondly, because of the distress and, in a minority of cases mental health problems, from which the suicide bereaved suffer.[2] Conservative estimates of the average ratio of suicide bereaved to suicides are between six and seven to one.[3] Yet applying this rule of thumb to the, on average, 400 suicides annually recorded in Ireland in recent years, results in an estimate of between approximately 2,400 and 2,800 newly suicide bereaved individuals in one year alone.

The suicide bereaved – frequently referred to in the literature as suicide survivors – are not limited to the family of the person who has died by suicide. They also include friends[4] and more recent definitions have broadened to include work colleagues, school peers, teachers, family doctors, therapists and any person who would have known the suicide well. The suicide bereaved have been loosely described as '...people in the life of a person who... [died by]... suicide who were close to him or her'[5] and as '...those who have experienced the death by suicide of someone that they care about'.[6]

Suicide bereavement is, in itself, a risk factor for suicide, although this is also true of bereavement from other causes of death.[7] In particular, those bereaved by the suicide of a family member are at greater suicide risk.[8] One psychological autopsy study of 173 suicides in people under twenty years old in metropolitan New York over a two-year period, found that suicides were almost three times more likely to have a first or second-degree relative who had previously either attempted or died by suicide, than a comparison group.[9]

The Grief Process

There has been extensive theoretical elaboration of stages associated with grief. Kubler-Ross, in her book *On Death and Dying*,[10] has described the following stages: denial and isolation; anger; bargaining; depression and acceptance. As the suicide bereaved generally follow the same grief process as those bereaved by other modes of death,[11] it is important that any person working with those bereaved by suicide has a thorough knowledge of 'normal' grief reactions.[12]

Despite efforts to 'fit' grief into a stage theory, grieving is an individualised process and this also seems to be the case for those bereaved by suicide. Grief stages do not always proceed in a predictable order and reverting to previous stages is common.

Is Recovery From Suicide Bereavement More Difficult?

Recovery from suicide bereavement was once seen as particularly problematic,[13] yet more recent studies using carefully selected comparison groups have indicated little, if any, evidence that suicide bereavement is more difficult than bereavement following other modes of death.[14] Research findings have indicated that suicide survivors are no more likely to develop pathological reactions or a prolonged or complicated grief reaction than survivors of other forms of tragic bereavement. [15] One major problem is that the families of those who die by suicide are more often trying to cope with pre-existing problems, which may complicate the grieving process.[16] This is particularly important, given that past experience of the suicide bereaved influences grief outcome.[17] For example, one study has shown that those who have experienced depression in the past are more likely to develop a depressive grief reaction following a suicide.[18]

There are more similarities than differences in the mental health problems of those bereaved by suicide and those bereaved by other types of death, as the exact mode of death has little or no quantitative difference in bereavement outcome.[19] However there is evidence that particular qualitative aspects or themes of suicide bereavement may complicate the grieving process.[20] These can include anxiety, guilt, shame, anger along with rejection and a sense of responsibility. Other particularly salient grief reactions among the suicide bereaved include numbness, shock, guilt, shame and anxiety.

In one Irish study comparing people bereaved by suicide with those bereaved by other forms of sudden death, those bereaved by suicide were more concerned with a perceived lack of social support following the death.[21] Levels of distress – obtained using standardised measures – did not differentiate between groups.

Normal Versus Abnormal Grieving

Therapeutically, the desired outcome in grieving a suicide is to be able to remember the deceased person without being painfully pre-occupied with the circumstances of their death. Having identified particular aspects of the grieving process that may be problematic in those bereaved by suicide, it is important to try to differentiate between normal and abnormal grief reactions (see Table 1).[22] Given that the length of time taken to mourn the loss of a person varies widely from one individual to another, this exercise can be particularly difficult for the teacher, counsellor, therapist or concerned family member or friend.

Chronic grieving, and delayed or inhibited grief reactions are important in the context of a sudden, tragic death like suicide. Chronic grief describes persistent grief that is experienced in full from the beginning, with significant depression, for an extended period. Delayed grieving is characterised by prolonged shock and numbness, with the grief experienced much later, often more severely and at a time when others expect the bereaved to have resumed normal activities. Clinical depression – as distinct from a normal depressed mood – is one of the commonest affective disorders associated with abnormal grief reaction (see Table 1), and requires the diagnostic skills of a trained GP.

Maladaptive coping may take the form of alcohol or tranquilliser dependence, in an effort to avoid painful thoughts and emotions.[23] If this is used as a long-term means of coping, it can further undermine coping ability, by jeopardising the process of grieving and may even cause depression.[24] Alcohol and/or substance abuse also increase the risk of self-harm.[25]

Table 1. Normal V Abnormal Grief Reactions

Normal Reactions	Abnormal Reactions
Physical Arousal	Chronic Grief
Guilt	Inhibited Grief
Anger	Delayed Grief
Depression	Mood Disorders (e.g. Clinical Depression)
Hostility	Alcohol & Tranquilliser Dependence
Loneliness	Panic Disorder
Somatic Illness	Psychosomatic Disorders
Suicidal Thoughts	
Loss of interest in living	
Loss of the ability to enjoy things	

Taken from O'Flaherty (1998)

ECHOES OF SUICIDE

Reactions of Children and Young People

As with adults, there is great variability in the reactions of children and adolescents to a suicide. Some may cope well with the traumatic experience, while others are overwhelmed by it. The National Task Force on Suicide in Canada (1994) recommends that children of all ages be told openly and honestly from the start about the suicidal nature of the death, using age-appropriate language. They also recommend that children be allowed to participate in funeral rituals. While grief reactions of children are similar to adults, they tend to express them differently. An atmosphere of open communication about the suicide allows children to ask questions about the death.

Adults need to be prepared for both the type and repetitive nature of the questions asked by children, bearing in mind that children also suffer from feelings of guilt, responsibility and anger, while often being unable to express them directly. For concerned teachers, parents or other carers, the effects of a suicide may only manifest themselves in the child's non-verbal behaviour, relationships, school performance or play. The child may experience the full impact of the suicide much later or they may hide their reactions from others. Guidelines from the Irish National Teachers' Organisation and the Ulster Teachers' Union recommend that teachers look out for changes in behaviour following the traumatic event; excessive reactions uncharacteristic of the person or inappropriate for the situation; patterns of distress; and persistent problems or lack of progress as evidenced in repetitive play.

Adolescents... experience of grief may be complicated, because they are also engaged in the development of self-esteem and values.

Adolescents also experience responses of similar intensity to adults. However, their experience of grief may be complicated, because they are also engaged in the development of self-esteem and values. Adolescents are particularly vulnerable to imitation as they learn by modelling the behaviour of others. They may develop the belief that suicide is a solution to their problems.

Gender Differences

There is a dearth of research into gender differences among those bereaved by suicide. In Ireland, male suicides outnumber female suicides by a ratio of approximately four to one, resulting in considerably more suicide bereaved female partners, wives and girlfriends. Fortunately, females have less difficulty in seeking help from family, friends or statutory and voluntary services. Males bereaved by suicide may need special attention, given the general male propensity to resist seeking help for emotional problems. In a study of 214 cases of individuals and families attending a suicide survivors' program at a Crisis Intervention Centre in the US, it was found that 65 per cent of females had already received counselling in comparison with 43 per cent of males.[26]

Differences have also been reported between male and female therapists who have had patient suicides.[27] Female therapists more often stated that they felt ashamed and guilty following a patient suicide. They also needed more consolation and suffered more doubts about their professional knowledge. More males than females continued working as usual following their patient's suicide. The findings are particularly important given that there were no significant differences between males and females in either discipline or years of work experience.

Members of the caring professions are not immune to the effect of a suicide in their practice. In a survey of 155 rural GPs in Ireland, one-third indicated that they felt guilty after a patient's suicide, while one in five suffered from disturbed sleep. The overall impact was considerably less than that reported in studies of psychiatrists and psychologists, which is thought to be related to the intensity of the therapeutic relationship.[28]

The Question 'Why?' and the Search for Meaning

One of the most commonly recognised reactions among the suicide bereaved is the preoccupying question: 'Why?' While this is common in most newly bereaved people, in suicide bereavement it may precipitate a prolonged search for an explanation. The person's need to reframe past events is an important part of coming to terms with what has happened and deriving some meaning from the experience.[29] It can also alleviate the burden of self-blame. However, this search for an explanation may strain family relationships, as family members can have very different perspectives and may blame one another.

The grieving process for survivors of suicide can become a persistent pursuit of an answer to the question 'Why?' In an attempt to answer it, many try to collect as much general information about suicide as possible. While this may be helpful at first, many become 'stuck' at this stage. There is a struggle to find meaning in what has happened, and the survivor may be unable to separate the deceased person's life from their mode of death.[30] It is usually in accepting the impossibility of an answer why that suicide survivors come to resolve their grief.[31]

This search for an explanation for the suicide may also precede a search for meaning and a questioning of formerly held values.[32] Such questions may include: 'What is the meaning of life?' or 'Why am I here?' Teachers and caregivers need to take into account that this search is an important component in grieving.

Suicidality

Suicidal thoughts, although a normal response in those bereaved by suicide,[33] should always be taken seriously and enquired about further. One study found that 50 per cent of a group of suicide bereaved who attended a support group had considered suicide as an alternative for themselves, in comparison with 0 per cent of a non-bereaved control group.[34]

Suicide goes against many of the assumptions people have formed about life prior to the event. These beliefs and assumptions are important, as they are the personal rules by which people live, helping to give life meaning and a sense of control to the individual. If the deceased chose suicide as an acceptable solution to a problem, it is not surprising that survivors may begin to consider suicide as an option for the dilemma in which they have been left. Identification with someone who has deliberately ended their life can endanger the bereaved person's sense of safety.[35] This is particularly important in the case of young people, given that they acquire many of their coping strategies through modelling the behaviour of others.

> All verbal or behavioural hints, suggestions or threats about death – whether implicit or explicit – should be taken seriously.

Survivors are at particular risk if they become anxious, hopeless or begin to entertain suicide as the only solution.[36] This is further complicated by other coping problems that may have developed, such as substance abuse or depression. All verbal or behavioural hints, suggestions or threats about death – whether implicit or explicit – should be taken seriously. Suicidal ideation needs to be monitored continually throughout bereavement counselling, and caregivers and teachers need to be prepared to deliver suicide intervention procedures where necessary.[37]

Needs and Help

The needs of those bereaved by suicide vary. Most individuals bereaved by suicide do not develop psychological disorders. Some people do not require outside help and may be happy to rely on the support of their family and friends, although this may be compromised if the death has adversely impacted on an already vulnerable family or social situation. Others may wish to talk to their GP, who may listen, offer emotional support, help with problems such as insomnia, anxiety or depression, prescribe medication where necessary, provide information about other sources of help or refer the bereaved on to others. Some may benefit from peer support through suicide survivor groups, and still others may require individual counselling.

Even within a single family the impact of a suicide affects people in different ways, as the following case shows: One middle-aged woman explained during a research interview that she had survived the suicides of two sons. The first son's suicide had elicited three very different reactions in her family. Her own reaction was to speak with her GP when she began to entertain thoughts of throwing herself under a bus. She was treated for depression by her GP and subsequently attended a support group for the suicide bereaved. Her husband, on the other hand, had never sought outside help, relying instead on his own coping ability. Another son – who had been very close to his dead brother – started to abuse alcohol and died by suicide within a short time. There are a number of valuable implications from this case. Those working with families bereaved by suicide need to be skilled in risk assessment, intervention and referral, while at the same time maintaining a flexible approach that accommodates the variation in grief reactions within a single family.

People surviving a suicide should be allowed to decide what help is best for them. Unfortunately, they perceive a lack of social support more often than those bereaved by other modes of death.[38] For this reason, it has been recommended that services for the suicide bereaved become more proactive in notifying survivors of their existence, rather than depending on word of mouth.[39]

It is important not to 'medicalise' the grieving process, unless psychological disorder warrants treatment.[40] Doing so may lead people to lose confidence in the support available from their families, colleagues, neighbours and friends in the aftermath of the suicide. This is particularly important given that social stigma – whether real or perceived – can complicate the grieving process in those bereaved by suicide. In addition to personal resources, support from others is one of the most important means of coping with a suicide loss.

When to Get Help

Given the considerable variation between people's grief reactions following a suicide, it can be difficult to decide when outside support might be appropriate. There are a number of useful cues, including when a person:

☞ continues to feel numb and empty some months after the suicide
☞ cannot sleep or suffers nightmares
☞ feels they cannot handle intense feelings or physical sensations such as exhaustion, confusion, anxiety or panic, chronic tension
☞ feels overwhelmed by the thoughts and feelings brought about by a loved one's death e.g. guilt, anger, rejection
☞ has no-one with whom to share their grief and feels the need to do so
☞ keeps constantly active in order not to feel (e.g. working all the time)
☞ finds they have been drinking or taking drugs to excess
☞ finds they have been worrying or thinking about suicide themselves
☞ feels afraid that those around them are vulnerable and not coping

(Taken from Hill, Hawton, Malmberg & Simkin, 1997)

Postvention

What is so special about the needs of suicide survivors? Certainly people who experience a traumatic loss of this magnitude are worthy of care and attention. Research findings are also offering compelling evidence that this response needs to be carefully planned.[41]

'Postvention' is a form of prevention after the act of suicide and it is applied to all activities aimed at the survivors of a suicide that help them to return to functioning as before the loss. Shneidman was the first to coin the term 'postvention', describing it as 'prevention for the next generation'.[42] He has argued that postvention is an integral part of any comprehensive suicide prevention strategy. The justification is that it consists of all preventive measures taken after the event of suicide and so it should be treated with the same importance as all other aspects of suicide prevention work.

The aims of postvention are threefold. Firstly, it tries to minimise the distress of survivors. Its second purpose is to help survivors to adapt to a life without the deceased; and thirdly it aims to reduce the likelihood of imitation.[43] The third aim is particularly important in institutional settings, such as hospitals and schools. The incidence of imitative acts of suicide has become so serious, particularly among adolescents and young adults, that the Centers for Disease Control (1988) in Atlanta, Georgia, have issued recommendations for preventing and containing suicide clusters in the aftermath of a suicide. Arising out of the recognised importance of postvention, special programmes have proliferated in school settings, although their effectiveness and safety have not yet been well established.[44]

There is an urgent need to evaluate postvention programmes in specific settings.[45] The main consideration is whether such programmes provide helpful intervention, by minimising dangerous after-effects without harming anyone; one case study reports on a school where postvention inadvertently added to the hysteria among students by glorifying the suicide.[46] Well intended responses can go wrong and the implementation of postvention programmes needs to be informed by best practice.

Formulating a postvention protocol
The most important part of postvention is the development of an agreed-upon protocol, upon which all the recommended steps

of a response hinge. Any traumatic event hinders the human capacity to manage its impact, making it less likely that it will be managed effectively. In addition to this, the Centers for Disease Control (1988) note that potential opportunities for prevention are often missed in the early stages of a community response, because community leaders are searching for information on best practice in responding to suicide clusters.

The following is an outline of CDC Recommendations for those who wish to develop a community plan for the prevention and containment of suicide clusters:

☞ A community should review these recommendations and develop its own response before the onset of a suicide cluster.
☞ The response to the crisis should involve all concerned sectors of the community, and should be co-ordinated by a Co-ordinating committee, which manages the day-to-day response to the crisis, and host agency, whose responsibilities would include 'housing' the plan, monitoring the incidence of suicide, and calling meetings of the co-ordinating committee when necessary.
☞ The relevant community resources should be identified.
☞ The response plan should be implemented under either of the following two conditions: when a suicide cluster occurs in the community, or when one or more deaths from trauma occur in the community, especially among adolescents or young adults, that may potentially influence others to attempt or complete suicide.
☞ If the response plan is to be implemented, the first step should be to contact and prepare those groups who will play key roles in the first days of the response.
☞ The response should be conducted in a manner that avoids glorification of the suicide victims and minimises sensationalism.
☞ Persons who may be at high risk of suicide should be identified and have at least one screening interview with a

trained counsellor; these persons should be referred for further counselling or other services as needed.

☞ A timely flow of accurate, appropriate information should be provided to the media.

☞ Elements in the environment that might increase the likelihood of further suicides or suicide attempts should be identified and changed.

☞ Long-term issues suggested by the nature of the suicide cluster should be addressed

(Centers for Disease Control, 1988)

Institutional response to the suicide of a student, patient or member of staff or community, needs to be delivered quickly to minimise any adverse impact. A timely response requires a protocol, agreed-upon in advance, that outlines appropriate action, is understood by all participants at the onset of a crisis, and is incorporated into procedural guidelines that can be drawn upon when such a crisis occurs. Most importantly, efficiency in managing the aftermath of a suicide will depend on how well-prepared staff are to deal with the crisis, which ultimately impacts on the welfare of patients, students or community members.

Once the cause of death has been verified, it is important to appoint a crisis management team from among the staff to organise the dissemination of information, and a meeting for all staff in which they are given the correct facts. Patients or students also need to be given standard information, while special attention must be paid to those considered at risk. This includes those with a history of self-harm, substance abuse or mental illness, those who have known someone who died violently, those who have recently broken up with a girlfriend or boyfriend, those who are dealing with family instability, those who had a close relationship with the person who has died and those particularly vulnerable to imitation.

While useful recommendations have been made by the CDC,

among others, and familiarity with these models is to be encouraged, they merely provide a framework for community leaders or administrators to develop their own response plans, tailored to the specific needs, resources, and cultural characteristics of the community in question. In order to be effective, it is essential that a community develops its own response plan.

Conclusion

The suicide bereaved are a larger group than those who die by suicide, and are now understood to include those outside of the immediate family and friends. The number of suicide bereaved and the associated risk of imitation in vulnerable groups are important justifications for a planned response to suicide in communities. While current evidence suggests that the suicide bereaved are no more likely to develop complicated or pathological grief reactions than those bereaved by other modes of death, there are particular themes or aspects that characterise grieving following suicide. Those who work with the suicide bereaved need to be familiar with normal grief processes. Attention also needs to be paid to special groups, such as children, adolescents, teachers and carers.

It may be that what we do following a death by suicide is as important for survivors as what we do to prevent a potential suicide. Postvention is multifaceted and includes consultation, assessment crisis intervention, community linkage, education and liaison with the media. Comprehensive postvention necessitates the development of a protocol specific to the organisation or setting.

Notes

1. McIntosh, J. L. (1996). Survivors of suicide. *Newslink, 22(3)*, 3, 15.
2. Clark, S. E. & Goldney. R. D. (1995). Grief reactions and recovery in a support group for people bereaved by suicide. *Crisis,* 16(1), 27-33.
3. Shneidman, E. S. (1969). Prologue. In E. S. Shneidman (Ed.), *On the nature of suicide.* San Francisco, CA: Jossey-Bass
4. McIntosh, J. L. (1994). *How many survivors of suicide are there?* The Georgia Coalition General Information Packet, p. 19 The Georgia Coalition for Youth Suicide Prevention.
5. Grad, O. T. (1996). Suicide: How to survive as a survivor? *Crisis, 17(3),* 136-142.
6. Bailley, S. E, Kral, M.J. & Dunham, K. (1999). Survivors of suicide do grieve differently: Empirical support for a common sense proposition. *Suicide and Life-Threatening Behaviour. 29(3),* 256-271.
7. Kavanagh, D. J. (1990). Towards a cognitive-behavioural intervention for adult grief reactions. *British Journal of Psychiatry, 157,* 373-383.
8. Ness, D. & Pfeffer, C. (1990). Sequelae of bereavement resulting from suicide. *American Journal of Psychiatry, 147,3,* 279-285.
9. Shaffer, D. & Gould, M. (1987). Study of completed and attempted suicides in adolescents. Progress Report: National Institute of Mental Health.
10. Kubler-Ross, E. (1969). *On Death and Dying.* London: Tavistock.
11. Van der Wal, J. (1990). The aftermath of suicide: A review of empirical evidence. *Omega, 20(2),* 149-171.
12. Task Force on Suicide in Canada. (1994). *Update of the Report of the Task Force on Suicide in Canada* Minister of National Health and Welfare
13. Clark & Goldney (1995). Op. cit
14. Bailley, S. E, Kral, M. J. & Dunham, K. Op. cit.
15. Van der Wal, J. op. cit.
    McIntosh, J. L. & Kelly, L. D. (1992). Survivors' reactions: Suicide versus other causes. *Crisis, Journal of Crisis Intervention and Suicide Prevention, 13,* 82-93.
16. Clark, S. E. & Goldney. R. D. (1995). Op. cit.
17. Parkes, C. M. (1972). *Bereavement: Studies of grief in adult life.* New York: International Universities Press.

18. Brent, D., Perper, J., Moritz, G. et al., (1993). Bereavement or depression? The impact of the loss of a friend to suicide. *Journal of the American Academy of Child and Adolescent Psychiatry, 32,6*, 1189-1197.
19. Clark & Goldney (1995). Op. cit.
20. McIntosh, J. L. & Kelly, L.D. Op. cit.
    Bailley, S. E, Kral, M. J. & Dunham, K. Op. cit.
21. Gaffney, P. & Greene, S. (1997). A comparison of the effects of bereavement by suicidal and other sudden death. Proceedings of the 11th Order of St. John of God research study day, 4th November 1997. Pp. 53-69. Dublin: Order of St John of God Research Unit.
22. O'Flaherty, A. (1998). Bereavement: Separating the normal from the abnormal reaction. *Modern Medicine of Ireland, Vol 28*, No 10 pp 19-20
23. Kavanagh, D. J. Op. cit.
24. Hill, K., Hawton, K., Malmberg, A., & Simkin, S. (1997). Bereavement Information Pack: For those bereaved through suicide or other sudden death. London: Royal College of Psychiatrists.
25. Kelleher, M. J., Keely, H. S., Lawlor, M., Chambers, D., McAuliffe, C. and Corcoran, P. (2001) Parasuicide in F. Henn, M, Sartorius, H. Helmchen and H. Lauter (Eds.) *Contemporary Psychiatry, Vol 3*, pp. 143-59
26. Bland, D. (1994). The experiences of suicide survivors. 1989-June 1994. Unpublished paper.
27. Grad, O. T., Zavasnik, A. & Groleger, U. (1997). Suicide of a patient: Gender differences in bereavement reactions of therapists. *Suicide and Life-Threatening Behaviour, 27(4)*, 379-386.
28. Halligan, P. and Corcoran, P. (2001). The impact of patient suicide on rural general practicioners. *British Journal of General Practice, 51*, 295-6
29. Kelleher, M. J. (1994). Therapeutic and administrative help for those bereaved by suicide. *The Irish Doctor*, March, 66-72. Gaffney, P. (1999). An investigation into the psychological effects of bereavement by suicide. Thesis submitted in partial fulfilment of the requirements for the degree of Doctor of Clinical Psychology, Trinity College Dublin.

30. Clark, S. (1996). Finding meaning from loss. Letter. *British Medical Journal, 312,* 1103.
31. Farberow, N. L. (1992). The Los Angeles survivors-after-suicide program: An evaluation. *Crisis, 13(1),* 23-34.
32. Task Force on Suicide in Canada. Op. cit.
33. Clark, S. E. & Goldney. R. D. (1995). Op. cit.
34. Battle, A. (1994). Group therapy for survivors of suicide. *Crisis, 5(1),* 48-58.
35. Hill, K., Hawton, K., Malmberg, A., & Simkin, S. Op. cit.
36. Shneidman, E. S. (1996). *The suicidal mind.* New York: Oxford University Press
37. Task Force on Suicide in Canada. Op. cit.
38. Farberow, N. L. Op. cit. Gaffney, P. & Greene, S. Op. cit.
39. Campbell (1997) Changing the Legacy of Suicide. *Suicide and Life-threatening Behaviour,* Vol 27
40. Kelleher, M. J. (1994). Op cit.
41. Centers for Disease Control (CDC). (1988). CDC Recommendations for a community plan for the prevention and containment of suicide clusters. *Morbidity and Mortality Weekly Report, 37 (Suppl. No. S-6).* Washington DC: Author.
42. Shneidman, E. S. (1972). In A. Cain (Ed). *Survivors of suicide.* Springfield, IL: Charles C Thomas.
43. Kelleher, M. J. (1997). Suicidal behaviour within schools: Prevention and response. Unpublished manuscript. National Suicide Research Foundation.
44. Goldney, R. D. & Berman, L. (1996). Prevention in schools: Affective or effective? *Crisis, 17(3),* 98-99.
45. Shaffer, D., Garland, A., Vieland, V., Underwood, M., & Busner, C. (1990). Adolescent suicide attempters: response to suicide prevention programs. *Journal of the American Medical Association, 264:* 3151-3155. Callahan, J. (1996). Negative effects of a school suicide postvention program. A case example. *Crisis, 17,* 108-115. Leenaars, A. A. & Wenckstern, S. (1999). Suicide prevention in schools: The art, the issues and the pitfalls. *Crisis, 20(3),* 132-1142.
46. Callahan, J. Op. cit.

YOU ARE NOT ALONE

Mary Begley

*Mary works with the Mid-Western Health Board.
In this article she focuses on the particular experience of those
bereaved by suicide. She offers an insight to the special
circumstances and also outlines some advice.*

Worldwide, six million people are bereaved by a suicide death annually. In Ireland, almost two funerals a day are as a result of a person taking their own life. In 1999, 439 individuals chose to end their lives prematurely, without saying goodbye to their families and friends.

Although the effects of suicide on the bereaved are similar to other forms of natural death, they do differ in a number of ways. For the suicide bereaved, making sense of the death and coping with strong feelings of rejection, anger, guilt and disbelief become real issues for families. Typically, the act of suicide affects a wide circle of people, many of whom feel isolated and burdened after the event.

Immediate Reactions
Why?
Death by suicide is an overwhelming loss that can leave families and friends besieged by a range of emotions and many unanswered questions. While the pattern of grief is unique to

ECHOES OF SUICIDE

individuals, many families experience similar reactions. The need to understand why a person took his or her own life is one of the questions that a surviving family will face. Making sense of the death, trying to find an explanation and dealing with 'Could I have prevented the death?' or 'Am I to blame?' are all part of the emotional turmoil that the bereaved can experience.

Unfortunately, it is not always possible to understand – to fully piece together – the person's unique story. Although a stressful event may appear to have been the trigger, it will seldom have been the sole reason for death. Ultimately, the bereaved will have to live with their loss, in their own individual way, albeit without having all the answers. What is important is to grieve and to come to a state of acceptance. While grieving never completely ends, the pain will soften over time. Sometime over the course of grieving, a conscious choice to fully live life again may need to be made. Asking why is important, but sometimes the answer may never be found.

Suicide is often the result of a complex combination of several significant factors. In the end, there may be no way to fully understand the deceased's frame of mind at the time of death. Getting through the experience, moving beyond the puzzlement of why and learning to fully function again are important challenges in the grieving process.

Am I to blame? Could I have prevented it?
No, it is not your fault. It is now known that those who die by suicide are particularly vulnerable to stress. The majority of them have suffered from some form of an emotional illness that may not have been detected prior to their death. It is often not possible to have known that a loved one might take their own life. Even professionals acknowledge the limitations of making such predictions.

After a suicide, family and friends often go over the pre-death circumstances and events, blaming themselves for the things they think they should or should not have done. This common

Over time, the intensity of pain will lessen, but for some, it may be important to seek help outside the family in order to make personal sense of the tragedy. experience is a natural reaction, but varies in intensity within families and among the different members of the family.

Often, in trying to cope with the impact of the death, family members are unable to offer one another support. Individual family members respond differently to the death, depending on their relationship with the deceased. Frequently, feelings of hostility and bitterness towards one another may surface. For others, withdrawal or excessive talking may be their way of coping. Essentially, the common denominator in such communications is the need to put things into perspective. To express feelings and deal with the hunger for information and inner emotional turmoil.

Over time, the intensity of pain will lessen but for some, it may be important to seek help outside the family in order to make personal sense of the tragedy. For many, talking through one's feelings with a trusted friend or relative provides sufficient support in working through grief. For others, meeting people who have had a similar experience brings tremendous relief and a sense of comfort and healing.

Natural Responses
Feelings you may be experiencing now or in the future
The aim of this section is to describe some of the most common feelings experienced by the bereaved shortly after discovering the death. The intention is to reassure you that you are not going crazy and that such a state of mind is both understandable and to be expected at this time.

The aftermath of a death by suicide leaves family and friends with the most painful of emotional legacies. The loss of a loved one is sudden and alarming. Complete shock often masks the full realisation of what has happened. Images and painful memories may intrude by night and day.

As shock gives way to painful reality, there may be feelings of guilt and great mental anguish. Unfortunately, there is much ignorance and confusion surrounding a death by suicide. This is one reason why suicide survivors may find comfort in being with other individuals bereaved by a suicide death. It is advisable to obtain reassurance and support in order to maximise one's ability to get through this very dark time.

Grieving is a long, lonely road, marked by times of complete hopelessness and despair. There is no way of avoiding this pain. Losing someone by what may appear to be a deliberate decision will heighten specific aspects of grief. It is essential that you are aware of some of these feelings and how they may manifest within yourself, or your family and friends. It is important to remember, however, that each person will grieve in their own way, and that not everybody will experience the same feeling.

Guilt

In the face of such tragedy, there may be an overwhelming sense of regret, self-doubt or deep shame, characterised by a gnawing sense of persecution. These feelings may feel deeply rooted in your mind and body and may allow you little relief or personal solace. You may feel that your breathing is affected and may experience waves of panic. The questions that will shape in your mind will include:

'Why didn't I listen?'

'Why didn't I prevent this from happening?'

'Why didn't I give him/her more time?'

Such questioning usually takes the form of self-reproach and self-blame, whilst removing all responsibility from the person who has ended his or her life. Time and support is needed in order to come to the understanding that suicide is an individual act. No one person is in control of another person's fate.

Anger

Anger is an extremely physical emotion that grinds away at whatever strength you may be clutching on to. Anger makes you tense, extremely irritable and prone to huge swings of emotion. At times, there will be feelings of rage directed at yourself, the person who has died, family, friends and, very often, God. You may want to blame someone, and that scapegoat may be anyone who crosses your path. In a grieving family, several members will be experiencing these emotions at the same time. Most families have their secrets, and in times of trauma these may well surface. This death may be the latest in a series of stressful life events. The relationship may have been ambivalent. At times the deceased person's behaviour may have caused great frustration and you may have wished for them to go away. Please remember that this is not the reason for their death. This may well be the opportunity to seek out confidential support and enable some personal healing to take place.

Depression

Depression has often been described as anger turned in on oneself. Depending on your individual make-up, you may feel greater amounts of depression than anger, or alternatively you may swing widely between the two.

Depressive feelings include a sense of being pressed into a dark space, a sense of not being able to move or see any light at the end of the tunnel. Physically, you may feel totally exhausted during the day and lie awake at night, tossing and turning into the early hours. Your appetite may completely diminish or you may find yourself eating indiscriminately or bingeing in a self-punishing way. Alcohol abuse, gambling, drug or other compulsive behaviours may all take an upward spiral. You may be worried about yourself or other close relatives or friends of the deceased. This may be the time to visit you family doctor or contact the local Samaritans.

These are just some of the stronger emotions that characterise the early stages of mourning. There is, of course, a whole spectrum of feelings and actions associated with this time. Denial of what has happened is a form of self-protection, and it will take time, care and listening to come to terms with the reality of life without a loved one. You may wish to avoid outside communication for fear of stigma, family shame or to protect the loved one; you may feel people are avoiding you for the same reasons. Remember, you have complete control of how much information you wish to share with others. You are not expected to provide reasons or explanations as to why the person is dead. A simple statement, such as 'They ran out of steam or energy', is enough to suffice.

This is an extremely vulnerable time; it is important to take personal care and allow yourself to reach out and expect appropriate help.

What Do I Say to the Children?

The death of a sibling or parent is a very confusing experience for a child. Often, parents feel the need to cover up or communicate only part of the truth in order to protect their children. Parents worry that the child will not be able to cope with the reality of a death by suicide in the family. However, this approach fails to consider how resilient children actually are. It is extremely important that a child's feelings and questions are acknowledged in a supportive way. Such a response augurs well for their healthy emotional development in the future. Trying to hide the reality causes an unnecessary burden on adults and only postpones the resolution of grief in the child to later years.

Honest and truthful communication, shared in a loving and caring way, helps a child to deal with, and recover from, the traumatic experience. The key is to share the truth gradually, but always with respect to the age of the child. Gradual disclosure allows the child to ask questions and talk about worries as they arise. It also enables them to embrace the sadness of never seeing their loved one again.

A very young child may be satisfied with the fact that the relative had an accident and, because of it, died. However, an older child may need to know more details and will usually ask if they do. In answering, it is important to be as honest as possible by stating the facts as known.

Children initially respond to a death with shock and denial. Depending on their age, some children may react by screaming, crying or with withdrawn behaviour. Others become angry and fearful that the remaining parent might also leave them, or they may blame themselves for the death. Adults can help the young person by acknowledging their feelings, by listening and offering them the time and space to talk about the dead person and about themselves.

However, should a child continue over a long period to exhibit ongoing outbursts, sleep disturbance or withdrawn behaviour, professional help may be required.

How Do I Deal with Neighbors?
Remember that a death by suicide happens to all sorts of families and impacts on many people. The shocked family may find it hard to face the world and talk about the death. Alternatively, friends and relatives may feel uncomfortable and unable to offer consolation. While all kinds of loss are painful, the issues are different when dealing with a death by suicide. Generally, friends and neighbours are well meaning and want to give support, but may feel uncomfortable. They may be afraid to upset the family or think it's best to leave them alone.

It may be helpful to take the initiative, by simply stating that the death has happened and asking for practical help. If you are uncomfortable with talking about the death, don't. When ready, talk about the event and the feelings of loss and pain, with family, close friends or other survivors.

SUICIDE: THE FACTS — A WHOLE COMMUNITY RESPONSE

Barry McGale

Barry is the Suicide Awareness Co-ordinator for the Western Health & Social Services Board (WHSSB), Northern Ireland, Suicide Prevention Stategy. In this article he outlines the nature of this strategy – its relevance and applicability to other regions becomes clear in the description.

Suicide has become a major issue, with few communities untouched by it. Worldwide, an estimated three-quarters of a million people take their own lives each year. In Britain, approximately 84 do so each week. The number of suicides in Ireland in 1998 was equivalent to the loss of four Boeing 737s.[1]

The Conservative Government's White Paper 'Health of the Nation' (1992) identified a clear target for the reduction of suicide by 15 per cent by the year 2000, and the Labour Government have extended this target to a further 17 per cent by 2010 in their White Paper 'Our Healthier Nation' (1998). The important point to note, is that we can all play a part in achieving this target. Edwin Shneidman, the esteemed American suicidologist, describes suicide as a multi-dimensional malaise;

therefore, a multi-agency approach is required. This should be a co-ordinated approach involving government, health and social services, local authorities, voluntary agencies, the private sector and the media. In response to this, the WHSSB set up the multi-agency Suicide Prevention Steering Group in May 1996 to address this difficult and challenging issue.

An essential part of the Group's work is the dissemination of accurate information. Unfortunately, a taboo still surrounds suicide and this can perpetuate a lot of myths and misunderstandings. The Suicide Prevention Steering Group, therefore, feels that it is important that these myths and misunderstandings are corrected with research based factual information.

For examples of some of the myths surrounding suicide, you might like to look at Dr John F. Connolly's chapter, 'Suicide in the Media' (p. 117-8).

The Facts

- Suicide accounts for approximately 1 per cent of deaths annually

- It has risen by 85 per cent since 1980 in young males in the 15-24-year-old age group[2]

- The rate for women has remained stable or, in some areas declined

- There has been a 4 per cent decrease in the UK rate of suicide since 1993

- Suicide accounts for 19 per cent of all deaths amongst young people and, in the UK, is second only to road traffic accidents

- The highest suicide rates per 100,000 are still found amongst older people, particularly those aged over seventy-five

- Males tend to use more aggressive methods of suicide

- Of those who have engaged in deliberate self-harm about 1 per cent take their own lives the following year, a rate one hundred times that of the general population

One difficulty with suicide rates is that they may be influenced by factors outside health service control, such as employment levels and divorce rates.[3] Changes in suicide rates may therefore reflect changes in these factors rather than the success of any health service interventions.[4]

Help and Support
The Steering Group has identified four key areas within their Strategy for action.

1. Education
The Public
The Strategy suggests that the public should be more informed about mental ill health and how to access services. Indeed, research would indicate a link between suicide and depression, and a more informed public would be more likely to seek help earlier for this very treatable condition.

Two major mental health campaigns are held each year: The National Depression Campaign Day in April and World Mental Health Day in October. These help to create awareness of various mental health conditions and provide information on how to obtain help.

It is planned to establish a website that will outline the Suicide Prevention Strategy, and research based on aspects of suicidal behaviour.

A Mental Health Directory, highlighting the range of services available in the area, has been produced and distributed widely.

A leaflet entitled *Concerned About Suicide*, highlighting the warning signs, risk factors, facts and how to respond is being piloted later this year in the North Western, Western, Southern and North Eastern Health Board areas and, depending on its success, may be launched throughout Ireland.

Health Care Professionals
All staff working with potentially suicidal clients require training in suicide risk assessment and management.[5] The importance of this training has been reaffirmed in the UK National Confidential Inquiry into Suicide and Homicide report 'Safer Services' (1999) where it is stated that this training should be updated every three years. As a response to this, a 'rolling' programme on suicide risk assessment is delivered to both statutory and voluntary agency staff by the suicide awareness co-ordinators and the Western Area In-Service Training Consortium.

Depression awareness training has been delivered within the Board area to GPs, in keeping with the recommendations of a study carried out in Gotland, Sweden.[6]

An information leaflet entitled *Everybody Hurts, Sometimes…* has been designed for distribution to all people admitted to the General Hospitals, in the Board area, through deliberate self-harm. These leaflets highlight local and regional self-help organisations that relate to stressors identified in deliberate self-harm.

The Steering Group recognised the important role the clergy have to play in the area of suicide, and organised an interdenominational training day for all clergy called 'Facing Up To Suicide'. This training looked at the risk factors and experiences of the bereaved, and at how the clergy can enhance their role during such a difficult time.

Schools and Colleges of Further Education
Funding has been obtained from various bodies, both statutory and private, to develop a drama project called 'Under Pressure' targeting 14- to 16-year-olds. The 'Under Pressure' project aims to explore necessary skills that will enable young people to deal

with personal trauma, low self-esteem, personal and family crisis and conflict resolution.

Unfortunately, we can't remove the problems that our young people may face, but the least we can do is prepare them to cope with them, should they arise.

The project has three phases:

PHASE ONE OBJECTIVES
- To enable young people to discuss mental health issues that encroach on their every day life.
- To encourage young people to share experiences and to develop skills and confidence in a co-operative and dynamic way.
- To develop and implement a school-based programme of creative activity.

PHASE TWO OBJECTIVES
- To select four representatives from each of the pilot schools to participate in a cross-school drama project.
- To develop an after school project (two sessions per week over six weeks) that will lead to the creation of a performance, produced and directed by the young people.
- To tour with the performance, initially in the Foyle area.

PHASE THREE OBJECTIVES
- To set up an advisory group from both the statutory and voluntary sector involved in education and health and social services.
- To produce a resource pack for teachers and professional advisors, with lesson plans, classroom-based activities and details of support services.
- To produce an interactive CD-ROM package with support materials and learning programmes for schools.

2. Environment

The Strategy stresses the necessity to remove, reduce or make less accessible the means of suicide. One popular method used is that of Paracetamol overdosage. As a result of continued lobbying, the government introduced new legislation in September 1998 limiting the over the counter sale of Paracetamol to twelve tablets in blister packaging.

A multi-agency group has been set up in Derry to look at ways of making the River Foyle safer and less accessible to those contemplating taking their lives. This is building on the success of the Foyle Search and Rescue service that has reduced the numbers of people using this method.

3. Media

Evidence exists that the depiction of suicide in the media leads to increases in both method specific and overall suicide rates.[7] In response to this, the Steering Group produced Media Guidelines, entitled 'Working Together, Preventing Suicide' (1999) and The Irish Association of Suicidology and The Samaritans produced national Media Guidelines in 2000. The aims of the guidelines are to make the media aware of the complex issues surrounding suicide and to give guidance on how to report suicide in an effective and responsible way.

The 'Changing Minds: Every Family in the Land' campaign was launched in 1999 by the Irish Division of the Royal College of Psychiatrists. This is a four-year campaign to reduce the stigma and discrimination associated with mental health problems. The college will work collaboratively with other organisations to seek changes, not only in attitudes and behaviour, but also in legislation.

4. Research

The Prevention of Suicide Strategy shows that there is a need to further investigate the causes of suicide and deliberate self-harm.

To date, a number of studies have been carried out in Northern Ireland: a two-year psychological autopsy study[8] that provides a profile of individuals who are at risk of suicide, and two studies into deliberate self-harm in Altnagelvin Hospital.[9]

The research sub-group, consisting of members from statutory and voluntary agencies, has identified the following aims and objectives:

- to provide an information base to the Steering Group in terms of collation of local information on suicide and deliberate self-harm, evidence of effective interventions and information on other work going on elsewhere

- to provide a framework for evaluation of projects initiated by the Steering Group

- to assess available audit tools for voluntary and statutory services and develop strategies for incorporating them in the above services

- to develop a database of research projects, identify locally useful research projects, prioritise these and develop possible strategies of achieving completed research

The WHSSB is also taking part in the three year INSURE (Ireland North South Urban Rural Epidemiological) Project. This is an all Ireland collaborative epidemiological study of suicidal behaviour. The study is aimed primarily at estimating risk of suicide in psychiatric disorder, which, it has been hypothesised, will be age-dependent and may display regional variation.

The Project Board is also keen to ensure that those people who have been bereaved by suicide have input into the Strategy. The views of families, close relatives and friends who have direct experience of the trauma of death by suicide and its impact – both short and long term – are taken into account. Two ladies, bereaved by suicide, have been particularly valuable to the Steering Group; one who lost her son in 1996, completed her dissertation for her BSc (Hons) Degree into services for those bereaved by suicide and this has been useful in helping us review services. The other lady, who lost her husband, has written extensively on her personal experiences and regularly contributes to articles the media.

As a direct result of this input from those bereaved by suicide, a Bereavement Group has been set up in the area. This group is co-facilitated by trained staff from both the statutory and voluntary sector.

Future Initiatives
A questionnaire is to be distributed to all post-primary schools to ascertain the staff's knowledge on mental health issues, and to identify training needs. All-Ireland school guidelines, on how to manage the issue of suicide, are being designed by the youth section of the IAS and a booklet for families bereaved by suicide, looking at the feelings they might experience and at providing practical information, is being produced.

Conclusion
The work described in this paper is but a small contribution to the fight to reduce suicide, and it is hoped that the evaluation of this work will help to provide impetus and direction to those working within the field of suicide prevention.

Notes
1. IAS Media Guidelines 2000
2. Charlton, J. et al (1992). 'Trends in Suicide Deaths in England and Wales', *Population Trends No. 69* ONS, HMSO
3. Charlton et al. Op. cit.
4. Gunnell, D. (1994). 'The Potential for Preventing Suicide. A review of the literature on the effectiveness of interventions aimed at preventing suicide.', HCEU University of Bristol: Department of Epidemiology and Public Health Medicine

5. DHSS 1994

6. Rutz W, von Knorring L, Walinder J (1989). 'Frequency of suicide on Gotland after systematic postgraduate education of general practitioners.', *Acta Psychiatr Scandinavica.80:*151-4.

7. Schmidke A. and Hafner, H. (1988). The Werther effect after television films: new evidence for an old hypothesis. *Psychol. Med; 18:* 665-676.

8. Foster, T., Gillespie, K. and McClelland, R. (1997). Mental disorders and suicide in Northern Ireland. *British Journal of Psych., 170,* 447-452

9. Brown, T. (1996). An Analysis of Referrals for Deliberate Self-harm to the Social Care Department, Altnagelvin Hospital Trust. *Foyle Health and Social Services Trust:* (Unpublished)

SUICIDE: FROM A CRIME TO PUBLIC HEALTH IN A DECADE

Dan Neville TD

*Dan is President of the Irish Association of Suicidology.
In this contribution, he gives an overview of the development of
legislation in the area of suicide and its impact. He goes on to
chart the many challenges that still lie ahead to action the
suicide strategy effectively*

On 1 July 1993, President Mary Robinson signed into law the Criminal Law (Suicide) Act of 1993, which decriminalised suicide. For centuries, suicide had been a crime, and those who attempted it were charged with a criminal offence. Hanging for attempted suicide took place in London up to 1860. The last charge in our courts of attempted suicide was in 1967, the same year as suicide was decriminalised in the UK. Until suicide was decriminalised, the issue was a matter for the Department of Justice and was not regarded by the State as a public health issue.

In the first half of the nineteen sixties, an average of 64 people per annum died by suicide. In 1999, 439 people – 349 males and 90 females – died. This represents a seven-fold increase since the sixties.

Towards Legislation

The debate in the Dáil and Seanad in the early 1990s on the decriminalising of suicide was the first comprehensive examination of the subject by the Oireachtas. It played a key role in bringing suicide out of the hidden Ireland, and facilitated political debate on this serious public health issue. That Ireland was one of the last western democracies to have suicide and attempted suicide as a criminal act had a very serious implication for the bereaved.

In June of 1991 I published a Private Members Bill – 'The Suicide Bill 1991' – that proposed to decriminalise suicide. Even though this Bill fell at the second stage, a promise by the Government of the day to introduce its own bill did not occur until 1993, following a further two attempts in the intervening period.

On the morning of 28 April, the Minister for Justice, Mrs Maire Geoghegan-Quinn, published a Seanad Bill – the Criminal Law (Suicide) Bill 1993. This was almost word for word identical with my first 1991 Bill. Both Houses of the Oireachtas finally passed the Bill on 3 June 1993.

The decriminalisation of suicide has helped to reduce the stigma surrounding the subject, and has removed the added stress of knowing that a loved one who suffered death by suicide or those who attempted suicide are treated under the law as criminals.

National Task Force on Suicide

Papers on suicide prevention, presented to the Association of Health Boards in Ireland in April of 1994 by Dr John Connolly, Chief Psychiatrist, St Mary's Hospital, Castlebar and Secretary of the Irish Association of Suicidology, and Dr Ann Cullen, a psychiatrist and Director of the Association of Suicidology, received unprecedented attention from delegates. On the information outlined, I introduced two Adjournment Motions in Seanad Eireann, one responded to by the Minister for State, Mr

Tom Kitt TD of the Fianna Fail/Labour Government on 24 May 1994 and the other by Mr Brian O'Shea TD, Minister for State at the Department of Health on 13 February 1995.

In the course of his contribution Minister O'Shea stated:

> My colleague, the Minister for Health, and I are open to suggestions on how, as a society, we can reduce the incidence of suicide in this country.

This prompted me to initiate contact with experts in the area.

I received a proposal from Dr Michael J. Kelleher, Clinical Director of Psychiatry in the Southern Health Board and Director of the National Suicide Research Foundation, to set up an expert group to examine the situation. We had meetings over the summer of 1995 and finally met the then Minister for Health, Mr Michael Noonan TD, on 25 August 1995. Dr Kelleher's proposals were discussed at this meeting, and the Minister fully took on board an established a National Task Force on Suicide on the lines Dr Kelleher had proposed.

The Report of the National Task Force on Suicide was published in January of 1998. This was the culmination of detailed analysis, discussions and consideration of the factors and causes of suicide and attempted suicide. An interim report had been published in September of 1996, which defined numerically and quantitively the nature of the suicide problem, and also the problems of attempted suicide and parasuicide in Ireland. In his foreword to the final report the Minister for Health and Children, Mr Brian Cowen TD stated

> In order to tackle the growing tragedy in our society it is essential that a clear, systematic approach aimed at the prevention of suicide and suicidal behaviour is put in place.

Task Force Recommendations

The Report made recommendations on how service providers can most cost-effectively address the problems of attempted suicide and parasuicide. It identified the various authorities with jurisdiction and suicide prevention strategies, and their respective responsibilities and outlined a National Suicide Prevention/Reduction Strategy.

While many of the recommendations have been introduced, I am deeply dissatisfied with the level of urgency in introducing a comprehensive suicide reduction strategy. Many of the Task Force recommendations require continuous development, particularly in the area of training and in the development of services relating to suicide and suicide prevention.

The National Suicide Review Group was established in response to the final report on the National Task Force on Suicide. It first met in June of 1998 and reports directly to the Chief Executive Officers of the Regional Health Boards. It has broad terms of reference that effectively give it responsibility to oversee implementation of the recommendations of the Task Force.

> Many of the Task Force recommendations require continuous development, particularly in the area of training and in the development of services...

The Group has established contact with different agencies in the area of suicide prevention. It has been encouraging initiatives in research and intervention and it has been actively supporting the efforts of all those attempting to deal with the burden of suicidal behaviour in Ireland. The group includes experts in the areas of mental health, public health and research.

Health Boards have established working groups to examine the implementation of the recommendations of the Task Force. The working groups are multi-sectoral and multi-disciplinary and engage in the promotion of positive mental health and the destigmatisation of suicide, to provide information in relation to suicide and parasuicide, liase with the media and provide training requirements for staff in relation to all aspects of suicide and parasuicide.

Resource Officers with responsibility for implementing recommendations of the Task Force have been appointed in all Health Boards. Their responsibilities include the recruitment of additional staff, the provision of staff training in risk assessment, production of information literature and events aimed at creating public awareness of suicide and parasuicide.

The Task Force also recommended that steps be taken to make the mental health services more accessible to the public, particularly to young people. Concern was also expressed at the risk of suicide in older people. In 2001, £830,000 has been provided towards suicide prevention and towards suicide research aimed at improving the understanding of this issue. Additional funding has been made available to further develop consultant-led child and adolescent psychiatry and old-age psychiatry services to assist in the early identification of suicidal behaviour and provide the necessary support and treatment to individuals at risk.

This year an additional £100,000 has been allocated to the National Suicide Research Foundation in Cork to support its work in the development of a National Parasuicide Register.

The National Task Force identified that a multi-department approach should be taken to deal with the problem. Contact is maintained between the Departments of Health and Children, Justice, Equality and Law Reform, Education and Science, Environment and Local Government with a view to implementing the Task Force's recommendation.

All the statutory agencies identified in the Report with jurisdiction and suicide prevention strategies have been approached by the Department of Health and Children requesting that the necessary measures be put in place to ensure implementation of the recommendations that relate to their respective areas.

Data on mortality is routinely published in the annual and quarterly reports on vital statistics compiled by the Central Statistics Office. Recording of the instances of suicide by the CSO is dependent on information set out in Form 104 completed by the Garda Síochána in respect of each inquest and forwarded to the CSO.

Ongoing Challenges

I believe that there is urgent need for a more proactive approach in introducing the recommendations of the Task Force on Suicide. It is not acceptable that the State has failed to set up an extensive network of community based psychiatric services, bringing specialised multi-disciplinary psychiatric services within easy reach and accessibility of all citizens and referral agencies to their psychiatric services which are readily available and acceptable to all.

The Department of Health must introduce training for the relevant health care personnel and give continuing education in matters relating to suicidal behaviour.

It is not acceptable that the Department of Justice, Equality and Law Reform has failed to ensure that coroners receive special training in psychological management of highly sensitive issues, with particular reference to adjudicating on matters such as suicide. The coroners hearing is one of the most traumatic experiences of the suicide bereaved.

It is not acceptable that the Department of Education and Science has failed to support teachers in respect of psychological and social dimension of their work through undergraduate and continued professional educational courses.

Inadequate progress has been made in initiating programmes teaching children about positive health issues, including coping strategies and basic information about positive mental health, at an early age as a natural part of their health education.

No move has been made whatsoever to cater for young people in the out-of-school sector. There is a higher rate of suicide amongst early school leavers than amongst those who remain in school. The Department of Health and Children has made no effort to work with youth services, or to develop a social and personal health education programme, which should include modules on depression awareness and anger-control skills.

The State must provide access to appropriate support services for children and young people in crisis and should provide them with a comprehensive range of psychological and counselling services.

No consideration has been given by the Department of Health and Children to the psychological needs of older people often due, for example, to isolation or bereavement. These issues must be separately addressed by counselling and social intervention, and by the provision of specialised psychiatric services for older people.

Inadequate research has been done with regard to the removing of the means that are used to commit suicide. A strong programme of teaching children to swim should be introduced as part of their general education. A programme of life-saving should be made available at all places where there is easy access to water, and all applications for firearms should be more carefully scrutinised.

> The State must provide access to children and young people at a time of crisis to appropriate support services and a comprehensive range of psychological and counselling services.

I welcome the recent decision of the Minister for Health and Children, Mr Mícheál Martin TD, who has ordered that, from 1 October 2001, supplies of Paracetamol, sold in shops other than pharmacies will be limited to pack sizes not exceeding twelve tablets, and these to be contained in a blistered pack. There will also be limitations on pharmacists, unless an authorised person has interviewed the customer requesting the product and is satisfied that it is safe. In such circumstances, the quantity must not exceed fifty tablets. The Minister has further ordered that the paracetamol products must be clearly marked with advice on usage. I welcome the decision of the Minister to make this order,

Concern over how individual suicides are reported in the media has arisen from studies that have indicated a risk of copycat suicides, particularly amongst adolescents and young adults...

however, it falls far short of what is required. I believe that the sale of all paracetamol products should be restricted to chemist shops only.

In 1999 there were 3,406 cases of self-inflicted poisoning. Of these 1,003 were poisoning diagnosed as paracetamol poisoning. Of these, 350 were male and 688 were female. A reduction in the number of poisonings could be effected by controlling paracetamol products.

Association of Suicidology

A welcome development in suicide prevention occurred in January of 2000, when President Mary McAleese, Patron of the Irish Association of Suicidology launched media guidelines on the portrayal of suicide that were compiled jointly by the Irish Association of Suicidology and the Samaritans.

During the early 1990s, Dr Michael J. Kelleher spoke about his intention to establish a National Association dealing with suicide. In 1995, he contacted me and confirmed his intention to establish this association, and invited me to be the founding President.

The Irish Association for Suicidology had its inaugural meeting in Adare on 26 October 1996. Dr Kelleher was appointed Chairman and Dr John Connolly was elected Secretary/Treasurer.

We felt there was no doubt of the need for an organisation such as this to act as a forum and meeting point for all those interested in suicidology. For too long, the many groups – professional, voluntary and self-help – involved in this field have ploughed a lonely furrow, each in isolation. No one group has an answer to the tragic, multi-faceted problem of suicide. It is only by the concerted efforts of all acting in unison that it will be possible to achieve the objectives of the Irish Association of Suicidology which are:

- to promote awareness of the problems of suicide and suicidal behaviour in the general public by holding conferences and workshops, and by the communication of relevant material through the media
- to ensure that the public is better informed about suicide prevention
- to support and encourage relevant research
- to encourage and support the formation of groups that help those bereaved by suicide

The Association is affiliated to the International Association for Suicide Prevention, this means that it is protected from parochialism, and will allow its members both to influence developments on a larger stage and benefit from innovative work done in other jurisdictions. Through its public meetings, its publications and the publications of its members, it intends to influence the media in its reporting of suicide, so that the Irish community at large will benefit from the endeavours of those who, in their diverse ways, are tackling suicide and its aftermath.

Our Association and its individual members have played a leading role in highlighting this sad and tragic issue, and focusing attention on the need to introduce suicide prevention programmes based on comprehensive research and responding to the cultural and societal circumstances. The present Chairman of the Irish Association of Suicidology is Professor Roy McClelland of Queens University, Belfast.

Suicide visits an extreme and unique trauma on the bereaved. In former times, this grief was borne in an unspoken and very isolated manner. While the loss has not diminished, in more recent times at least suicide has been given a voice and those who have suffered this bereavement are coming together and supporting each other. Our society has moved to address the isolation and to provide a range of resources at a personal and professional level. While there is much work still to be done, a beginning has been made.

SUICIDE AND THE MEDIA

Dr John F. Connolly

*John is Chief Psychiatrist,
St Mary's Hospital, Castlebar, Co Mayo.
He is also Hon. Secretary, Irish Association of Suicidology.*

Suicide contagion, copycat suicides or the so-called 'Werther Effect' have been of great concern to all involved in the field of suicidology. The book *The Sorrows of Young Werther,* a novel by Goethe, set off a number of copycat suicides in Europe after its publication in 1774 and, as a result, was banned in many countries. The role of the media in such phenomena has been known for a considerable time. The media can have a positive or negative effect in the way they report mental health issues and suicide. They can educate and promote growth and health, or they can sensationalise and promote unhealthy stereotypes and a view of mental illness and mental health that may make the public slow to seek treatment for their problems.

The effect of the media, however, is only one factor involved in some suicides. Suicide is a complex phenomenon and the paths to suicide are varied and many. There is no single cause for suicide but many interweaving influences and factors that come together to shape that final horrific act. Factors that are highly associated with completed suicide are well documented, and all are important in devising suicide prevention programmes. Of great concern, is the role of the media in promoting suicide and in causing copycat suicides and suicide clusters, in particular. In this chapter the scientific evidence for the effect of the media is discussed and some points proposed, that after discussion with all parties involved, might form the basis for the development of ethical guidelines for the reporting of suicides and matters relating to suicide. This is an important issue, as in suicide prevention it may be one factor that is relatively easy to control.

There is no single cause for suicide, but many interweaving influences and factors that come together to shape that final horrific act.

Clustering of suicides is a not uncommon phenomenon, and has been well studied. Suicide clusters are most common among the young but become very rare in older age groups. There is however, increasing evidence that copycat suicide may be more common in the elderly than previously realised. The young and the elderly are perhaps less integrated into society than those at work.

Research Evidence

Clusters are difficult to define and there is no universally agreed definition of a cluster. Suicide clusters represent a dramatic increase in observed over expected suicides in a community.[1] A working and acceptable definition may be three or more suicides that occur in a defined period in a particular area. Copycat suicides and clusters may occur following direct exposure to the suicide of a friend or acquaintance, as in cases where the victims were known to each other, or through indirect exposure where the victims knew of the initial suicide in the cluster only through accounts in the media or by word of mouth. It has been noted that persons attempting suicide had an unusually large number of suicidal friends.[2] Sometimes suicide clusters are compared to an epidemic or outbreak of a disease, which will end when all those susceptible to the disease will have contracted it or, in this case, have completed suicide. The precise nature of the imitative process is not understood.

Some risk factors or indicators of susceptibility for suicide clusters identified by researchers are common to suicides in general. These included emotional illness, previous suicide attempts, loss, family instability and family dysfunction, problems of alcohol and drug abuse. Those with a history of interpersonal violence, previous suicide attempts or self-destructive actions may be at greater risk for imitating an earlier suicide in the cluster. Others at increased risk include teenagers whose lives are disrupted by more frequent changes in residence, schools, or parental figures.

Romanticised or sensational media coverage of suicide may foster an affinity with those who completed suicide and confer an aura of celebrity on them.

Their experience with suicide and interpersonal violence were more likely to have included damaging self, threatening suicide, attempting suicide, injuring others and being close to others who die violently. They were more likely to have been arrested, have an emotional illness or substance abuse problem serious enough to have required hospitalisation, were more easily hurt and more likely to have lost a boyfriend or girlfriend in the year they died.

Individuals are more likely to imitate a model's suicide if they identify with the characteristics they attribute to the model. During a cluster of suicides, potential suicides may identify more closely with those who die violently if their own past includes similar violent experiences, such as suicide attempts, threats or interpersonal violence.

Since teenagers susceptible to suicide in the cluster did not show greater exposure to suicide, those teenagers who killed themselves may have been more vulnerable to the effects of exposure to suicide. Thus small degrees of exposure could have had a large effect on susceptible persons.

Romanticised or sensational media coverage of suicide may foster an affinity with those who complete suicide and confer an aura of celebrity on them. Many of these findings are confirmed in other studies.

Studies show that significant clustering of suicides occurred mostly among teenagers and young adults with minimal effect after the age of twenty-four. The magnitude of the clustering effect is in the order of 1-2 per cent with a range of 1-13 per cent. They conclude that the relative risk of suicide, following the suicide of one or more persons, may be relatively greater than normal. They also conclude that though the number of youth suicides that occur in clusters is small, they represent a class of suicides that may be particularly preventable.[3]

The studies of Philips (1974) and Philips and Carstensen (1985) prove the contagion effect. Many had held that news coverage of suicides only served to bring forward suicides that would have occurred anyway. If this precipitation theory were correct, then a post-story rise in suicides should be followed by an equally large drop below normal expect rates caused by people moving up their death dates. No such drop was found.

Philips found that following suicide stories, single death motor vehicle fatalities increased by about 9 per cent in the week after a suicide story. Single occupant motor vehicles 'accident' fatalities are frequently disguised suicides and account for about 6 per cent of all suicides. Most of the observed increase occurred on the third day. The increase was greatest on the area where the story was most heavily publicised, and the more publicity the suicide received, the greater the increase of such 'accidents'. The drivers involved in these 'accidents' were unusually similar to the person described in the story. No such similarity was found between the publicised suicide and the passengers who died just after the story or indeed drivers who died in multiple vehicle crashes after the story.

The impact of these stories usually lasted for about seven days. The effect on suicide rates was small, except for teenagers where the increase was in the order of 22 per cent. This study was carried out in California and if the results were to be extrapolated for the USA as a whole, the suicides of this nature would have increased by just under 2000.

Interestingly, the authors compare suicide stories with advertisements and conclude that, as with advertisements, the more dramatic the suicide story line, the more prominence it gets, the more frequent the repetition and the more people can identify with the subject of the story the greater the effect. This is particularly so if the negative consequences of the suicide – pain and disfigurement – are not mentioned.

One study looked at suicide in Portsmouth in England, following newspaper stories of suicide. They compared the number of observed suicides with the expected suicides for two, four and seven days after the story. They found that violent suicides were more likely to be given longer and more detailed multiple reports.[4] Violence, it seems, is always newsworthy

An Model of Good Reporting Of Suicide
More recently a series of articles on the 'Kurt Cobain Suicide' crisis was published in Suicide and Life Threatening Behaviour (1996) and the conclusions therein may form a worthwhile basis for the development of a code of practice for the reporting of suicide.

The impact of the suicide of Kurt Cobain on suicide and the use of the crisis clinic in Seattle were scrutinised. The expected Werther effect or suicide cluster did not occur. There was an increase in the suicide crisis calls. The lack of a copycat suicides may have been due to various aspects of the media coverage, the method used in Cobain's suicide, and the crisis centre and outreach interventions that occurred.

A legend in his time, the lead singer and song writer for Nirvana could not adjust to his success. As a child, he had treatment for hyperactivity and had problems of conduct. He had a long history of alcohol and substance abuse. In addition, as a child he suffered from chronic stomach pain and severe depression. There was also a history of chronic suicidal preoccupation and interest in guns. In March 1994 he overdosed on champagne and tranquillisers. Eventually he killed himself with a shotgun wound to his head, at a time when he had high blood levels of valium and heroin. Needless to say, the suicide of such a celebrity received great publicity. The local crises centres feared a great increase in suicide in the immediate aftermath of Cobain's death.

The crisis centre acknowledged Cobain's suicide along with the thousands of others that occur each year and hosted a press conference. At a special vigil Cobain's wife made an impassioned speech, making clear to all the awfulness and needlessness of what had happened and the hurt and anger it had caused those close to the deceased. All of this succeeded in de-romanticising the event.

Only one suicide in a seven-week period was linked to Cobain's suicide and was a typical copycat suicide. Fewer suicides occurred immediately following Cobain's death than in the same period in the previous year.

The articles raise many interesting points:

- news coverage of suicide cannot be prevented as such stories are often newsworthy and will be reported

- all parties should understand that there is a scientific basis for concern that news coverage may contribute to the causation of suicide

- some characteristics of news coverage may contribute to contagion and other characteristics may help prevent suicide

- public officials and the news media should carefully consider what is to be said and reported regarding suicide

In the aftermath of Cobain's death, reportage showed a high degree of professionalism and responsibility and succeeded in separating Cobain the musician from Cobain the drug addict and suicide. His violent death by use of a shotgun served to remove any romantic image of a misunderstood lonely star. His wife's action and impassioned speech made the death disturbing and real, and showed it to be tragic, selfish and wasteful, as are all suicides. The news coverage increased public awareness about suicide and gave information about outreach and helping services, available treatments and means of accessing them.

The risk factors for suicide are:

- easy access to means of committing suicide
- a history of psychiatric illness, particularly major depression
- a previous suicide attempt
- a history of suicide in the family
- a history of personality or behaviour disorder
- drug or alcohol abuse
- family breakdown or conflict and other relationship breakdown
- physical or sexual abuse
- absence of a confiding relationship
- unemployment
- physical illness

Cobain had many of these risk factors: depression, substance abuse, gun ownership, non-compliance with treatment, family breakdown, a previous suicide attempt and a history of personality and behaviour disorder.

Myths About Suicide

The media must take on board and help to dispel the common myths about suicide held by the general public and unfortunately, also by many in the helping professions. All of these myths have been disproved by scientific research. The myths include:

- Those who talk about suicide are the least likely to attempt it – *not true about 80 per cent of those who take their lives will have talked about it to some significant other in the few months before hand*

- If someone is going to complete suicide they are going to do it and there is nothing you can do about it – *the majority of those who take their own lives are ambivalent about doing so until the end. Most people who complete suicide do not want to die they just want to end their pain*

- You can get a good idea how serious someone is about a suicide attempt by looking at the method used – *not true. Most people have little awareness of the lethality of what they are doing. The seriousness of the attempt is not necessarily related to the seriousness of the intent*

- If some one has a history of making cries for help then they won't do it for real – *not true. The group of people at highest risk for suicide are those who have attempted it in the previous year*

- Only the clinically depressed make serious suicide attempts – *not true people are also at risk suffering from other forms of psychiatric illness and emotional distress*

- Those with personality disorder attempt suicide to manipulate others – *a commonly held belief. Many a patient is alienated and an ideal opportunity for therapeutic intervention missed because of the reception the receive in some emergency departments*

- If someone is going to commit suicide they will not tell anyone of their intentions and prepare well in advance – *not true. Many suicides are completed on impulse*

- Talking about suicide encourages it – *not true. Raising the issue of suicide with those who are depressed or distressed may open the door to therapeutic intervention*

- Suicide can be a blessed relief not just for the individual but those surrounding him or her – *not true. Bereavement by suicide is a very heavy cross to bear; those bereaved by suicide have special needs and need special support. Bereavement by suicide is itself a risk factor for suicide.*

Some Guidelines For Reporting Suicide

While education in matters relating to suicide is important, we must refrain from repetitive reporting and preoccupation with such matters. There is a danger that such preoccupation may make it appear that suicide is an acceptable solution to problems of living.

In summary then, the media can help by paying attention to the following points in the knowledge that they arise from valid research:

- avoid simplistic explanations of suicide: completed suicide is the end result of a process involving many complex, interwoven factors
- debunk the common myths about suicide, the most common of which are detailed earlier
- highlight the underlying factors involved in suicide and avoid creating stereotypes and, particularly, try to break down gender stereotypes
- include information on further sources of support and advice, including general education about public health issues
- avoid 'how-to' descriptions of suicide in reports: the less detail of the mechanisms used the better
- avoid repetitive, ongoing coverage of suicide stories, especially of youth suicides as this may promote an

unhealthy preoccupation with suicide among the young

- don't romanticise or glorify suicide: some reports may seem as if the community is honouring suicide
- don't over-emphasise the positive characteristics of the deceased person, the mistaken impression can be created that suicide is an acceptable response to an everyday life crisis; left out may be all the problems, which the deceased experienced
- the media should exercise vigorously its right to question: for example, by questioning bad practice

Professionals in the health services and personnel from voluntary organisations working in the field of suicidology need special training in dealing with the media. This must start with an examination of our own prejudices about mental illness. The fashion in which the media portray mental illness, and the stereotyped negative view of psychiatry, are reasons why many people fail to seek help for what are, in effect, life threatening – though in most cases treatable – illnesses. It is important that we use appropriate language. The majority of guidelines for the portrayal of suicide in the media suggest to journalists the sort of wording they should use in reporting suicide such as:

- a suicide
- die by suicide
- a suicide attempt
- a completed suicide
- person at risk of suicide
- help prevent suicide

Many professionals use language in interviews that may stigmatise. How many of us talk about 'committing suicide' rather than completing suicide or dying by suicide? Crimes are committed, suicide is not a crime, and by using the word committed we may perpetuate stigma.

The fashion in which the media portray mental illness and the stereotyped negative view of psychiatry, are reasons why many people fail to seek help for what are in effect life threatening, though in most cases, treatable illnesses.

In addition, we must challenge the myths, which we share with the general population, about suicide. In many respects, organisations such as health authorities try to control the media too much and are to slow to respond to requests for information. This often happens because we are unaware of the pressure and deadlines under which the media work. Many matters, suicide included, are newsworthy and will and must be reported. If health officials are not to impart information, the reporters must do the best they can with the data available to them. The United States Centers for Disease Control and Prevention, in its guidelines for the reporting of suicide, states that 'when information is provided for the media, it should be given in an efficient and accurate manner.' In addition, they point out that 'no comment or a general refusal to speak to the media is not a useful response.' Responses such as these may create an adversarial relationship with the media and miss the chance to influence and shape the information that is made known to the public.

Growth of the Internet

In discussing the media, we must not forget the Internet. There are numerous sites on this medium devoted to the promotion of mental health and the prevention of suicide. Some of these are aimed at the dissemination of information and the education of professionals. A number of organisations, such as The Irish Association of Suicidology (www.ias.ie), The American Association of Suicidology (www.suicidology.org), The Samaritans (www.samaritans.org.uk), The World Federation For Mental Health (www.wfmh.com) and The International

Association for Suicide Prevention (www.who.int/ina-ngo/ngo/ngo027.htm) have very useful data. Many pharmaceutical companies have developed useful sites disseminating information on everything from depression, schizophrenia and Alzheimer's disease to promotion of their own products.

We must be alert to the fact that there are other more sinister sites available, which appear to actively promote suicide. Young men are the group most vulnerable and the most likely to complete suicide in western society at the present time, and there is a danger that they may be too influenced by such sites. They are also the group that uses the net most. It is a worrying thought that these most vulnerable in our society are the most likely to come across these sinister sites, and that little can be done to control or limit access to them.

Conclusions

The media have a duty to promote positive mental health, demystify psychiatric illness and help combat public prejudice and misconceptions about it. There is ample evidence that the effects of the negative and discriminatory stereotyping of the mentally ill acts to deter people from seeking appropriate psychiatric help for their problems. This is tragic, as suicide is associated very frequently with depressive illness, which is eminently treatable.

In relation to suicide and mental health issues, the media can be a powerful influence for good, encouraging education and positive attitudes and promoting collaboration between community groups to take us some way along the road to a healthier society.

Professionals and volunteers dealing with suicide and suicidal behaviour must learn to foster good relationships with the media and foster an alliance with them based on mutual trust and understanding.

The World Wide Web and email need further study and may prove to be very therapeutic tools in suicide prevention

Notes

1. Davidson, Rosenberg, Mercy, Franklin and Simmons (1989). 'An Epidemiological Study of Risk Factors in Two Teenage Suicide Clusters', *JAMA 262* pp. 2687 et seq.
2. Kreitman et al (1969). Attempted Suicide in Social Networks
3. Gould, Wallenstein, Kleinman, O'Carroll and Mercy (1990). *American Journal of Public Health, Vol 80,* pp. 211-2
4. Barraclough, B., Shepherd, D., Jennings, C. (1977) 'Do Newspaper reports of coroners' inquests incite people to commit suicide?', *British Journal of Psychiatry* 131:528-32

REFLECTIONS ON A SOCIETY

John Lonergan

As Governor of Mountjoy Prison in Dublin, John is in a unique position to reflect on Irish society at a time when, in our apparent success, so many are left behind, isolated and ignored. He challenges us to pick away at the veneer of the economic Celtic miracle and look to the state of the person, the family... what is being lost... what is worth fighting for... It is in this context that the connection with suicide becomes clear.

We live in an era dominated by economics, when almost everything is measured or valued in monetary terms. How much the job pays, or how much the task is worth are all too often the first questions asked nowadays. What the job actually involves, or the issue of job satisfaction are very much secondary considerations. Money is put forward as the solution to most of our human problems and needs. We educate, coach and encourage our children to be competitive, engraining in them a philosophy of winner takes all. The TV programme 'The Weakest Link' illustrates this particular approach and, in my opinion, it is not just a coincidence that it is so popular. It very clearly reflects some of the most prominent values of our modern society. There is no room in our materialistic, driven society for those who fail to measure up. They are not only seen as liabilities, but are made to feel like embarrassments, social rejects, spongers, and, all too often, are treated as failures – if only we could vote them out of existence.

We all contribute to this culture. We readily take credit for the successes of our society and we are only too willing to boast of those within our own families who are seen as high achievers. How often do we compare one of our children with another, 'I wish you were as good as your brother, or your sister…' Do we ever consider how grossly unfair such comparisons are? First of all, if we love all our children equally there would be no room for this insensitive and hurtful attitude. Secondly, every child is totally unique and special and each one deserves the same respect as the next. Also, if we feel justified in claiming credit for our successes we must surely accept responsibility for those labelled as our failures.

The booming economy is presenting us with a wonderful opportunity, but also with a huge challenge. We must decide our priorities: people and their needs or the economy. This requires much soul-searching for all of us. Put bluntly, the economy must be managed to serve our society, and not the other way around. Of course, we should rejoice in our economic success, but we must reassess the priorities we give to human needs. We must ensure that the economy does not become a monster and, above all, we must made sure that people are not forced to become slaves to it.

Space for Human Needs

On reflection, therefore, it is not surprising that many young people feel under great pressure to meet the very high expectations we have of them. Those who fail to measure up often feel isolated, unwanted and rejected. Do we hear their cry for help or are we completely out of touch, are we much too busy even to think about their human needs, or worse, do we really care anymore? Loneliness and rejection are two of the most hurtful and traumatic of all human experiences. Young people are particularly vulnerable when they experience rejection. Their self-esteem takes a battering, and they are convinced that they are 'no-hopers'. As adults we must be very sensitive during such crisis periods and we must be most generous in giving our time to help them cope and overcome these negative experiences. I cannot over-emphasise the importance of this – we have a real responsibility not to be found wanting at such times. One of the most disturbing and negative consequences of our modern materialistically obsessed society is that we all feel too busy to spend time with those in need. We may be very generous financially, but money, which is usually the soft option, is definitely no substitute for personal attention. In our pursuit of materialism we have developed a hardness of heart which is preventing us from even noticing the pain around us. We are all social beings, and we need to have ongoing contact with other people for a variety of reasons. Certainly, we all need to be heard and this is particularly true in the cases of those in emotional distress, those located at the periphery of our society and those who feel broken and lost. How available and open are we to hearing those who are crying out for help? Is our first defence a refusal to hear based on the strategy, 'What I don't know won't trouble me'?

Hearing the Human Cry
The challenge facing all of us is this, how do we establish and maintain contact with those in our society who feel left out, unwanted and marginalised? How can we do it within our own families? Do we want real people with all the human vulnerability that goes with them, or people with a successfully created image with robot-like characteristics? Children have lots and lots of human needs, which can only be met if they are given the space and opportunity to be normal, displaying both their strengths and weaknesses. We adults are the only role models available to them. Fundamentally, what sort of a role model am I? The answer will be found only when I look into my own heart.

3

THE RESPONSE OF
THE SCHOOL
COMMUNITY

SUICIDE: PRACTICAL RESPONSES IN THE POST-PRIMARY SCHOOL

Siobhán Foster-Ryan

In this chapter, Siobhán explores how the school community can respond to the particular challenges and concerns raised by suicide. She examines the place of a Crisis Response Team at the time of a suicide and offers a comprehensive range of practical suggestion to support the school. Siobhán is a post-primary teacher with a Masters degree in Guidance and Counselling. She is currently on secondment to the Department of Education and Science, in the area of Social, Personal and Health Education. She is also on the national executive of the Irish Association of Pastoral Care in Education.

The death by suicide of a student is a devastating event for the school community. Research shows that the group in society most at risk to suicide is the young male. While significantly lower in number, the death rate for young females through suicide has more than doubled in recent years. Another startling fact is that half of all paracides in Ireland are aged under twenty-five. Adolescents are especially vulnerable, due to the particular physical and emotional changes that are occurring and the stresses that accompany this developmental period. Therefore it is clear that the school community cannot ignore suicide, but rather must explore how it can address the issue in a constructive manner.

The School Community

This chapter will explore a comprehensive framework to guide the school in its multi-dimensional response involving all partners in the school community. This framework will be outlined under the three major phases widely recognised in the research in this field:

Prevention – what the school community can do to create a preventative environment around suicide.

Intervention – strategies the school can employ when a tragedy occurs.

Postvention – supports to put in place over the medium and long term following a suicide event.

Central to this framework is the establishment of a **Crisis Response Team** that will form the core of the whole-school approach to suicide. This approach is built upon the relationship that teachers have with their students. They are in a unique position to offer specific support to students in a time of tragedy. While there is no claim that what follows is in any way exhaustive, it is hoped that the range of areas addressed and the strategies suggested will provide a practical framework for a school community to address issues of suicide in a sensitive and effective manner. With this in mind, it may help the reader to reflect on the following questions as they consider the situation in their own context:

- what is effective in the areas of prevention, intervention and postvention?
- what areas need to be addressed?
- what specific steps can be taken?

PREVENTION

So often, the focus around suicide is about intervention at the time of the tragedy. It is vital to step back from the event and explore how a school can contribute to an environment that will be resourceful in the prevention of suicide. While the school on its own cannot take responsibility for the ultimate decision of the individual, it can be a resource to support the person in crisis. Before programmes or structures are put in place in terms of prevention, we must articulate the values and attitudes that ground them. These values will influence the school's ability to provide a healthy, safe and respectful environment for the student, a place that offers a range of 'connection points' that will be especially helpful in times of difficulty. Therefore, a co-ordinated approach that is directed to the whole school community is required, in tandem with a focused response to students most at risk.

Policy Development

Having a comprehensive approach to suicide will provide an important source of guidance when a crisis occurs. It needs to be part of the overall policy on Social, Personal and Health Education, (SPHE) drawn up in a consultative process involving all the relevant partners in the school community – management, staff, parents, students, educational and community agencies. This policy should also address such related areas as substance misuse, anti-bullying, relationships and sexuality. Specifically, the area of the policy dealing with suicide should address:

- suicide Prevention Programmes
- whole-staff inservice
- roles and responsibilities of a Crisis Response Team
- collaboration with support agencies and professional personnel
- communicating with parents

- referral structures
- ongoing support for students at risk

Suicide Prevention Programmes

Research shows that one of the ways to decrease the incidence of adolescent suicide is to empower the student to cope with everyday stresses of adolescence. Any suicide prevention programme or strategy is best placed within the SPHE framework that seeks to develop the well-being of the whole person. SPHE aims to:

- enable students to develop skills for self-fulfilment and living in communities
- promote self-esteem and self-confidence
- enable the students to develop a framework for responsible decision making
- provide opportunities for reflection and discussion
- promote physical, mental and emotional health and well-being

(Department of Education & Science Guidelines on SPHE)

It is in this context that the programme developed by Michael Ryan – detailed later in this publication – will provide a very specific guide to dealing with issues of bereavement, loss and suicide in the school setting. One of the values of this programme is the manner in which it promotes links with community mental health agencies and support groups. These links are an invaluable resource to the teacher facilitating the programme. The Irish Association of Pastoral Care in Education (IAPCE) offers training for teachers in this programme nationwide.

It is important to recognise also that there are other areas in the school curriculum where opportunities for dealing with bereavement, loss and suicide present themselves. In particular, Religious Education provides a valuable context to deal with these issues from a faith perspective.

Identifying Students at Risk

Normally it is a small group of suitably trained teachers who facilitate the preventative programmes, however, every teacher can contribute to identifying students at risk. Because they are in daily contact with their students, teachers are best placed to observe potential warning signs of suicidal behaviour. In outlining the following signs, it is important to remember that no one factor can offer conclusive evidence, but rather may be indicative of a student in need:

- significant change in behaviour, particularly if the student becomes withdrawn
- a fall-off in school performance
- substance and alcohol abuse
- episodes of anxiety and depression
- withdrawal from favourite activities
- risk-taking or aggressive behaviour evident in the classroom context
- recent loss or break-up of a close relationship
- expressing feelings of failure, uselessness, hopelessness or loss of self-esteem – these may be manifest in the written or art work of the student
- unusual neglect of personal appearance and hygiene
- preoccupation with or statements about suicide
- change from depression to sudden elation and no longer preoccupied with suicide

Dealing with a Suicidal Student

A dilemma that teachers may face is the student in crisis who says, 'I want to kill myself', 'I wish I was dead'. The intention in any response is to bridge the importance of being a supportive presence for the student while helping him or her move forward to seek more appropriate professional help. This help will come from the pastoral team, in particular the guidance counsellor.

The following steps act as a guide to teachers in such a conversation before a referral:

- Be aware of your own responses and feelings, but keep them in check.
- Be calm – panic will only increase the student's distress and may jeopardise your own ability to respond.
- It is important not to ignore the expression of suicidal thoughts or intentions by the student. At the same time, try to recognise the often temporary nature of these thoughts, as impulsiveness is a common feature of adolescent suicidal behaviour.
- Be reassured by the fact that the student is talking. It demonstrates, at some level, that he or she is not yet at a point to carry out this threat. Suicidal students are often relieved to find someone willing to listen to them.
- Begin by asking an open question like 'What has you so upset?' Encourage the student to verbalise their feelings and thoughts.
- Explore how long they have been feeling this way, and accept what they have to say without judgement. Show that you care by making it clear that you understand and are really concerned for the student.
- Ask if they have spoken to anyone else. Through this question you are trying to discover if there are any other trust figures in the student's life.
- In this situation, a student will often paint a bleak picture of every aspect of their life. It would be worthwhile to try to check this out, as the reality is rarely as bleak as they perceive it to be. You could ask about some of the following: school, exams, friends, boyfriends or girlfriends, home, parents, siblings.
- The most important reassurance to offer is that you recognise their pain, while at the same time communicating that they can be supported through it.

- Do not make false promises that things will get better immediately.
- Do not get tied into any confidential pacts.
- Ensure that the student is not left alone.
- Arrange for the student to meet with the guidance counsellor as soon as possible.
- Where appropriate, support the follow-up steps agreed with the guidance counsellor.
- You may find it helpful to talk with a colleague or friend about the experience and its impact on you.

Referral Issues

Each school community will need to have a referral plan in place for such situations. It is a crucial part of the school's role in prevention, intervention and postvention. The referral procedure needs to be very well communicated to the staff, so that when a crisis occurs they are confident in the back-up support that is available to them.

Referral is best arranged in consultation with the distressed student. Where possible, the teacher should seek their agreement for the next step in the process, which will normally be a meeting with the guidance counsellor and/or the principal. Contact with some family member is crucial as soon as possible. If the student refuses and the risk is sufficiently high, then the school may have no other choice but to consult the student's family regardless. The school may also decide, in consultation with the student's family, to refer the student to more specialist care. In terms of primary prevention, the GP is an important resource both in advising the school and treating or referring the student. Their knowledge of the medical, family and social history of the student can be invaluable in these situations. In the case of an emergency, the casualty department of the local hospital is the appropriate place of referral – they will attend to the immediate physical needs of the student and also may refer on to the psychological services for either out or in-patient psychiatric care. If there are difficult social circumstances then the intervention of a social worker may be required.

INTERVENTION

At the centre of the intervention process will be the work of the Crisis Response Team whose role and function will be outlined below. In addition, there are some issues, essential to explore in terms of intervention, that will be an important resource particularly to teachers dealing directly with students:

- When a Suicide Occurs – Guidelines for School Intervention
- Breaking the News

Crisis Response Team

The purpose of a Crisis Response Team is to deal with any significant trauma that may occur in the life of the school. Suicide is clearly one such trauma, and will require the activation of the team. It is recommended that this team be in place on an ongoing basis. It is important to clearly outline the roles and responsibilities of the team members and to provide appropriate training and resources, so that the team is prepared to offer a prompt and effective response. A possible framework for such a team now follows – schools can adapt it according to their own particular context. At the core of the framework are the members of the team who carry out the following roles:

- leadership
- counselling
- family liaison
- chaplaincy
- communication

Leadership Role

The principal, who would normally be in this role, is the heart of the school and therefore carries an enormous weight of responsibility for every area of school life. In the case of a suicide, the burden of carrying the school will be all the more keenly felt as the principal endeavours to co-ordinate the response of the school. The particular role of the principal lends itself most clearly to being a supportive presence to others in the school. This is shown through acknowledging the feelings of those in any way affected and providing informal or formal opportunities for people to chat and discuss the incident and its impact on them. The active participation and sensitivity of the principal can set the tone for the manner in which the entire school responds. The following responsibilities are proposed to help the principal consider his or her role in advance of a suicide event and his or her role as part of the Crisis Response Team:

Prevention Responsibilities
- Develop and implement a policy on suicide prevention, intervention and postvention
- Have in place a trained Crisis Response Team
- Provide inservice to staff around issues of loss and trauma
- Promote the inclusion of programmes that deal with bereavement, loss and related issues in the curriculum
- Put in place a resource list of personnel and agencies, including school psychologist, mental health professionals, clergy, Gardaí, local doctors and relevant voluntary agencies

Intervention Responsibilities
- Confirm that the death has occurred
- Express sympathy to the family and assure them of the school's support
- Identify a contact person for the family with the school, explain their role and how the family can make contact with them
- Clarify the facts surrounding the death
- Activate the Crisis Response Team by organising a meeting

- Prepare an announcement for staff and students
- Decide on when, how and who will break the news
- Organise special staff meetings as required
- Devise a process to deal with telephone enquiries, particularly from concerned parents
- Notify the Board of Management
- Prepare a media statement

Postvention Responsibilities
- Ensure the provision of ongoing support to students, staff and parents
- Hold a meeting of the Crisis Response Team to evaluate the effectiveness of the response
- Facilitate any appropriate memorial events

Counselling Role

A pivotal person in the crisis team will be the school counsellor who will have responsibility for managing the range of counselling services required during times of trauma. Integral to the role of the counsellor is the relationship that is built up with students, particularly in the area of social and personal development. They have a role in supporting those students at risk and are also best placed to be a resource to staff and parents in a variety of ways. In the event of suicide, the experience and expertise of the guidance counsellor will be essential.

Prevention Responsibilities
- Assist with the development of programmes dealing with bereavement and suicide prevention
- Support and resource those teachers involved in the facilitation of such programmes within the Social, Personal and Health Education programme
- Contribute to the organisation and delivery of in-service to staff around issues of loss, crisis management and suicide

- Co-ordinate a panel of personnel, from within the staff, who will assist in the support of students and staff in distress. Any staff member who has received training in the area of bereavement counselling can be a member of this panel.
- Develop a network of, and a working relationship with, the school psychologist, mental health professionals, clergy, Gardaí, local doctors and relevant voluntary agencies

Intervention Responsibilities
- Clarify their role as co-ordinator of the counselling services to be offered throughout the school community
- Outline the specific services available in terms of what, who, where and when –
  What: individual and group support
  Who: the panel of trained support staff
  Where: the rooms available
  When: the times allotted
- Put in place a clear referral procedure to support staff in dealing with students in distress
- Address immediate needs of staff –
  Information: on grief responses, signs of students at risk, referral and support strategies
  Counselling: alerting staff to opportunities for personal support as required
- In conjunction with the year head and class tutor, attend to the needs of the class group to which the deceased student belonged
- Be available to students to support them, assess their needs and refer on as necessary. A referral will involve contact with individual parents.
- As required, make contact with relevant educational and community support personnel and agencies

Postvention Responsibilities
- Ongoing support to vulnerable students, with a particular eye to the concern around copycat incidents. An effective

identification and referral strategy will be a significant resource in this area.

- Continue to monitor the bereaved class group
- With the Crisis Response Team, evaluate the overall effectiveness of the school's response and put in place any changes necessary. In particular, the counsellor will be concerned with the effectiveness of the referral procedures; the support panel of staff; the liaison with outside personnel and agencies and the programmes dealing with loss, bereavement and suicide.

Chaplaincy Role

The chaplain's special contribution cannot be overestimated as the faith presence in the school community. He or she has a core pastoral role to play in supporting the family, students and staff. The chaplain will be an important member of the Crisis Response Team as they address such issues as school liturgies, liaison with local clergy and support of students and staff.

Prevention Responsibilities
- Contribute to the various programmes for students dealing with bereavement, loss and suicide
- Annual liturgy to remember deceased friends and relatives

Intervention Responsibilities
- Visit the home of the bereaved when appropriate
- Assist with any prayer services that may be arranged
- As required, work with the panel of trained staff dealing with distressed students
- Make contact with local clergy and offer support, particularly in relation to funeral arrangements and the involvement of the school
- Be available as a personal and spiritual support to the staff
- Be a resource to religion teachers as they address any religious issues that students may have surrounding the suicide

Postvention Responsibilities
- Take part in the evaluation of the Crisis Response Team - the chaplain will be especially concerned with the liturgical and spiritual aspects
- Provide follow-up support to the families in conjunction with the Home-school liaison
- Work in partnership with the religious education team

Family Liaison Role
The link and involvement of the school with the suicide-bereaved family is essential. The designated staff member in the family liaison role is an important resource in the response of the school to the bereaved family – and to other families who may be distressed. In many schools this role will fall to the Home-School Liaison Co-ordinator. Their knowledge of, and relationships with, families and community groups will be invaluable in shaping the school's response. The impression the family forms from their meeting with this person will influence their perception of the entire school's response to the death of their child. This underlines the importance of communicating in a sensitive manner.

Prevention Responsibilities
- The relationships this person has developed over time with families will be of great benefit in times of crisis
- In developing working relationships with support personnel and agencies in the community he or she will assist the Crisis Response Team in putting together a contact list of such people and groups
- Organise bereavement, loss and suicide awareness seminars for parents in addition to parenting programmes which aim to develop overall parenting skills

Intervention Responsibilities
- Following a first contact by the principal with the family, the

family liaison person will co-ordinate any further contact as families can feel very confused and pressurised having to address the same issues with too many people
- With the chaplain, consult the family about the involvement of the school in the funeral services
- Assist with all communication dealing with parents of any student affected by the crisis – this may involve drawing up a letter to parents, guidelines for telephone enquiries and meeting with distressed parents

Postvention Responsibilities
- Provide ongoing support of the bereaved family – a visit in the weeks following the funeral and at significant times in the following year
- Involve, as appropriate, the family in school liturgies or memorial ceremonies for their child
- Offer to link the family with community support groups such as Beginning Experience, Barnardos, Rainbows, Samaritans
- Participate in the evaluation of the crisis response strategy

Communication Role
In times of crisis, there may sometimes be media interest that will need to be sensitively managed so that the media involvement becomes part of the support effort rather than an unhelpful intrusion. The person in this communication role will also have a major responsibility to support the other members of the Crisis Response Team involved in communicating with staff, parents and students. The person selected needs to be comfortable with appearing on television and radio as they, with the principal, should be the only points of contact with the media. It is also recommended that this person should have good written communication skills, as they will be responsible for preparing and updating press releases and statements to the school community.

Prevention Responsibilities
- Establish contacts with various media representatives before a crisis occurs. This will make communication easier and procedures smoother during a crisis.
- Determine the nature of access that will be offered to media in a crisis situation
- Gather templates of statements that could be adapted to a particular context

Intervention Responsibilities
- With the Crisis Response Team, prepare a concise statement that expresses the school's sadness at the tragedy and outlines the steps in the school's response
- The protection of the bereaved family's privacy is paramount and therefore underlines the importance of discouraging teachers and students independently communicating with the media
- Put in place a designated room where reporters can gather and be addressed as a group by a school representative. It is important to ensure that the media do not have free access to the remainder of the school community.
- The school needs to respond promptly, as to delay may allow the media to obtain misinformation elsewhere
- Provide assistance in drawing up the written and oral communication with parents, students and staff
- Co-ordinate the approach taken to telephone enquiries from parents and others

Postvention Responsibilities
- Review and evaluate the effectiveness of the communication role in the crisis response of the school. Part of this review may be to take the opportunity to help educate the media about responsible suicide reporting in order not to sensationalise the event, given the potential danger to adolescents at risk.

When a Suicide Occurs – Guidelines for School Intervention
The following is a suggested outline guide to the major tasks that will have to be undertaken in the school on the day of the tragedy.

- The principal, having confirmed the death, makes contact with the bereaved family to offer sympathy and to offer support.
- The Crisis Team meets, if possible, before the school day begins. The key tasks at this early stage are:
  - ☞ Clarify the roles of each member of this team
  - ☞ Decide on a plan for the conduct of the day
  - ☞ Prepare an announcement for the staff
  - ☞ Put together guidelines for teachers on how to communicate the news to students
  - ☞ Agree a process for informing parents
  - ☞ Outline a statement to be used for telephone enquiries
  - ☞ If required, a media statement should be prepared
- Hold a staff meeting as early as possible in the school day. All school staff should attend – teaching, administrative and support. At this meeting:
  - ☞ The principal informs the staff of the death, or updates them on developments since the information was made public
  - ☞ The Crisis Response Team clarify their various roles and outline a plan for the day
  - ☞ Allow some time for staff to express their feelings on hearing the news. It may be appropriate to invite the guidance counsellor to outline the range of grief responses that may be experienced.
  - ☞ Outline the suggested procedure for breaking the news to students (see below). In many schools the class tutor takes on this responsibility.
  - ☞ Explain the referral structures – at this time the counsellor introduces the panel of trained staff who will assist him or her in dealing with distressed students – rooms and times are clarified

- ☞ Put in place a time for a further meeting at the end of the school day to update staff
- ☞ Perhaps the chaplain may conclude the meeting with a quiet moment of prayer for the deceased student and bereaved family
- The family liaison and/or the chaplain visits the bereaved family
- The Religious Education Team meet with the chaplain to discuss and organise the school's involvement in the funeral liturgies and any in-school services that may be deemed appropriate
- Details of the funeral arrangements are clarified for the school

You may find it helpful to refer to Luke Monahan's article, as he describes how his school coped with such a tragedy.

Breaking the News to Students

There can be few more difficult tasks for a teacher than to have to break the news to a class than that a fellow student has died by suicide. Therefore it is important that the teacher is personally prepared and has discussed the approach in advance with the Crisis Response Team. Some useful information to bear in mind:

- It's important to note that you cannot term a death a suicide unless the bereaved family have consented. Instead refer to it as a tragic death.

- Research and experience have shown that many people who die by suicide are not thinking properly – this can be due to depression or excessive use of drugs or alcohol.

- While in hindsight friends and family may be able to point to signs that were given, it is very often the case that no clear signals were evident.

- It is imperative to communicate that the act of suicide does not solve anything, rather it is a devastating event in the lives of all connected to the person.

- For the class group most affected by the tragedy it is suggested that the class tutor be supported by the chaplain and guidance counsellor when breaking the news.

The following steps may be taken in breaking the news:
- Prepare the class by telling them that you have sad news and that it is difficult for you to have to do this. The purpose of this is, in some small way, to prepare them emotionally for what they are about to hear.

- The next stage is to let them know who the news is about.

- Now, gently and sensitively, tell the class that 'N. has tragically died and the facts as we know are...' It is important that you give all the accurate information you can to the class, in order to prevent rumours from circulating. The class need to trust the teacher and feel they are able to check out any stories that may circulate around the tragedy.

- Encourage questions to ensure that everybody has truly heard the news. It may now be appropriate to take some quiet time for reflection and prayer.

- Then you can let the class know all the range of reactions they may have to this news and the various ways that the school will support them and how they can be a support to each other. There is no right or wrong emotional response. It may be helpful for you to share your own feelings.

- Allow time for students to talk to each other, circulate among them – being attentive to those particularly upset or shocked by the news. You may need to connect with a member of the pastoral team (e.g. guidance counsellor, chaplain, and year head) both as a personal support and to refer students in need.

- A useful exercise to consider is to invite the students to spend some time writing about how they feel – this will help them to articulate their feelings. Then, divide the class into groups to write a prayer for one or more of the following:
    the student who has died by suicide
    the bereaved family
    the class group
  These prayers may be useful at an assembly, a retreat day, a class Mass or a memorial service.

Some of the above points will be very helpful if the subject of suicide is raised during a class discussion. You will also find the article by Michael Ryan in this volume useful in this regard. Remember that you should only address this issue if you are confident in your ability to deal with it.

POSTVENTION

Care of students, teachers and parents does not end at the intervention stage. Experience shows that support offered in the post-tragedy phase is crucial in addressing the needs of all of those affected in the school community – this phase is termed 'postvention'. This section will address the following areas:

- Days and Weeks following the Suicide – Guidelines for Schools
- Evaluation of the School's Response to Suicide
- Pastoral Care of Students
- Pastoral Care of Families
- Pastoral Care of Staff

Days and Weeks following the Suicide – Guidelines for Schools

- The guidance counsellor, with the help of the pastoral team, provides ongoing support of students at risk, with particular attention to be given to any siblings or relations who attend the school. Also, special care needs to be given to the class group of the deceased student.
- The chaplain, in liaison with the religious education team, organises memorial services as appropriate
- The class tutor or other staff member arranges for a book of condolences to be sent to the family
- The Home-School Liaison ensures ongoing contact and support to the bereaved family, and also to concerned parents
- Attend to ongoing needs of staff – refer to Pastoral Care of Staff section below
- Evaluate the overall school response to the tragedy – refer to Evaluation of the School's Response to Suicide section below

Evaluation of the School's Response to Suicide

Only by analysing the results of the school community's effort to cope with such a tragedy can the school hope to improve and ensure a more effective response in the future. The role of the Crisis Response Team will be a particular focus for any evaluation, as they will have carried a significant responsibility for co-ordinating the school's response. The purpose of the review is to acknowledge and build upon the effective elements of the strategy, and to identify areas for improvement and restructuring. As well as the members of the Crisis Response Team, others who need to be consulted are those teachers most involved – including tutors, year heads, the guidance counsellor's panel of support staff and the religious education team. If possible, it will be helpful to have a whole-staff review. Parents and students will also have very pertinent feedback to offer.

Pastoral Care of Students

Many of the elements of the pastoral care of students have been addressed above, such as, prevention programmes, the identification of those at risk and breaking the news of the tragedy. A further area to recognise, especially in the postvention phase, is the support students offer each other. This is especially important at traumatic times, and can be an important part of their own grieving and healing process. Teachers need to facilitate ways in which peer support can occur. This may involve encouraging students to:

- be a friend and look out for each other
- be sensitive to those who may feel isolated in the class group
- be supportive of each other in the expressing of emotions about the tragedy
- be vigilant – bring concerns about classmates to the attention of teachers
- be respectful of the needs of the bereaved family
- be open to ways of participating in the funeral liturgies

Refer to the article by Martin Daly where he addresses the area of how the school leadership working with staff and parents can care for students at risk.

Pastoral Care of Parents

Throughout the above framework, the needs of parents – including the bereaved family – have been attended to in various ways. In particular, the role of the family liaison person has been emphasised, it is he or she who co-ordinates the school's contact with parents in terms of home visitation, providing relevant information and organising talks. The effectiveness of the lines of communication between home and school are vital, especially in terms of knowledge around roles, structures and procedures. It is important to note that pastoral support for families can come from students as well as from staff. Nonetheless, it needs to be acknowledged that those students closest to their deceased friend may find it very difficult and distressing to approach their friend's parents. This is all the more traumatic in the case of a suicide, as they themselves may be carrying feelings of guilt, confusion, helplessness, anger and intense sadness. Teachers may assist students with the following advice in terms of what students need to know in order to support the bereaved family:

- in most cases, the bereaved parents find it comforting to spend time with the friends of their deceased child
- your respectful presence may be all that is needed – do not be afraid of silences or not knowing what to say
- on the first occasion of meeting the parents, simply offer your sympathy by saying: 'I'm so sorry about N's death'. You may wish to add something about the deceased that was special to you: 'I'll miss his sense of humour'.
- ask if there is any practical help you can offer
- don't talk in clichés, such as, 'He's better off now since he has no pain'

Consider making an occasional visit to parents in the weeks following the funeral.

Pastoral Care of Staff
In caring for the students, it is important not to neglect the needs of the teachers, who will also be deeply upset by the tragic death of one of their pupils. Addressing the needs of the staff obviously requires sensitivity to each individual as well as care for the whole group. Some elements of this care are as follows:

Information – at all stages, it is essential that staff are aware of key facts and how they can access relevant information.

An agreed approach – having a common stance on how to deal with the suicide event is a great support. The Crisis Response Team are a central resource here.

Identifying needs – in order to ensure that the range of concerns that staff may have are addressed it may be helpful to invite staff to complete a brief and simple questionnaire and/or informal staff meeting to allow issues to be expressed, such as the need for inservice on bereavement and counselling opportunities.

Opportunities to talk – a variety of formal and informal opportunities to support staff needs to be provided. The provision of informal social time together, such as a break from normal class routine, allows staff to share their feelings and concerns. In terms of formal responses, confidential access to the chaplain and guidance counsellor may be very supportive. Links with professional support agencies or individuals can be called upon if required

Needs of key teachers – particular care needs to be taken of those teachers more closely associated with the tragedy, particularly the Crisis Response Team. It is important to ensure that responsibility is shared in a team approach, that there is time out for them individually and collectively to debrief. However, it is also important to recognise that individual teachers may have very good reasons to excuse themselves from direct involvement.

Inservice – an important resource for teachers will be inservice on issues of grief and loss. Additional training should be provided for those teachers particularly interested in this area.

Staff Ritual – it can be very healing for staff to come together to place the event in a faith context. The chaplain and the RE team, working with the staff, can facilitate different events – for example a staff Mass, a simple prayer service or an evening of prayer and reflection followed by some social time together.

Care of Self – at all stages of a trauma, staff need to

acknowledge and attend to their own personal needs – particularly in knowing limits and valuing the contribution they make to the well-being of colleagues and students.

Conclusion

This chapter has sought to offer practical guidelines for the school context in relation to suicide. Underlying this contribution has been a clear approach to education in Irish society today. This approach is a life affirming one, where the person is valued, self-esteem is fostered, respect, tolerance and fairness are evident. In particular, there is support for those in difficulties. It is in such an atmosphere that the best conditions prevail for the development of the young person – where the personal, social and health education needs of all in the school community are paramount. Although the school cannot in any circumstances take full responsibility for the young person, it needs to recognise, and indeed celebrate, the contribution it can make. The challenge for the school is to articulate this contribution and to allocate adequate resources to ensure this contribution can be delivered upon.

LISTENING AND HEARING — THE COUNSELLOR'S ROLE

Tony Hanna

Tony, a school chaplain and counsellor, has long experience in education and in pastoral ministry. In his contribution, he explores both an understanding of, and a response to, those touched by suicide. Names and situations have been altered to protect the identities of those involved.

'Every morning I knock on her door and I wait for her to answer. You have no idea what it feels like, waiting for her to answer. Those thirty seconds each morning are an absolute nightmare.'

These are the words of the father of a sixteen-year-old girl who attempted suicide last year. The watching, the waiting and the ever-present fear of another attempt has placed an intolerable strain on both him and his wife, to the extent that it almost led to the break-up of their marriage. The father told me, with compelling honesty, that he looked forward to next year when, 'Hopefully she will be at university and we won't have the daily physical reminder of this threat.'

His hope is that, to some extent, out of sight will mean out of mind. He is a good father, one who loves his daughter very deeply, yet his own resources have been stretched to the limit. He feels exhausted, with nothing more to give.

Why, Why, Why?

A seventh year student arrived in my office a few weeks ago looking tired and shaken. His seventeen-year-old girlfriend had taken a serious overdose the previous night and he had just returned from the hospital. He was distraught, because apparently nothing had been wrong in their relationship; on the contrary, it was very good; they had been on a date the night before and – from his perspective – there were no warning signs. Her action was a total, earth-shattering shock. He needed to talk, to try to make sense of it all, to deal with his pain, his confusion and – in his words – his 'sense of betrayal'.

Experience and skills are useful prerequisites when confronting brokeness. Allied with compassion and empathy they usually equip the chaplain/counsellor to be at least a comforting presence and possibly an effective instrument of healing.

Above all, he wanted to know how he should relate to her. Without saying it explicitly, he knew that this event had forever changed the nature of their relationship. It was now radically different than before. As I explored the situation with him, he expressed huge sadness that she could not tell him, even now, what drove her to this attempt. He felt anger that she had betrayed his trusting relationship with her, that her action was a rejection of him and his love. He also acknowledged his fear of the future and his uncertainty that he had the resources to support her. He wanted to know how he should talk to her; should he do anything differently, should he raise the issue or leave it alone and wait for her to talk about it?

I have been in my new post as chaplain/counsellor to large boys' grammar school in the North of Ireland for just over six months, and the issue of suicide is a depressing reality. Less than a week after my appointment, I received a call informing me of the death of an 18-year-old student from the school.

ECHOES OF SUICIDE

He had taken his own life. My first act as chaplain was to visit his mother.

Experience and skills are useful prerequisites when confronting brokeness. Allied with compassion and empathy they usually equip the chaplain or counsellor to be at least a comforting presence and possibly an effective instrument of healing. On this occasion, confronted with the controlled despair of a mother, one was left bereft, with a feeling of total uselessness. Words seemed inadequate, and even one's presence was like a guilty intrusion. The awful magnitude of her loss was crushing and her gentle disposition merely accentuated the tragic poignancy of the moment.

I had not known him, but it was easy to sketch a good outline of Stephen from the stories told by his friends, teachers and parents. Life had not always been easy for him, and he suffered from bouts of depression and an acute sensitivity that was both his gift and his cross. He was a talented musician and raconteur, popular and likeable. He had recently completed his three A Levels and his posthumous results, issued in August, would easily have secured him a place in a host of universities for a wide variety of courses. Their subsequent arrival compounded the family's grief because it reinforced the incomprehension.

'Why? Why? Why?' screamed across the mind of all who knew him. Family, friends, teachers – all struggled to comprehend. Stephen rejected life as he experienced it, and those who were part of that life were traumatically affected by his demise. Could I have made a difference? If I had been more alert could I have recognised telltale signs that forebode disaster? Could I have befriended him more?

We probe in order to understand, and the tinges of guilt that assail us remind us that we are our brothers' keepers, that one person's tragedy affects us all. We are all diminished by the futility of suicide. Yet guilt and mourning, however those two emotions mix, cannot be allowed to fester and corrode our own zeal for life. Life is to be lived, and one of the most difficult tasks for the survivor is to re-engage in life. Naturally, there is a time span in all of this and it will vary according to the depth of the grief experienced. Yet there is an inescapable truth that the bereaved have to let go and move on. With a natural death, be it sudden or expected, there is within us a rational and, eventually, an emotional acceptance that such is life. In time we learn to adapt, to filter the pain through new lenses and we are able, however reluctantly at first, to recommence our living.

Responding

Suicide is profoundly more difficult to accommodate. Suicide is an ugly word that does not fit into any emotional or rational framework. It screams failure, it points the finger, it accuses, it condemns and it haunts – like a spectre from which there seems to be no exorcism. Time is needed, but so too is compassion, tolerance, support, encouragement and, from time to time, a firm but gentle and persistent challenge.

The pastoral response is to be there, waiting and listening. It doesn't seem much comfort. You are apparently not doing anything, and yet you are doing the one thing necessary. You are absorbing the pain, lancing the boil, allowing the anger, frustration and guilt to be released. Creating space for the griever to be honest, to rant and rave, to weep and to reminisce, to cry out and to struggle for answers – this is a holy place. It is not an easy place for either the bereaved or the counsellor, but I have no doubt that it is a privileged place, that it is holy ground; God is present in these moments because as the psalmist says, 'The Lord hears the cry of the poor'.

Language

In moments like these there is no one poorer or more deprived than the parents or family of the one who has taken their own life. They are often bankrupt of reasons or resources to cope with the horror that confronts them.

Language becomes critical. Somewhere, I picked up the phrase 'completed suicide' rather than 'committed suicide' – because the latter has explicit connotations of a criminal act. Sensitivity such as this in the area of language is not avoidance, but sympathetic exploration of an unspeakable horror. By way of parallel, on one occasion I inadvertently used the phrase 'handicapped' in referring to a client's sister. Although he was young, he quickly corrected my terminology, explaining tersely that his sister had a learning difficulty, but she was not handicapped. We who practice in the healing ministries need to be ever so careful of the fragility of the people whom we encounter. Language needs to be empathetic and secure. The horror has to be confronted by the mourners sooner or later. They need to know that there is no negative judgement of them, that this is a safe place in which they can own and face their feelings of guilt, anger and frustration.

> Sometimes the mourner needs permission of a significant other to lay aside these feelings of guilt, anger etc. before they can forgive themselves and move on with life.

A Healing Presence

When a young person rejects life because it is too painful, those closest to the deceased interpret this as a rejection of them. Inevitably it leads to regrets: 'I didn't do enough' or 'I didn't love enough' or 'I am not good enough'. It helps when the counsellor can accept these feelings and then place them into the wider picture. We can't live on feelings alone; they are part of us; we live by our reason and our will, which are there to help us to integrate feelings. Sometimes, the mourner needs the permission of a significant other to lay aside these feelings of guilt, anger etc. before they can forgive themselves and move on with life. They need to own the reality that they cannot be in control of what others do, they can only be in control of what they do. What they choose to do in dealing with the pain becomes the focal point of the therapy. The counsellor encourages them to grieve and to give concrete expression to that process, but at the opportune moment, they are challenged to move on, to take control of and responsibility for their actions, not for what someone else has done or may do. This requires, firstly, an intellectual disengagement from being responsible for another, then an emotional disengagement that recognises and accords autonomy to the other.

Attempted Suicides

This is not to be misinterpreted as a removal of all support from someone who has attempted suicide and survived. Such potential suicides need the loving support and acceptance of family, friends and significant others as they recover and try to rebuild their lives. However, as part of their therapy, it is vital that they accept responsibility for their actions, accept that the choices they have made are not caused by others, but by their own personal decisions. Over-dependence on others is not the solution to their problem, and it can be too heavy a burden for others to carry because they just do not have the resources, personal or professional, to provide adequate support. Those affected by suicides need to discover the delicate balance between being a befriender and supporter and being held responsible (by themselves or the suicides) for what the other person does. This repositioning of relationships and responsibilities for the survivors is a delicate but crucial task in the aftermath of an attempted suicide or a completed suicide.

A Faith Perspective

Finally, it can help to look at the witness of others who have survived past horrors. In a concentration camp in the Second

World War where millions of Jews were executed a prisoner had carved the words,

> I believe in the sun, even though it doesn't shine,
> I believe in love, even when it isn't shown,
> I believe in God, even when he doesn't speak.

As a Catholic chaplain and therapist, I believe in the healing power of Christ's redemptive love – especially for the broken-hearted. Life always conquers death, and it is the Christian belief that Christ came that we 'would have life and have it to the full.' I encourage survivors to hear the invitation of Christ, 'Come to me all you who labour and are heavy burdened and I will give you rest.' Integrating pain, and all the accompanying emotions, becomes significantly more attainable if one has a religious outlook, if one can – through faith – accept that 'God's grace is made perfect in weakness.'

SCHOOL:
MINDING THOSE AT RISK

Martin Daly

Martin is principal of Catholic University School, Leeson Street, Dublin. He is a family therapist and a consultant to and facilitator of groups and organisations.

When a suicide occurs in our midst, it raises questions for us that we are unable to fully answer, and often cannot even partially answer. Without the comfort of explanations, we are left with feelings of helplessness, with which, if we are honest, very few of us are comfortable. The helplessness and powerlessness of not understanding, not knowing why this has happened is very difficult to handle. What could be worse than knowing that you were aware of the person's decline – only too well – but found your best and continued efforts thwarted? What must it be like for parents and loved ones to watch as the apparently inevitable eventually happened? Or, on the other hand, what must it be like to be confronted with suicide apparently without any warning, and all the wondering afterwards as to how you could not have noticed? In the aftermath, there is hardly a deeper abyss for those left behind. There are things we can do long before we get to this point. In saying this, I am under no illusions that we can prevent the tragedy of suicide occurring in our midst, but we can try to create environments where things get noticed, where children are minded, and where sensitivities are acknowledged.

Needs

I am frightened by what is happening to our students as they grow up. They appear to have so much frustration and anger in them, and so little facility to handle these feelings. Feelings of hurt and diminishment register, leave their mark and mould their personalities. They have not the words to explain what is going on and often there is no one to explain these things to them. They bottle it up, but whatever 'it' is leaks out sooner or later in anger and aggression. If it doesn't leak out, it leaks in and the anger turned in on the self leads to depression. Cut off from their feelings, they wander around in what feels like being lost in a familiar place. Philip Larkin's poignant words about home as 'a joyous shot at how things ought to be long fallen wide' describes evocatively the despondency that can hit teenage boys when their inner and outer world no longer seems like a place in which they can feel at home. As principal of both a primary and secondary school for boys, I feel that the environment in which they spend so much of their formative years can make a world of difference if it provides the kind of minding and holding that they need now more than ever.

> For boys, the need to provide a sensitive holding environment becomes daily more important so as to counteract the disservice our culture does to them in blunting and, ultimately, denying their sensitivity.

A Holding Environment

The notion of a 'holding environment' was first described by Donald W. Winnicott, in explaining the connection between mother and child and the conditions that would enable the child to grow up into an emotionally secure adult. When parents come to see the school for the first time, I ask them about how they mind their son and the kind of minding they want the school to provide for their son. Sometimes, people are surprised at the emphasis, but increasing numbers of them will describe their sons as 'very sensitive' and are attuned to their temperaments. 'Aren't we all sensitive?' I hear the reader ask. Sure we are, but do our schools and the ways in which they 'handle', 'relate to', 'draw out' and 'educate' boys place the minding of this sensitivity to the fore? The language I am using may seem 'soft' and appear like I am suggesting boys need to be mollycoddled. I remember one father, on hearing me use these terms, asked me if the boys in the school were competitive and got stuck in on the sports fields! I was able to allay any anxieties he had in that regard. He wanted him to be able to 'stand up for himself.' The best way of ensuring that children can do so is to build up their emotional self by providing an environment that is respectful of their feelings, affirms their sensitivity and encourages a sensitivity towards others. For boys, the need to provide a sensitive holding environment becomes daily more important so as to counteract the disservice our culture does to them in blunting and, ultimately, denying their sensitivity. To use a phrase that at this stage has become hackneyed, there has to be a 'whole school approach' if sensitivity is to be fostered in the students.

Sense of the School

Parents will tell you – if only you would ask them – that they could get a 'feel' for a school when they walk in the gate, or even by standing outside the gate! In those moments, the living prospectus of a school can be read. As teachers and principals, we might usefully ask prospective parents and pupils what feeling they get about the school when they first arrive. They are uncannily accurate in their sense of the place. Some questions that might be posed:

ECHOES OF SUICIDE

- Do they sense that the children are happy, full of life and relaxed, but not out of order?
- What sense do they get when they walk into the school office?
- Is the atmosphere warm, welcoming, down-to-earth, and un-intimidating?
- What do they notice about how the boys are treated if they come into the office?
- Do they seem at ease talking to the teachers and the principal and deputy principal without being over-familiar?

A similar exercise could usefully be carried out with students:

- How do pupils who are at the school talk about the other pupils, about the teachers and the authorities?
- Do they like coming in each morning?
- Would they say that the teachers 'in there' are interested in them?
- Would they say that they are strict, but fair?
- Would they go so far as to say that they could talk to some of them?
- Would they and the parents find the school approachable if they had a problem?
- Is there that kind of 'at-ease-ness' in the school?
- Do the boys feel respected?
- Are they called by their first names?
- When they are asked to do something, are they asked or are they barked at as though they were in the Marines?
- In return, are they courteous to each other and to the teachers? The Litmus test of courtesy is whether or not they approach a visitor who comes into the schoolyard to see if they can be of any help!
- Do the teachers know the names of the pupils?
- How do they talk about them to each other in the staff room, at staff meetings and at parent-teacher meetings?

These questions are not an exhaustive list, but a litmus test, as I mentioned above, of the quality of relationships in the school, the feel of the school – whether it is a joyous shot at how things ought to be or possibly falling wide of the mark.

In summary, when parents or visitors walk into the school, do they get a sense that it is child-centred and child-sensitive?

The principal has the task of setting the tone and of ultimately holding what is valuable. He or she has to model this child-centredness in their way of speaking to pupils, and about pupils, in their behaviour and in their decisions. He has to ensure that all discussions about pupils with parents and/or staff are informed by what is best for the children. In any discussions about pupils, he must invite parents and staff to consider the meaning of pupils' behaviour in the context of all that is known about them and about their circumstances.

Role of Staff

Staff can be helped to keep in mind the wider context if there are ongoing meetings with teachers of particular classes or years, at which they are kept informed – as appropriate – of the personal circumstances of children, be they issues of background, learning difficulties, peer issues, bullying and, where possible, vulnerabilities. The staff need to be encouraged to discuss pupils within this wider context, with a view to understanding the meaning of their behaviour. This type of conversation opens up the possibility of gaining the cooperation of teachers in a more nuanced, less reactive and punitive approach to discipline. It develops in staff a sensitivity to the signals that pupils may give that all is not well, that they are going off the boil or are distressed. It also provides an opportunity for them to voice their frustrations with particular pupils, or groups of pupils, and feel that they have been heard. It provides an opportunity for them to feed back information on how they are observing pupils. This is crucial for the ongoing minding of those who may be more vulnerable.

The leadership has to stay in touch with the staff, as they are interacting everyday with the pupils in a classroom context. They pick up the signals that something is amiss. The school that notices what is going on for pupils is the one best situated to anticipate possible difficulties. The quality of noticing depends on how attuned staff are to the pupils. This depends on how much they value this aspect of their role as educators, and on how much this role is grounded in the school by the leadership and at meetings with individual staff, groups of staff and at staff meetings. The leadership must invite them to attend to the pupils. By offering them opportunities to discuss the meanings of children's behaviour, asking them what they have noticed, valuing their perspectives on the children, they become more mindful of those signals and meanings that might otherwise go unnoticed. In thinking about their role – and about the children – in a context of mindfulness, their descriptions of the children become richer, and their responses are likely to be more sensitive to the wider context within which the children's behaviour can be viewed. The staff will be more likely to involve themselves as carers:

- if they are addressed as and treated as carers
- if they are involved in conversations about how best to care for the pupils entrusted to them
- if they are given information that persuades them of the appropriateness of taking up this position
- if they feel their perspective and experience is being respected

We become the people we are addressed as. In addressing the staff as carers, the leadership is drawing on the capacity to care that motivated many of us to enter, and remain, in the teaching profession. Developing this sense of care and minding in a school in no way undermines or is opposed to discipline.

Principal and Staff

The principal should model to the staff a way of relating to the pupils that privileges their sensitivity and that is seen to work. Issues of discipline have to be dealt with head on, but in a context of care that is mindful of the family and peer context within which the disciplinary issue has arisen. The blunt instrument of discipline, divorced from a perspective that situates a child's responses within this wider context, is ultimately insensitive. While it may be understandable that a teacher out of tiredness, helplessness, frustration or inadequacy wants certain pupils 'nailed' or put on a hit list, the principal's job is to hold the teachers in their helplessness, and help them work through their issues around what a particular child may be triggering for them. The teachers need to develop an awareness that they are part of the system. They need to begin to ask questions about how they might respond differently to the children in order to evoke different responses from them, to observe their participation in the situations that arise. This will only be possible if the staff feel that the boundaries for pupils are clear and unambiguous, and will be observed and held by the principal. You cannot expect a teacher to open up to such questions except within a context where the principal has shown a commitment to containing the aggression of pupils and demanding a respectful, sensitive attitude to the staff.

Principal and Pupils

The principal again has to model this to the pupils. All of us have heard stories of schools where staff have felt undermined by a principal who confused caring for the pupils with a disowning of his or her role to monitor and enforce the boundaries in the school. For staff to feel able to consider a more nuanced approach to caring for pupils, they need to know that the environment in which they are being held with the pupils is secure. Pupils need to know exactly where the principal stands, and where they stand in relation to the principal and the staff.

Discipline only makes sense in a context where there is a felt sense of care.

Andrew

Perhaps an example from my own experience of dealing with one boy may illustrate the responsibility we need to develop in our schools. At several meetings, the staff had begun to talk about Andrew. He was seventeen, quite intelligent and had been a solid worker, but seemed to be 'slacking off', to use one teacher's words. He promised he would knuckle down and did for a few weeks, but then went off the boil again. His parents were brought in by the class tutor and the situation was discussed with Andrew present. Andrew seemed uncomfortable, not surprisingly, and gave more promises that he would turn over a new leaf and get back into the work. He was asked if there were any difficulties, and he said there weren't. He said he had just got out of the habit of studying. Nothing changed. He wasn't the sort who gave trouble, so people didn't complain much about him, except to say on reports that he could do better, needed to work much harder and so forth. During the Christmas exams, several of the teachers noticed he was writing very little, just staring into space. Between exams I met him and asked him how he was getting on. Initially, he was slow to disclose anything. As with many fellows of his age, he found it hard to get talking about himself, but then he began to cry. He said that things were getting on top of him: sometimes he couldn't get up in the morning and he couldn't get started on the study. During the exams, he found himself sitting looking at the paper feeling that there was no point in trying it because he knew so little. There was so much study to do that he did not know where to start. He couldn't tell his parents, because they just became more anxious, which made matters worse and made it more difficult to talk to them, and he felt he was letting them down – so he just went up to his room and pretended he was studying. He had missed a number of days in school because he told his parents he wasn't feeling well. When he did come in, he found himself sitting in class, but not paying attention. He was really down in himself.

In response to a question I asked him, he sort of half said that he had thought about doing something to himself, but didn't want me to tell his parents, because they would get completely wound up and that would only make things worse. I persuaded him to agree to meet his parents with me, outside of the school, because he didn't want the other lads seeing his parents arriving in. At the meeting we told them between us what was going on, and my job was to fill in the gaps for him and to contain his parents' anxiety. They, very helpfully, stated sincerely and spontaneously that they just wanted him to be happy and that if he didn't manage to do well in the Leaving Certificate this year, they could live with that. We decided between us that he would only attempt one or two exams in the Pre-Leaving and that the parents would arrange for a grind in one subject in which he felt unable to structure any study. We agreed that staff would be told that there were 'things going on for him', and that he wasn't able to do much study at the moment. More importantly, we agreed that if he woke up in the morning and didn't feel up to coming into school, he was to ring me or his parents would and I would ring back. I undertook that either myself or the deputy would meet him for a cup of coffee. If he wished he could go home after that, or if he felt able he could come in for a while. I would have a word, discreetly, with his class tutor. This happened on several occasions over the next few months. I also gave him the name of a counsellor whom I knew and whom I thought would be able to establish a rapport with a young fellow of seventeen. He agreed to go to him once and see what he was

ECHOES OF SUICIDE

like. He went two or three times, and then occasionally afterwards. As he said to me later, he knew he was there if he needed to contact him. In my terms, it provided a holding environment outside of the school and of the family. It meant that he didn't have to talk to anyone in the school about himself, but could go on about his business, and his parents were relieved of the responsibility of feeling they had to 'get him to talk'. Paradoxically, this freed him up to talk to them somewhat more than he had been doing.

The following November I got a card in the post. It was a picture of a small sailing boat anchored in a calm inlet. When I opened the card, it was from Andrew and all it said was: 'Things have settled down. Give my regards to all the staff.' The picture spoke volumes.

He didn't do as well in the Leaving Certificate as he might otherwise have done, but he got through it and decided to take a year out afterwards from studying. The following November I got a card in the post. It was a picture of a small sailing boat anchored in a calm inlet. When I opened the card, it was from Andrew and all it said was: 'Things have settled down. Give my regards to all the staff.' The picture spoke volumes.

Responding to the Signals

It is so important to have children in an environment where things get noticed. Fortunately, in Andrews's case, we picked up the signals. When you get the signals, you have to try to keep the child active around their feelings of being fed up or down or depressed, and find someone to hold them in that and help them articulate what is going on. We need to do everything we can to keep in touch with them, to remain connected to them. Other objectives – laudable in themselves – like getting the points for medicine may have to be left aside. Parental and teacher expectations may have to be revised. Structures, within reason, need to be flexible and demands made must be such that there is a possibility that they can be met, because when a child begins to get pulled out by undercurrents and can't tread water, saving them from drowning is really all that matters.

BEREAVEMENT AND TRAGEDY: LEARNINGS FOR THE SCHOOL

Luke Monahan

In this contribution, Luke highlights some issues around bereavement and, in particular, the impact of loss on the young person. He goes on to outline one school's response to a sudden death and indicates some of the supports that are available to school communities. Luke is Head of the Centre for Education Services at Marino Institute in Dublin and National Co-ordinator of the Irish Association of Pastoral Care in Education. He has published a range of books on educational practice.

Approaching issues of such a sensitive nature as suicide, bereavement and loss requires a range of qualities, but in particular: respect, courage and honesty.

Respect as we are discussing some of the most traumatic events in people's lives and each responds to trauma in a unique manner that defies facile description.

Courage as it is important to counter the marginalisation of loss issues in ourselves, our communities and in our society. These concerns are real and must be addressed.

Honesty as one of the most treasured and essential qualities we have for looking at our own lives and how we can be a true support to others who cross our path.

I mention these qualities as I am so very conscious that when I am working with individuals or groups in this area I am walking on 'sacred ground'. My contribution to this volume will be to look at the concerns around suicide in youth, and how the school can respond. It is essential, in the first place, to situate suicide in a wider context of whole person development – of the importance of the range of skills needed to embark on the journey of life in a healthy and fulfilling way.

Bereavement
We need to go behind suicide, as it were, to look at bereavement and our ability to deal with loss. Our culture does not help us to face one of the most inevitable experiences of life – we will experience loss. Society today wants us rather to run away and hide from this reality, and lures us into the quick fix of materialism. In a book published recently by the Irish Association of Pastoral Care in Education (IAPCE) entitled, *Suicide, Bereavement and Loss: Perspectives and Responses*, Christy Kenneally writes that, to a great extent, 'We are today what we have made of our bereavements'. This is a very challenging statement that invites us to look again at:

- how we have weathered the inevitable losses of life
- what our patterned responses are
- how unfinished or suppressed the business of our bereavement is
- how we are supported in this area of our lives
- what internal and external resources we can draw upon

Moving Through
There is no scale that can accurately measure the amount of pain and distress that will be experienced by any of us through

any particular loss – that has to do with the depth of connection, of commitment, of investment. Moving to a new home for example – what is overwhelming for one is merely a mild disturbance for another. We can never categorise the impact of a loss on a person – rather we can seek to support that person in articulating its significance for them, and assist them as they move through the experience. It is the ability to move through the experience that is vital as the loss takes up its rightful space in the life of the person. The route of avoidance, of suppression, of neglect, places the loss in a 'holding' space, as it waits for its opportunity to be addressed. The good news is that life will give us many occasions to deal with our own losses. Notice how it is at the funerals of those whom we have not known well that we can become very 'upset' – some of this is undoubtedly our grieving for our own losses. These can be for occasions in the past, but also for losses we know await us. The quality we need here is awareness, to ask ourselves some of the following questions:

- what is going on for me?
- what is this experience reminding me of?
- have I issues to resolve?
- have I feelings to be conscious of?
- have I actions to take?

The Power of Denial

We must be very respectful of our ability to avoid pain, indeed, it is a necessary life skill as we attempt to deal with pain in manageable 'chunks'. This explains the very normal initial denial that accompanies the trauma of the death of a loved one – our body needs to 'shut down', as it were, to allow it slowly to process the news. The difficulty arises when the natural denial becomes a habitual state of being. As friends to the bereaved we have to ensure that we do not collude with denial over a long period. We can so often allow our own discomfort to determine how we acknowledge a loss. It is important for us to find our own courage to – actually or metaphorically – hold the hand of the bereaved, a gesture that communicates that: yes the loss has occurred, yes it is traumatic and yes I am here to move through this time with you. This is where the power of ritual is so significant as we express the reality of the loss in a variety of ways – word, song, touch, and action – all ways to accompany the bereaved through the loss at its most consuming time.

Youth and Bereavement

In my many years working with young people who have been bereaved, their courage and their ability to take their own time in the grieving process strike me. I am also convinced of their need for a variety of resources in their dealing with loss. A story that illustrates this is that of a student of mine, Kevin, who lost his Dad at the age of thirteen. I chatted to him in the days after the funeral, and he made it clear that while he was grateful for the concern, he was not ready or able to talk about his loss. He said he just wanted to be with his friends and get back into the routine of school. It wasn't until he was seventeen that he returned to me to say he wanted to talk about his Dad, and how the loss had affected him. In the meantime, we had offered many opportunities, but he took his own time to address the loss. I asked him what made him come to me at this particular time – he replied: 'I always knew that when I was ready you would listen, my stalling did not put you off.'

Many Opportunities

One of the many lessons I learned from Kevin is the need to offer a variety of possibilities to young people to address the concerns they have. The issues can be experienced in a very intense manner and therefore a conclusion can easily be reached that there is 'no way out'. It is important to have available a range of 'connection points' for the young person – be they sports teams, clubs, hobbies, discussion groups, pastoral links in the school, extended family. We also have to recognise that, even with all these supports in place, a young person can still choose a self-destructive path. Working with youth, most especially with those at risk, requires many qualities:

- non-judgemental: yet clear on one's own values
- resourceful: able to help to imagine a variety of courses of action
- psychologically available: not consumed by one's own issues
- able to maintain a healthy distance and not become emotionally entangled
- honest: able to build a trusting relationship
- aware of the need for self-care: a support structure
- have a sense of humour: to take the many 'hits'!

Suicide

Examining the issues that arise for those who contemplate and complete suicide, we come across self-esteem, identity concerns, even our economic situation also contributes – if you're in a 'tiger economy' and you are unemployed, it says something very serious about you. You perceive yourself to be a failure with a capital 'F' in our society. For many people, the experience is that of being an island where the support structures of former times are lost – the family, the church, the local community. Communication is now more likely by text messaging than around the kitchen table. Gone, but not replaced, are the clear value and support systems. The time of uncle or granny or granddad being the counsellor is past. As a result, many young people are left unsupported in uncharted waters.

Sudden Death of A Student – A School's Response.

The following is an account of an experience in a Dublin school where I was chaplain before taking up my present post. In recounting this experience, I am not suggesting that the way that our school responded to the sudden and tragic death of one of our students is a blueprint for other contexts. It is merely our experience that I put before you for your consideration as you reflect on the issues and practical concerns raised by sudden death. Some minor details have been altered. This material appears also in the book *Suicide, Bereavement and Loss: Perspectives and Responses.*[1] As you reflect on this experience you may find it helpful to ponder the following questions:

- which aspects of this response are you at ease with and which would you seek to alter and how?
- what role could you play in such a case?
- how might your school community react to such a case if it were to occur tomorrow and what action does this reflection prompt?

First Responses

I was in my office talking with two senior students when the principal came in, his face ashen white. 'What am I about to hear?' I thought to myself as he was so clearly upset. He took me outside and told me that John (not his real name) had been found hanging in his garage at home. It was unclear if he had intended to commit suicide or was play-acting or giving a scare to his sister, with whom he had had a fight hours earlier. To this day, there has been no definitive answer to the 'why?' question. Myself, the principal and John's class tutor got together and began to talk, first of all, of our shock and then, slowly we began to discuss how we would communicate what had happened to John's friends and the entire school community.

John's Class

We agreed that the first concern was to talk to John's class. In talking about how we would do this, we were at the same time talking and listening to each other as we came to terms with the brutal fact that John, aged fifteen, was dead. We decided to bring the class to the oratory. We hoped that the very act of going to the oratory in the middle of normal class would begin to alert the students that something out of the ordinary had happened – to, in some small way, begin to prepare them for the shock. The class tutor, the principal, some teachers who were free and myself accompanied the class. The tutor, who had an excellent relationship with the class, was the first to speak, followed by the principal and myself. The effort was to:

- communicate the news in a sensitive manner
- give the facts as they were known
- create a safe space for the students
- begin to articulate the many ways they might react at the time and in the hours and days ahead
- highlight the support that would be available to them
- outline how they could help each other
- take time to pray for John, his family and friends

It goes without saying that the 'how' of the saying is at least as important as the content of the message being communicated. The class requested time together in the oratory to chat to each other. They also asked for time with their teachers and the chaplain.

The Remainder of the School

Between classes, the remaining staff were informed. A group of teachers undertook to visit each class in the following forty-minute period to notify the student body at large. This group spent a few minutes together formulating how they would break the news along the lines of what was said to John's own class. One of the teachers suggested that it might be helpful if all the staff could circulate in the yard during the upcoming break time. This proved very supportive to students, and indeed the staff themselves. Again, the variety of reactions was visible both in staff and students: disbelief, deep upset, curiosity, guilt, blame, anger, sadness, bewilderment and avoidance behaviour.

Assembly

The religious education co-ordinator organised a brief assembly for the whole school for later in the morning. This was a very simple occasion that allowed the school community to give some formal recognition to the tragedy. The principal opened the assembly and the chaplain spoke for a few moments recognising:

- the sense of loss
- the many different ways we respond to loss
- the importance of our prayer for those bereaved
- our need as a school community to watch out for each other in these days
- the support that would be available to students

A short reading from Isaiah was chosen:

> Do not be afraid, for I have redeemed you;
> I have called you by your name, you are mine.
> Should you pass through the sea,
> I will be with you; or through rivers,
> they will not swallow you up.
> For I am Yahweh your God,
> The Holy One of Israel, your saviour.
> It is because you are precious in my eyes,
> because you are honoured and I love you.
> Do not be afraid, for I am with you.
> (Is 43:1-3a, 4a)

This was followed by the singing, by one of the teachers, 'The Lord is My Shepherd'. Then some prayers for John, his family, his friends and the school were read.

John's Family

The principal, chaplain and John's class tutor visited the home in the morning. The family were delighted to know that John's friends were being supported and made it clear they were welcome to visit in the coming days, as John would be 'waked' in the house. Many of the students took up this invitation. In preparation for the visit to John's home the chaplain and tutor spoke to the students about what the experience might be like particularly for those who had not been in the presence of a dead body before or had not experienced a major bereavement in their lives. Time was taken, following such visits, to debrief the students and staff.

The Funeral and the Days Following

In consultation with the family and local clergy the school assisted with arrangements for the funeral, particularly in regard to guards of honour and choir. Students who were attending the services were encouraged to gather at the school beforehand – the vast majority did. Many arrived early and availed of the opportunity to talk together in small groups, or with teachers.

In the days following, John's class were reminded of the supports that were available to them. Many of the class came to see the chaplain or guidance counsellor in small groups and were encouraged to talk about their feelings and other issues that were being raised by the trauma. For many, this was the beginning of addressing significant personal concerns in their own lives. It was important that they were able to have the support they needed to begin to explore the issues raised.

Those staff members closely associated with John's class regularly met together informally in the days following to discuss the class – and also each other's – reactions. This proved an important support for all those involved. The group also sought the advice of outside professionals, so that they could have confidence in how they were addressing the overall situation.

Moving Through

An effort was made with John's class and his friends not to stay 'stuck' in the tragedy, but to recognise what was happening and aid the students absorb the experience as they continued with their lives. This was achieved in the individual conversations, in discussions held with the class and in the prayer times requested by the class.

This process of 'moving through' the experience was also helped by a day of reflection that was organised for John's class and friends – with parental permission – six weeks after the death had occurred. This was led by a trained retreat team who further supported the class and the individuals within it. The day ended with a liturgy organised by the students and attended by some of John's teachers. The class drew up a charter of how they would support each other in the months and years ahead – the charter dealt with issues such as:

- including everyone in class activities
- outlawing of bullying in any form
- rejoicing in each other's successes
- supporting each other in difficult times

The class agreed to review their charter regularly and asked their class tutor to support them in this review by setting aside tutor time for this purpose.

Final Thoughts

Careful consideration needs to be given to some further key aspects of a tragedy such as the one outlined above:

- support for teachers – a sudden death may raise painful issues in relation to the student concerned or other personal concerns
- parents of those students most affected by the tragedy may need some support

- those on the staff who have a key role in responding to a tragedy – such as the chaplain, guidance counsellor or class tutor – need to be helped in their dealing with the emotional load of such a tragedy

Postscript

It is now three years since John's death. Many of the students of John's class are in sixth year. There has been a special award in sport dedicated to John – one of his close friends was the first recipient. John's classmates have a special bond and are clearly 'moving through' their lives with the learnings of this loss as part of their experience. It is clear that their charter has indeed influenced their relationships with each other.

Notes

1. Monahan, Luke (ed.) (1999). *Suicide, Bereavement and Loss: Perspectives and Responses*, Dublin: Irish Association of Pastoral Care in Education

SUICIDE PREVENTION IN SCHOOLS

Michael Ryan

This chapter is based on an address to the Irish Association of Suicidology Conference, 'Suicide Prevention in Schools', held in Galway in December 2000. Michael highlights the research in the area of loss as it relates to the development of the young person. In particular, he outlines the programme for schools he has developed for the Irish Association of Pastoral Care in Education (IAPCE).

> 'Living With Change and Loss – A life-skills programme' was researched, developed and piloted by Michael Ryan as part of a post graduate study at Dublin City University. The Programme contains fifteen integrated units, including units on positive mental health and suicide prevention.
>
> In May 2000, the Irish Association of Pastoral Care in Education published the programme in a partnership with the Department of Education and Science, the Samaritans and the Dublin Lions Club. The first phase of programme piloting has commenced and programme facilitators from twenty-five second level schools nationwide have completed a mandatory in-service training module that accompanies the programme.

One of the consistent research findings associated with suicide relates to the issue of unresolved loss experiences. The purpose of this chapter is to examine relevant research findings that may help us understand the challenges for young people in coping with significant loss experiences. It is my belief that strategies for suicide prevention in schools will be more successful if we try to explore the complicated nature of adolescent life and how the adolescent perceives and experiences these losses.

A Philosophical Overview and the Pastoral School

Consistent attempts to define a philosophy of education in its fullest sense invariably refer to the promotion of spiritual, moral, cultural, aesthetic, mental and physical development of students and the preparation of them for the opportunities, responsibilities and experiences of adult life. If we accept the enduring wisdom of Heraclitus, that there is nothing permanent in life but change and nothing certain in life but loss, there are implications for our school curricula. How can we offer a balanced curriculum and an education and training for life without addressing such all-embracing issues as change and loss education? If we are committed to the education process in its fullest sense, then a central focus should be to enhance the psychological well-being of our students. Specifically, this involves improving mental well-being, reducing fears, and instilling a sense of self confidence to cope with life's crises. If so, then we will embrace the ethos of the truly pastoral school and the associated challenge of 'pastorally infused teaching'. To facilitate this, we require pastoral leadership, an appropriate ethos and vision, structures which facilitate the co-ordination of pastoral programmes, and a sense of coherence in actively promoting the school as a community of support for all its members.

The emergence of research on 'School Effectiveness' during the 1980s included explicit reference to pastoral care and the need for a strong sense of community. In an English context, the subsequent review of the national curriculum and its recommendations for social, personal and health education (SPHE) were that it cannot be left to chance, but needs to be co-ordinated as an explicit part of a school's whole curriculum policy inside and outside the time-table. Growing awareness was also expressed at formal policy level in an Irish context with the publication of The White Paper in Education – 'Charting our Education Future' (1995) – which stated in chapter thirteen that 'the promotion of the social, personal and health education of students is a major concern of each school.' In attempting to define how each school could give a practical dimension to the promotion of SPHE, the White Paper suggested that there were three main strands to be considered, these were:

- school climate
- the involvement of parents and the wider community
- positive interventions

A 'Living With Change and Loss Life-Skills Programme' could embrace all three strands, but primarily be a positive intervention for the pastoral school.

During my own initial research in developing the programme 'Living With Change and Loss' a colleague whom I interviewed had the following to say:

> From my experience, many of the students who experience low self-esteem and emotional trauma are frequently responding to significant losses in their lives. Many of these kids are under pressure and pre-occupied with their own internal turbulence.

Unresolved Loss and Mental Health Issues
Almost all available research findings suggests that emotional and psychological distress in adolescence is often linked with loss and disappointment, which was suffered in childhood and never adequately resolved. Recently, Dr Patrick McKeon, author of *Suicide in Ireland*, refers to losses in life as one of three cascading factors that influence suicide, the other factors being psychiatric illness and alcohol or drug abuse. An exploration of

the possible interrelationship between these three factors would be very interesting, but is not within the scope of this chapter.

Research on the theme of loss during the last two decades provides some valuable insights. Williams and Sturz (1990) describes the severe difficulties that adolescents may have in coping with the death of a parent, due to a less than perfect relationship with the deceased.[1] Subsequently, these adolescents experience prolonged feelings of guilt. Jewett explaines the consequences of complicated and unresolved grief for the adolescent in later life: 'Studies show that emotional distress in adolescence and adulthood including depression, alcoholism, anxiety and suicidal tendencies is often linked with bereavement suffered in childhood... which was not resolved.'[2]

Other authors, such as Bowlby, substantiate this view. Bowlby notes 'the communicative difficulties' experienced by the grieving adolescent, and terms such as 'Emotional Bottleneck' and 'Recycled Grief Syndrome' were characteristic of adults who had not resolved significant losses in their youth.[3]

Rebecca Abrams, when discussing the death of a mother during a son or daughter's early adolescent stage writes: 'It appears repeatedly in the literature on depression as a trauma sometimes likely to create nearly irreparable emotional havoc.'[4] While we must not generalise on the basis of such findings, seeking a meaningful and supportive response to the needs of such teenagers is surely a worthy psychological goal in a holistic curriculum.

Sandra Horn also addressed these factors when she describes:

> How a growing sensitivity in adolescents will result in a cover up of feelings so as not to cause additional distress to surviving parents and younger siblings... the young person may seem nonchalant, but poor school performance, withdrawal and awkward behaviour can be the outward signs of grief within.[5]

Horn also details the pressure on older adolescents to assume parental roles and the subsequent resentment of this by some teenagers.

Research findings, therefore, suggest that various factors combine in the effective isolation of some adolescents as they suppress, deny or silently grieve for a profound loss at a most vulnerable stage of their social and psychological development. This further accentuates the philosophical and psychological rationale for introducing a 'Living With Change and Loss' programme into a school context, where loss experiences may find a holistic and supportive educational environment. Further research, such as that of Holmes and Rahe's 'Readjustment Rating Scale', presents death as life's single greatest stress inducer. Therefore, there is surely a psychological imperative to address the theme of change and loss in our curricula?

Over a quarter of a century ago Elizabeth Kubler Ross, one of the most influential theorists regarding the need for change loss and death education, wrote:

> I hope to convey one important message to my readers; namely, that death does not have to be a catastrophic, destructive thing, indeed, it can be viewed as one of the most constructive, positive and creative elements of culture and life.[6]

Social Change

Previous generations of young people may have found support systems more readily available within the extended nuclear family or immediate neighbourhood. Today, however, we are living in an increasingly materialistic and secular world where individualism, academic achievement and material success are highly valued. If this trend continues, then our educational system will need to examine how best to prepare our young people to cope with the inevitable changes, losses and disappointments of life.

In recent years Ireland has become increasingly suburbanised, and the associated lifestyles, which are often disconnected from a sense of social community or place, may have an impact on the support mechanisms available. This movement from *gemeinschaft* type relationships, based on social cohesion and belongingness, to *gesellschaft* type relationships, based on impersonal, contractual arrangements, as elucidated by the German theorist Ferdinand Tonnies could help us understand the changing fabric of community bonds in an Irish context.

Mary Paula Walsh raises these concerns: 'Ireland up to two generations ago was a pre-industrial society, with a strong tradition of grieving and supporting rituals... Death was not denied, it was part of the natural order of things.'[7] She continues to demonstrate how death is being removed to hospitals, nursing homes and funeral parlours – creating further psychological alienation. Raising the issue of social change in an Irish context O'Rourke observes a

> More mobile nuclear family unit as the norm, and elderly people, among whom the vast majority of deaths occur, living geographically and psychologically apart from their children and grandchildren. This deprives the elderly of traditional assistance and reduces the impact of their death and dying on the day-to-day lives of their families.[8]

A consequence of this contraction of the extended nuclear family is that young people do not see the process of ageing take place and, since most people die in hospital, the process of dying can be hidden. Thus, according to O'Rourke, society has created a psychological taboo behind which death-related issues must hide, thus exacerbating anxiety levels and fear of the unknown.

Martin Desforges cites how many teenagers have lost touch with the realities and meaning of death, because of 'the way that death is trivialised and distanced in the media... and [in] computer games where characters 'die' several times.'[9] It would therefore seem that our post-modern world attempts to conceal and distance death from view, while also trivialising its impact as a profound psychological experience. If it happens then that young people experience a significant loss, they can be desensitised and unable to process the associated grief. Many of these changing attitudes towards death are seen as the psychological catalyst for 'Change and Loss Education', which has the potential to confront the fear, emancipate us from anxiety and positively sensitise us to the profound nature of change and loss.

At a wider level, communication within families and communities has greatly changed as work patterns and technological developments seem to reduce the time available for family communication. Televisions, computers, videos walkmans and mobile phones have become the pervasive communication media in many homes. We may have the technology to exchange messages and communicate at a global level, but the danger associated with this electronic message syndrome is that it will further de-skill the affective communication domain if listening and interpersonal sensitivities are not appropriately nurtured.

Suicide and the Adolescent

Throughout the Western World, the rate of suicide is increasing, particularly in the 15-25 year age group. In Ireland 33 per cent of the 439 reported suicides in 1999 were completed by people under thirty years of age. The National Suicide Research foundation is also reporting signs of an increase in young female suicide.

An extensive market research survey of the attitudes, behaviours and beliefs of young Irish adults in 1999 showed that 27 per cent of young males and 23 per cent of females saw suicide as sometimes justified, whereas only 6 per cent of the same sample thought driving with alcohol was ever justified.[10] In discussing these results, Dr Anthony Clare subsequently warns us of 'a tolerant view of suicide, which contrasts sharply with other findings in this national survey of six hundred young adults.'[11]

Researchers in Ireland have sought to understand the nature of increasing suicide rates in this young age cohort. Their ongoing research points toward endogenous depression, chronic schizophrenia and manic depression as still the most commonly influencing factor on suicide rates. Commentators such as Dr Michael Kelleher warn, however, that there are no universal or biological processes that invariably result in suicide. Each death is the result of an individual combination of personality and circumstances.[12]

Research work by Dr Alan Apter of Tel Aviv University Israel, presented at a national conference on suicide in Ennis in September 2000 concludes that there are three clusters of traits associated with suicidal behaviour. These clusters he identifies as:

- Impulsive Aggression – sensitivity to minor life events perhaps associated with abnormalities of serotonin and genetic factors, including polymorphisms of tryptophan hydroxylase. The tendency to frequently abuse drugs and alcohol is associated with this cluster.

- Narcissm and Perfectionism – low tolerance of failure and imperfection.

- Psychopathology – various affective disorders, such as schizophrenia, and depressive symptoms of helplessness and feeling overwhelmed by the psychiatric illness.

The McDonagh and Fitzgerald survey of Irish teenage depression in 1994 (although confined to just four Dublin secondary schools) concluded that: 'depression is much more common among teenagers than is generally realised.' Research shows that loneliness, isolation, low self-esteem and poor communication attributed to the high percentage of suicide among young males. By 1996 suicide in Ireland in the 15-25 year age group was the single greatest cause of death after road traffic accidents. This view is realised by the Irish organisation, AWARE, who state in relation to depressed teenagers:

> It is important to get the message to these young people that they are suffering from an illness – a treatable one. There is no better way of making information available than making it part of an integrated education programme in all schools.[13]

In a more recent study Dr Patrick McKeon, author of *Suicide In Ireland*, reports that 10 per cent of all Irish teenagers in the 13-18 year age cohort have clinical depression, and that 50 per cent of these cases are not recognised in the family home. Assuming that these findings are accurate, schools may need to be more pro-active in recognising and responding to depressive symptoms.

Emergent research findings also suggest that young homosexual men are a high risk-group. In an American context, William reported that 30 per cent of gay and bisexual men had attempted suicide,[14] while in Ireland, it was reported that 'thirty percent of youth suicides in Ireland are amongst gay adolescents'.[15] Considering these research findings, and the recommendations of the 'Suicide Task Force' report (1998) that pro-active programmes be introduced in schools to assist students maintain positive mental health, further procrastination is unwise. However, the challenge to design effective, sensitive, proactive, response-initiatives, cannot be underestimated.

Adolescents and Peer Death

For the adolescent, the death of a peer forces a very profound confrontation and premature acknowledgement of one's own mortality. The loss is particularly profound due to the intensity of adolescent peer relationships. Other authors also emphasise the sense of 'dislocation' and 'disconnectedness' that adolescent bereavement can present at a time of great transition. Adolescents are also heavily reliant on their peers for support, but Harris highlights how this support may be unavailable as 'the joint experience of suffering may render network members unable to support the individual for whom the loss is most immediate and profound'.[16]

Adolescent Loss and Changing Family Structures

While unresolved loss associated with death has been acknowledged by most people as a significant factor in the overall mental health debate, there is now growing awareness of the impact of loss experiences associated with parental separation and divorce.

In Ireland, an estimated sixty thousand marriages had ended in separation prior to the enactment of divorce legislation in 1997. Despite a smaller than anticipated uptake on divorce in the first year after its introduction, there were still eight thousand divorce applications and four and a half thousand judicial separations sought between 1997 and 1999. However, unofficial evidence might suggest that the rate of marital breakdown and subsequent new parent partnerships might be on the increase.

Despite the absence of reliable research in an Irish context, some international literature does raise interesting perspectives on parental separation and adolescent responses. In Britain, four out of ten marriages ended in divorce in 1996. Martin Desforges, when writing in a chapter entitled 'Separation, Divorce and the School' in the English context, stated: 'Within two years of parental divorce about 50 per cent of teenagers have lost contact with their natural father.'[17] According to the INTO, one in four children entering primary school was no longer from a traditional nuclear family.[18] Barbara Ward, when presenting the findings of observational research in English schools, validated my own intuition and that of many colleagues, based on our experience in Irish schools:

> Two thirds of all students showed some notable changes in school, subsequent to parent's separation... Teachers reported a high level of anxiety... described as new and unaccustomed restlessness... in the process interrupting classroom activities.

In earlier research Claudia Jewett alerts teachers to the complicated psychological responses of some adolescents as they blame either themselves or one parent for the separation. Jewett cites how some such adolescents: 'become stuck in the developmental process, unable to move past a particular developmental stage... repeating inappropriate behaviour over and over again.'[19]

Following longtitudinal research in an American context, Hetherington concluded that difficulties between custodial mothers and their teenage sons, and between teenage daughters and new step-fathers, emphasises the importance of schools playing a 'buffering' role for relevant adolescents.[20] Recent research carried out by the Californian Psychologist Judith Wallerstein, based on twenty-five years of research specialising on the effects of divorce on children, concluded: 'Children are better off living with happily separated or divorced parents than they are living with married parents in an ongoing atmosphere of strife and anxiety'.[21]

Regardless of the research findings, there is consensus that young people will frequently worry about such issues as custody, family finances, new partner parents and siblings, while also experiencing a sense of divided loyalties and self doubt.

ECHOES OF SUICIDE

In the Irish context, assumptions of traditional family structures demand more inclusive pastoral responses from our schools. A holistic change and loss programme could create positive awareness among teachers and students, while also providing opportunities for thoughtful and supportive responses throughout the pastoral dynamic of the school.

Grief Responses and Gender

In seeking to understand the particularly high ratio of young male suicides, some research on the theme of grief and gender responses may be helpful in exploring why males are less successful in negotiating around the feelings associated with loss experiences. Carol Staudacher's theory of gender and grief responses is one of these theories which highlights differences in gender responses.[22]

Staudacher's three-stage model of how loss should be dealt with could be summarised as follows:

- Phase One: Retreating, denial, confusion and temporary management of pain
- Phase Two: Working through the pain and disorganisation through a range of affective and cognitive responses
- Phase Three : Reorganising and Restructuring

Staudacher's research concluded, however, that many males did not complete or experience stage two. Instead of working through the pain of loss, they engaged in some or all of the following – remaining silent and engaging in secret grief, taking physical and legal action and becoming immersed in activity.
Subsequently J. Harper, when writing on grief and gender differences, states:

> Many men have been raised not to talk, cry or reach out. Therefore, their grief tends to stay inside and can create physical ailments, as studies have shown. Heart attacks,

ulcers, cancer are a few of the physical ailments that can be created when the grief stays within.[23]

Exposure to these theories in a life skills programme would focus attention on the consequences of unresolved grief for young men and invite further elaboration on socio-cultural aspects of gender responses. It would also prioritise the desirability of achieving 'emotional maturity', that is, the willingness to experience and express our feelings so that we develop a kind of resilience, a capacity to bounce back after facing stress. Whenever we face anything difficult without running away, we are courageous.

Points to Consider

Collectively, the theories and research outlined significantly elucidate the philosophical and psychological rationale for an appropriate change and loss education. Exposure to these theories in a school context may ameliorate the denial and fear among teachers and students, while also promoting positive awareness, support strategies and more optimistic integration of change and loss throughout life. It would also improve the cognitive and affective dimensions of the young person as proposed by Douglas Hamblin's seminal voice regarding pastoral care and the school: 'The two sides of school life are inseparable for what is good for moral development is also good for intellectual growth.'[24]

However, we must proceed with caution as Hamblin recommends: 'In no other subject are we so likely to cause harm through good intentions unbacked by careful thought.'
We should also consider Martin Desforge's more recent claim that 'most teachers err on the side of caution' and thus embrace the truly pastoral school as a means of instituting constructive, carefully planned curriculum innovations, rather than propping up the status quo and inhibiting change.[25]

In conclusion, there are many themes worthy of inclusion in

a positive intervention programme. Ultimately however a successful programme should help students deal with various crises so that they are able to build upon that foundation and emerge with increased self-confidence to cope with the various losses of life.

Living With Change and Loss– a life-skills programme

I will now briefly outline the programme that is currently being piloted in about twenty-five schools nationwide.

Core Programme Aims
- To facilitate participant understanding of change and loss as intrinsic to life itself.
- To develop communication skills.
- To develop coping skills for dealing more effectively with loss experiences.
- To facilitate an understanding of positive mental health.
- To help participants become better support agents to others throughout life.

Programme Themes
- Change Throughout Life
- Memories of Personal Loss
- Reactions and Responses to Loss
- Stages of Grief and Unique Personal Journeys
- Response Influencing Factors
- Different Types of Bereavement and Different Responses
- The Grieving Process and the Tasks of Mourning
- The Consequences of Unresolved Grief
- Gender and Loss
- The 'Dos and Don'ts' of Grief and Loss
- Adolescent Loss and Communication Issues
- Parental Separation and Loss Responses
- Mental Health Issues and Managing Feelings
- Helping the Anxious Young Person and Listening Skills

- Suicide a Proactive Response
- Universal Beliefs and Funeral Ritual
- Change and Loss as Catalysts for Fulfillment in Life

Each of these themes is presented within an associated unit that includes a range of appropriate resources, focused on the development of improved coping skills and positive approaches for programme participants. Each unit also includes practical guidelines on facilitation techniques and creating a positive learning environment.

Interactive Facilitation Methodology

The programme has been developed as a participative, experiental, activity-based model. Programme facilitators will have received some professional training in the process of facilitation, and will be familiar with relevant theories. The richness of the facilitation will emerge, however, as facilitators guide participants to engage in an exploration of relevant themes using reflective questionnaires, pair and group work, role plays, brainstorms, poetry, music, drama, case-studies, and meditation exercises.

An Ethical Framework

Given the potentially sensitive nature of the programme, it is appropriate that a rigorous ethical framework be put in place for facilitators and participants.

This framework is intended to provide for:

- the integration of the programme into the school's pastoral curriculum
- having appropriate support and referral mechanisms in place
- briefing the school community about the programme and its aims
- seeking the consent of parents
- observing the principle of appropriate confidentiality

ECHOES OF SUICIDE

- facilitating the participants right to withdraw from the programme
- ongoing programme evaluation

Programme Evaluation
A comprehensive three-tiered evaluation framework has been designed to ensure ongoing improvement of the programme. The evaluation is being coordinated by the Irish Association of Pastoral Care in Education and the programme author. It involves:

- evaluation of the in-service training module by participants and trainers;
- unit by unit evaluation by participants and facilitators in each pilot school;
- interim and summative evaluation by participants and facilitators.

The programme was previously evaluated in three pilot schools, where the author initially implemented the programme, and the responses were overwhelmingly positive:

- 94 per cent of participants described the themes as very interesting, worthwhile and comprehensive
- almost 90 per cent thought the programme would help them cope much more successfully with loss throughout life and
- 89 per cent felt they would now be much more successful in helping others cope.

Some interesting individual participant responses were as follows:

> I would now deal with loss better. I didn't realise it was so important to let out your grief. I would know how to get help...

I would be a much better listener now. I would know what to say and, more importantly, what not to say.

It helped us get closer as a class and get closer to our teachers. It was brilliant to talk about feelings and it should be really good for the future. It helped much more than one can say...

The programme resource book also received very favourable reviews from relevant personnel within the psychological service, the Department of Education and Science, from Barnardos and from the Samaritans, who are now actively involved in supporting the programme.

While these initial responses to the programme are very promising, I am fully aware that the successful implementation of the programme in any school setting will depend on many localised factors, including the availability of various resources.

The programme will continue to be evaluated so that future participants will benefit from the ongoing feedback from the pilot schools. Further in-service training for programme facilitators will integrate this feedback so that we can all contribute to the ongoing enrichment of an interesting programme initiative.

For further details regarding the programme contact:
Luke Monahan, National Co-ordinator, Irish Association of Pastoral Care in Education, Marino Institute of Education, Dublin 9 (Tel: 01-8057785)
Michael Ryan, Programme Specialist, Tipperary Rural and Business Institute
Nenagh Rd, Thurles Co, Tipperary (Tel 0504-24488)
Email: mryan@tippinst.ie
The book, *Living with Change & Loss* is available at £12.95 & £2 p + p from the IAPCE Office, Marino Institute of Education, Griffith Avenue, Dublin 9.

Notes

1. Williams, D. R and Sturz, J. (1990). *A Parent's Guide for Suicidal and Depressed Teens*, Minnesota: Hazelden

2. Jewett, C. (1984). *Helping Children Cope With Seperation and Loss*, London: Batsford Academic And Educational.

3. Bowlby, J.(1980). *Attachment and Loss, Volumes 1-3*. London: Hogarth Press

4. Abrams, R.(1992). *When Parents Die-Learning to live with the Loss of a Parent*, London: Thorsons

5. Horn, S.(1989). *Coping With Bereavement*, London: Thorsons Publishing Co.

6. Kubler Ross, E. (1991). *Living With Death and Dying*. London: Souvenir Press

7. Walsh, Mary Paula (1995). *Living After A Death, A guide book for the journey of Bereavement* Dublin: Columba Press.

8. O' Rourke, R. (1997). Thanatology-A Feasibility Study In the Irish Context, (Unpublished M.Ed Thesis)T.C.D. Berkley Library

9. Desforges, M.(1995). Separation, Divorce and the School, in Best, R. et. al. (Eds) *Pastoral Care and Personal Social Education*, London: Cassell

10. Wilson Hartnell Public Relations Group. (1990). *Market Research Survey on Attitudes of Young Irish Adults*

11. *Sunday Independent*, 21 November 1999

12. Kelleher, M. J. (1996). *Suicide and The Irish*, Dublin: Mercier Press

13. O'Reilly, S. (1997) AWARE

14. Williams, K.(1995). *Grief Counselling and Grief Therapy; A Handbook for The Mental Health Practitioner, (2nd Edition)* London: Tavistock/Routledge

15. *Irish Times*, 24 April 1999

16. Harris E. S. (1994). Adolescent Bereavement Following the Death of a Parent, *Child Psychiatry and Human Development*, Vol. 21, No.4

17. Desforges, Martin. Op. cit

18. INTO Conference (1997)

19. Jewett, C. Op. cit.

20. Hetherington, M.(1991). Coping with Family Transitions, in Woodhead, M., Light, P. and Carr, R.(Eds) *Growing Up In a Changing Society*, New York: Routledge.

21. *Irish Times*, 12 October 1999

22. Staudcher, C. (1991). *Men and Grief,* Philadelphia: Charles Press
23. Harper, J. M. (1998). Grief and Gender, in Grief Net Library (http://rivendall.org/)
24. Hamblin D. (1981). *The Teacher and Pastoral Care,* Oxford: Blackwell
25. Desforges, M. Op. cit.

4

FAITH
PERSPECTIVES

The Faith of Broken Hearts

My God,
What is faith anyway?

Faith is not
certainty of belief.
Certainly not!

Faith is a clinging on;
A hanging on,
When there is no longer
any logical reason to believe.

It is a spark,
A tiny voice within
That just would not allow me to let go of You.

All I could say for weeks and weeks –
'My God'
'Jesus'. 'Jesus'
'My God'.

I know that I repeated it a thousand times –
And more!

I know too
That You were with me all the time.
Neither would You let go of me.

You did not take away my pain.
You did not ease my awful ache.
Nor did you break the darkness of my life.

Yet now I know,
That, as I clung on in faith,
'My God',
You held me tightly through it all.

Stephen O'Gorman

HOPE IN THE FACE OF SUICIDE

Eamonn Walsh

Eamonn is auxiliary bishop in the archdiocese of Dublin. He has been chaplain in Mounjoy Prison for many years. In this article he articulates the Christian voice in the context of suicide.

'Is this the person you are looking for?' the man at the morgue said to me as he pulled back the sheet covering the open mouth of Jane. I nodded in silence. As he shoved the tray back along the runners of the large, metal fridge he muttered, 'That's life for you, Father'. I left the morgue that evening in November 1978 stunned, and studying Jane's note that told me who to say her goodbyes to and her scribbled instructions that all her belongings were to go to her friend, Peggy. They filled two plastic bags. When Jane had taken all her tablets and a bottle of wine, she took up her perch in the alley way at the back of the old Mater Private. As she lay dead in a doorway, all her money, her bits of paper, including her name, were stolen.

Philomena was hanging for eight days in her single-room bedsit in the August heat of 1987 before she was discovered. I was not there for her call. The 'if only's' are there in every suicide. As a child, I vividly recall hearing the adults talking of the terrible death of a friend who had deliberately taken strychnine.

I recall a broken-hearted mother reflectively saying, 'If only I could have reached out and told him he could talk, and he would still be a man.' What a burden for a mother who give birth with such hope and love.

These are just some of the memories that came back to me as I was invited to write this reflection. All of us have different instances of suicide that we all recall. Now it is more common. The statistics are worrying. The fall-out horrific. It is not for us to judge those who died from suicide. Only God can fully understand their tortured state of mind. Whatever occasions the final night, whatever blocks out the light of hope or reduces life's focus to an intolerable burden, somehow the natural instinct of self-preservation gives way.

It is a reality that many people actively contemplate suicide. They experience a deep sense of hopelessness and despair. In some way they reflect the experience of the poet, Robert Frost

> I have been one acquainted with the night
> I have walked out in rain – and back again.
> I have out walked the further city light.

How can we communicate hope to a person in their darkest hour? How can we communicate a motive for not turning off the light? How can we enable a person to spot the crack that lets the light come through? How can we encourage them again 'to pay out their nets even though they have laboured all night and caught nothing'? How can we bring them beyond the cry: 'My God, my God why have you abandoned me?'

As baptised members of God's family, we are entrusted with the privileged task of being Christ's ears, voice and hands to each other. We make our feeble efforts to walk with our heavily-burdened brothers and sisters along the hills and valleys of life's journey in the confidence that we are God's instruments and that his strength, wisdom and compassion will flow through us to our companions in need. God is calling each one of us to be the 'Hope in the Face of Suicide' to one another.

No one needs to face this frightening situation alone. It is up to you and to me to communicate that we care by thoughtfully asking, 'Are you alright?' and listening to the reply. Our concern must leave no doubt that our time is not precious, or more important than calming the storm in their heart or mind at that moment. It means living basic Christianity. 'When I was hungry you gave me to eat'. It has no price tag because it is priceless. Family, friends, organisations – for example, Aware, the Samaritans, the Suicidology Association – the companion on a bar stool or in the coffee dock all have been, and continue to be, lifelines to those in the depths of darkness, who believe, at a particular time, that there is no more to life than as seen now.

No words can capture the intense grief of those bereaved by suicide. At first, the deliberate nature of the act is difficult to accept or understand. There may be feelings of anger, guilt, anxiety and a sense of irreplaceable loss. Then there is the prolonged and painful search for explanations. Sometimes it is only with the benefit of hindsight that we reach understanding. In time it is only with support from people around them and God beside them, that survivors receive the inner strength to face the tragedy.

No one needs to face this frightening situation alone. It is up to you and to me to communicate that we care by thoughtfully asking 'Are you alright?' and listening to the reply.

We cannot ignore suicide and pretend that it is nothing to do with you or me. If people are walking off our world, then it is our concern. If we belong to a faith that makes us see each other as brothers and sisters in Christ, then they have an even deeper claim on us. If we can manage to give hope to one person it will have been worthwhile.

For the believer, there is a depth of experience and hope to be gained from those who have walked and survived in the valley of darkness.

> You O Lord are my lamp,
> My God who lightens my darkness
> With you I can break through any barrier
> With my God I can scale any wall. *(Ps 17:30)*

SUICIDE AND MORALITY

Sean Fagan

Sean, a Marist Priest, has more than forty years experience of teaching, counselling and writing in Europe, America, Africa, and Asia. He is author of Has Sin Changed? (1977), Does Morality Change? (1997), and over sixty articles on theology, spirituality and religious life.

The Jewish, Christian and Muslim religions have always condemned suicide as a moral wrong, as sinful. Indian and Japanese religions accepted certain types of suicide as part of their culture, almost as noble gestures (for example, suttee, the death of a Hindu widow on the funeral pyre of her husband, or hara-kiri, the ritual suicide by disembowelment with a sword, formerly practiced by Samurai to avoid dishonour), but these have declined in recent times. The Muslim Koran censures suicide as a more serious crime than homicide, and the Jewish Talmud condemns it as sinful, because of the sacredness of human life.

The Christian tradition, which condemns suicide as immoral, or in religious terms sinful, is rooted in the fifth commandment's solemn prohibition, 'Thou shalt not kill'. Church law reinforced this command by refusing ecclesiastical burial to those who committed suicide. This punishment was intended to stress the seriousness of the crime and to act as a deterrent to those tempted to take their own lives. The enormity of the penalty may well have given pause for thought to some would-be suicides, but it is less than helpful, indeed it is seriously harmful, in coping with our experience of suicide today. The Catholic Church has taken note of this in so far as this harsh penalty was dropped from the latest edition of its canon law in 1983. The only reference to suicide in the Church's current law is to state that people who have attempted suicide are barred from ordination.

Christian Tradition

It is instructive to see how the Christian moral tradition developed in its treatment of suicide. The standard textbooks for centuries were quite clear and consistent, beginning with the statement that 'the direct and voluntary taking of one's own life is a mortal sin,' an intrinsic evil that can never be justified. Whether one's death is freely caused by a positive act of self-destruction or by refusing to do something necessary for the preservation of life – such as failure to close an open bleeding artery – makes no moral difference to the seriousness of the sin. But there is a moral difference between direct and indirect suicide. It is direct when death is deliberately chosen for its own sake or as a means to an end, but indirect when it is not directly willed, but simply foreseen as the likely consequence of an act chosen for another purpose, for example when a driver turns a car over a cliff to avoid colliding with an oncoming school bus. Catholic theology has always regarded direct suicide as a violation of the divine law 'Thou shalt not kill'. This prohibition was also seen as a violation of natural law, going against a basic human instinct. The classic arguments backing up this position were formulated by St Thomas Aquinas as follows: The taking of one's own life is contrary to the inclination implanted by the Creator in every creature to love itself, to preserve itself in existence, and to resist whatever would destroy it. Suicide is also an offence against society, since human beings belong to the human family, to society, as parts to a whole, and the suicide who takes his own life deprives the community of something belonging to it. Life is a gift from God, given to be used and enjoyed, a gift entrusted to our stewardship, something for which we are accountable, over which we have no dominion. Only God has absolute dominion over life.

Direct and Indirect

Catholic moralists were agreed that direct and freely willed suicide is intrinsically evil, so that no circumstances could ever justify it. In the case of indirect suicide, one's death is not desired or intended, but is simply a consequence foreseen as probable or even as certain, of an otherwise lawful action. Moralists listed the following conditions which might justify indirect suicide: (1) if the action itself, apart from the consequent death, is morally good or at least indifferent, (2) that the evil effect is not intended, (3) that the good effect follows directly from the action and not as a result of the evil effect, and (4) that the good effect is of sufficient value to compensate for allowing the evil effect to happen. To evaluate the balancing of the good and evil effects, moralists pointed out that the common good may take precedence over the personal good of an individual, that helping someone in extreme spiritual need might be considered a greater good than saving one's own physical life, that one could risk life for the sake of a better livelihood, or risk death in a dangerous operation in the hope of relieving unbearable pain.

The *Catechism of the Catholic Church*, published in 1994, summarises this reasoning in two short paragraphs, and adds that if suicide is committed with the intention of setting an example, especially to the young, it also takes on the gravity of scandal. It also says that voluntary co-operation in suicide is contrary to the moral law. While going into great detail to evaluate the morality of suicide, the tradition was always careful to stress that the seriousness of the sin could be lessened by a lack of knowledge or of freedom on the part of the suicidal person. The Catechism expresses this with the words: 'Grave psychological disturbances, anguish or grave fear of hardship, suffering or torture can diminish the responsibility of the one committing suicide' (n. 2282). It makes no reference to the Church law, which until 1983 refused ecclesiastical burial to people who commit suicide, but tries to be compassionate by saying: 'We should not despair of the eternal salvation of persons who have taken their own lives. By ways known to him alone, God can provide the opportunity for salutary repentance. The Church prays for persons who have taken their own lives' (n. 2283).

Changed World

Theologians or historians may be fascinated by the painstaking moral analysis of our Catholic tradition. It was motivated by concern for the purity of God's law, and the effort to help people to understand it and be faithful to it. But we need to realize that there is no word of God in pure unadulterated form, atemporal and ahistorical. God's word comes to us in human words, and every human word, from the moment when humans first learned to speak, is culturally conditioned, reflecting the experience and the culture of the speakers. The Old Testament God exhorting his people to slaughter their enemies in thousands, or supporting slavery and polygamy, needs a special kind of interpretation to make sense in the modern world. Likewise, the culture and experience reflected in our traditional theological discussion of suicide is that of a world much simpler than the one we are familiar with today. Even allowing for occasional diminished responsibility, people committing suicide were judged as deliberately choosing to end their lives in defiance of God's law and therefore needing punishment. Even the Catechism's effort to be compassionate ('God can provide the opportunity for salutary repentance') seems to imply that many, if not most, people who commit suicide are sinners. This is weak and half-hearted in face of the huge numbers of suicides in

ECHOES OF SUICIDE

today's world. Until fairly recently, moral theology books claimed that suicide occurred less frequently in Catholic countries like Ireland and Italy than in the non-Catholic Scandinavian countries. Whatever about the past, modern statistics present a different picture. In fact, Ireland has one of the highest suicide rates in Europe, and suicide is the second most common cause of death in the fifteen to thirty-four year old age group of men. For this group the numbers are three times what they were twenty years ago, and they continue to grow.

While the moral principles and the discernment process used in the Church's traditional teaching are still valid, we need to be much more humble and tentative in our approach today. Perhaps we did too much lecturing and not enough listening in the past. We need to accept that the phenomenon is far more complex than a simple decision to opt out of problems by taking one's life. Research shows that no single factor can be identified as a common cause. Various psychological motivations can lead to suicide: frustration leading to hostility, which is turned inward upon oneself instead of outward to others; a loss of love, a feeling of inadequacy or rejection, feelings of guilt and a desire for revenge. These are further complicated by sociological factors, by religious beliefs and cultural influences. A new element is the discovery that suicidal people are deficient in a brain chemical called 5-HT, just as most male psychopaths are found to have an extra Y-chromosome. Indeed there are so many factors involved that we need to be hesitant about moral judgement of any individual case. There is a wealth of information on suicide now available that we need to study. The World Health Organisation has published a considerable amount of well researched material, and there are some excellent studies available on the Irish situation.

Today's Challenge

A first conclusion that emerges from current studies on the subject is that while the traditional moral principles and discernment processes are still valid, our judgement of individual cases needs to be much more carefully nuanced. Indeed since the act of suicide runs totally counter to the most fundamental thrust of human nature, the general presupposition must be that people taking their own lives are most unlikely to be fully responsible for their action. For many, if not most, the moral question is almost academic. The moral challenge is to the community, a challenge to pastoral care for those at risk, and appropriate concern and practical help for the family and friends left behind. A caring community needs to provide understanding and sympathy for the bereaved, but they need special skills to guide them through the bereavement process. A particular challenge is the help needed by people who have attempted suicide and failed. Over and above natural sympathy and concern, there are professional skills available to help them to adjust to their situation, to recover some sense of self-worth, to realise that they are not to be blamed for what they have done, to learn to cope with feelings of guilt, and to work towards a more positive attitude to life.

While understanding the Church's stand on the morality of suicide in previous generations, the Christian community must see that the moral challenge in today's more complex, fragmented and individualistic world is one of boundless compassion for people who are driven to suicide, and the practical challenge is that of preventive medicine, to work towards the creation of new communities of openness, sincerity and welcome, where all can feel at home, where people are affirmed, healed and enabled to grow, so that they have a feeling of self-worth, of being happy in their own skin, where they have nothing to be afraid of or ashamed of. How seldom do Christians in their gatherings – even at the Eucharist where they are told that they are one in Christ, sharing in his body and blood – really believe that they are infinitely precious in God's eyes, uniquely created in the image and likeness of Jesus? Even if they are told this in an occasional homily, how many feel it in practice in their daily lives? The big challenge to the Christian Church today is to stop thinking of itself as an elite society, a kind of club for the perfect, a reward for those who keep all the rules, and to reflect instead on the image that Jesus himself used for the community of his followers. Essentially, the Church is a sign, symbol and sacrament of the whole family of God, perfect and imperfect, saint and sinner, a community whose most telling image is the tiny grain of mustard seed that grows into a mighty tree to give shelter to all the birds of the air, where each can feel at home, loved and cherished, whatever their gifts, their weaknesses or their needs.

Essentially, the Church is a sign, symbol and sacrament of the whole family of God, perfect and imperfect, saint and sinner, a community whose most telling image is the tiny grain of mustard seed that grows into a mighty tree to give shelter to all the birds of the air, where each can feel at home, loved and cherished, whatever their gifts, their weaknesses or their needs.

APPROACHING GOD IN ANGER AND HOPE

Orla Phillips

Orla explores our relationship with God in the context of bereavement and trauma. She examines Scripture for hints as to how we might approach God as our true selves. She is a post-primary teacher of Religious Education, in which she holds a masters degree from Mater Dei Institute. She is currently on secondment to the Department of Education and Science supporting the new curriculum on Religious Education.

In the days and weeks following a suicide strong feelings of anger tend to surface in the bereaved. This anger can be with oneself, with the person who has died, with relatives or friends, indeed, with anyone who might have contributed to the death, or who could have acted to prevent it. Frequently, this anger is directed at God. The tragic fact that someone we love has taken his or her own life can cause us to rage at God. 'Why did God do this to me?' 'Why did God let my daughter die by suicide?' 'Where was God when my son took his own life?' – these are some of the questions that we hear from the lips of those bereaved by suicide.

Human Anger with God: A Genuine Faith Response
To some, such questions are unseemly. An instinctive reaction is to tell the speaker to keep quiet. However, such a reaction is misguided. Questions such as these are legitimate faith issues.

The anger that underpins them is a genuine faith response. We know from our experience of interpersonal relationships that there is a close connection between anger and love. Frequently, the people with whom we become most angry are those whom we most love. Is it any different in our relationship with God? Perhaps, it is precisely because they have set their hearts on God that those bereaved by suicide rage at Him. Their fury may have its roots in their very commitment to a particular vision of God. They may perceive that the God they love has let them down, and naturally, feel very angry.

Why, O Lord? How Long?
The Bible contains many examples of human anger with God. This anger finds clear expression in the many songs about suffering in the Old Testament Book of Psalms. In these prayers of lament or complaint, sufferers confront God with the pain-filled reality of their lives. They bring their shame, isolation and afflictions to the attention of God. In some cases, they affirm that their anguish is the result of God's absence and neglect (cf. Pss 10:1; 22:1, 19; 35: 22-23). In other cases, they angrily assert that God is the very agent of their distress:

> You have put me in the depths of the Pit,
> in the regions dark and deep.
> Your wrath lies heavy upon me,
> and you overwhelm me with all your waves.
> You have caused my companions to shun me;
> you have made me a thing of horror to them...
> Your wrath has swept over me;
> your dread assaults destroy me...

You have caused friend and
neighbour to shun me;
(Ps 88: 6-8a, 16, 18a)[1]

As we might expect, the idea that God either causes or permits
their suffering is a source of great puzzlement to the psalmists.
This is because it contradicts the ancient teaching that God
rewards the righteous and punishes the wicked. Guided by this
traditional doctrine, the psalmists frequently protest that they
are innocent and do not deserve such abuse from God (cf. Pss
26:1, 6, 11; 35:11-14, 24-25; 44:17-19). They also demand
answers from God. Since their experience of life contradicts the
traditional view that righteousness leads to prosperity and sin
leads to suffering, they angrily question God concerning the
purpose and duration of their troubles:

Rouse yourself! Why do you sleep, O Lord?
Awake, do not cast us off forever!
Why do you hide your face?
Why do you forget our affliction and oppression?
For we sink to the dust; our bodies cling to the ground.
Rise up, come to our help.
Redeem us for the sake of your steadfast love.
(Ps 44:23-26)[2]

How long, O Lord? Will you forget me forever?
How long will you hide your face from me?
How long must I bear pain in my soul,
and have sorrow in my heart all day long?
How long shall my enemy be exalted over me?
Consider and answer me, O Lord my God!
(Ps 13:1-3a)[3]

Like many people bereaved by suicide today, the psalmists of
Ancient Israel want to know why God allows or inflicts trouble

upon them. The fact that their experience of life goes against the inherited understanding of the divine causes them to angrily demand answers of God.

The complaint-psalms are remarkable for the boldness with which they address God. In these psalms, sufferers refuse to accept their situation quietly. They seek to have their passionate say with God. The fact that the psalmists regarded this as an appropriate way to relate to God is significant, and has important implications for speech about human anger in the face of suicide. However, before we consider these implications, it is important to note that frustration with God's ways is only one theme, albeit a central theme, in the complaint-psalms. An important counter-theme is hope and confidence in God. Alongside the many complaints and challenges to God are numerous expressions of hope and confidence in the divine. The God who is charged with negligence or destructiveness is also the God to whom psalmists turn for hope.

Hope and Confidence: Another Faith Response

A key characteristic of the complaint-prayers is that the psalmists call upon God to rescue them from their troubles. In almost every one of the complaint-prayers the speaker begs God to redeem the pain-filled situation:

> Incline your ear, O Lord, and answer me,
> for I am poor and needy,
> Preserve my life, for I am devoted to you;
> save your servant who trusts in you...
> For you, O Lord, are good and forgiving,
> abounding in steadfast love to all who call on you.
> Give ear, O Lord, to my prayer;
> listen to my cry of supplication.
> In the day of my trouble I call on you,
> for you will answer me.
> (Ps 86:1-2a, 5-7)

At the root of this and similar petitions is the belief that God will respond positively to the speaker's pleas. In this and other complaint-prayers, the psalmists call upon God for help precisely because they trust that God will receive and answer their appeals. Their petitions are simultaneously cries for help and confessions of confidence in God. In spite of their afflictions, the psalmists continue to trust in God's steadfast love. They trust that the God who is indirectly – or even directly – responsible for their troubles will assist in rectifying the unbearable situation. Inspired by this hope, they petition God for help.

Generally, the psalmists' hope in God is vindicated. In most of the complaint-psalms, God is moved, by the mixed cries of anger and hope, to engage in new rescuing activity. Typically, God responds to the passionate pleas of the psalmists by helping to redeem their pain-filled situation. As a result of God's activity, many of the complaint-psalms end on a note of thanksgiving and praise to God:

> Blessed be the Lord,
> for he has heard the sound of my pleadings.
> The Lord is my strength and my shield;
> in him my heart trusts;
> so I am helped, and my heart exults,
> and with my song I give thanks to him.
> (Ps 28:6-7)[4]

The complaint-psalms are an amazing blend of human frustration and hope in God. However, they are not unique in the history of Israel. Similar expressions of frustration with God and hope in God's ways can be found in other books in the Bible, such as Lamentations and Job. One particular text that deserves special consideration is Jesus' cry of abandonment from the cross.

Jesus' Cry from the Cross: An Expression of Anger and Hope?
According to the gospel writers Mark and Matthew, the final words of the crucified Jesus were: 'My God, my God, why have you forsaken me?' (Mk 15:34b; Mt 27:46b). These words are from the opening verse of Psalm 22 – a complaint psalm traditionally known as 'the psalm of the righteous sufferer'. The fact that Mark and Matthew place these words on the lips of the dying Jesus suggests that he experienced hurt, puzzlement and frustration with God's ways in the face of his own death. These words indicate that Jesus found it hard to reconcile the silence of God in the face of his sufferings with the intimate presence of God in his life. As the one who had performed mighty deeds in the name of God, Jesus was baffled and distressed by the apparent inactivity of God on Golgotha.

However, in spite of his pain and puzzlement at God's apparent inactivity, the crucified Jesus continued to hope and to trust in God's ways. At the time of Jesus, the saying of the opening verse of a psalm implied the saying of the whole psalm. Significantly, Psalm 22 moves from complaint to hope to praise in regard to the mystery of God. After a series of complaints and recollections of past care on the part of God, the speaker turns to God in hope and calls upon God to deliver him or her from the current danger. Apparently, his or her prayers are answered, because the psalm ends with an ode of praise and thanksgiving to God.

In view of the precise contents of Psalm 22, it is clear that the crucified Jesus did not relinquish hope in God. Despite his puzzlement and frustration with God's ways, the crucified Jesus continued to trust in the God who had initiated and sustained his ministry. He continued to hope and to have confidence in the answer that he had arrived at earlier – namely, that his shameful death was somehow bound up with the coming of the Kingdom of God (Mt 26:29).

However, at the same time it is clear that Jesus' faith was challenged by God's failure to rescue him. We should not let the final confident verses of Psalm 22 blind us to the fact that the crucified Jesus found it difficult to reconcile his God-forsaken death with the intimate presence of God in his life. While his faith in the reliability of God did not give way, Jesus did experience distress, puzzlement and disappointment with God. His protest on the cross is a mixture of frustration and hope in God's ways.

Ultimately, Jesus' confidence in God was rewarded. The Gospels indicate that God responded to the faith-filled protest of Jesus by raising him from the dead to new life. The God who answered the mixed cries of the psalmists also responded positively to Jesus' complaint.

Suicide and the Complaint-Tradition

The complaint-tradition that finds expression in the Book of Psalms and on the lips of the crucified Jesus combines frustration and hope in the same utterance. In this tradition, sufferers both protest to God about their troubles and turn to God for hope. The fact that the ancient Israelites, and more particularly Jesus, regarded this as an appropriate way to relate to God is significant. Even more astonishing is the fact that, in the Bible, these mixed cries of hope and complaint generally elicit a favourable response from God. In the complaint-tradition, the sufferer's assault upon God usually moves God to help redeem the situation. The precise nature of the exchange between God and the sufferer in this tradition suggests that authentic faith involves not only the worship and praise of God, but also the bringing of one's afflictions, challenges and anger to God. From this perspective, the faith valued by God is characterised not only by trust and hope, but also by the confidence to bring one's challenges, questions and frustrations to God.

The complaint-tradition in the Bible constitutes a rich resource for people bereaved by suicide. It opens the way for them to bring their protests, hurts and needs to God, and provides the language for them to do so. Contrary to the modern suspicion that human anger is an affront to God, the complaint-tradition reveals that God is One who receives – and takes seriously – our harsh complaints. From this perspective, genuine complaint-making is an aspect of human behaviour that finds acceptance from God. Therefore, there is no need for people bereaved by suicide to feel guilty about expressing anger with God. The God revealed in the complaint-tradition, especially in the prayer of the crucified Jesus, is big enough to understand and to receive one's hurts, doubts and complaints. There is no need to feel uncomfortable about bringing these issues to God.

The realisation that it is legitimate to express anger with God can be an important step in the healing process of people bereaved by suicide. We know, from lived experience, that when anger is suppressed or denied it eats away at the person and embitters one's relations with self, others and God. On the other hand, the responsible venting of anger cleanses the self and facilitates life-giving relationships with the self, the divine and others. In opening the way for people to bring their protests to God, the complaint-tradition may help those bereaved by suicide to face and to express their pent-up anger with God. Such a release of anger may help the bereaved to work through their grief to a healthier life- and God-affirming situation.

> The striking blend of human anger with God and hope in God in the complaint-tradition challenges people bereaved by suicide to hope and to trust in the God who is the focus of their anger. It invites all sufferers to turn to God for help, even while they express their exasperation with God's ways.

While indicating the legitimacy of expressing genuine anger with God, the complaint-tradition also reveals that anger with God and hope in God are not opposed. From this perspective, being angry with God does not mean having to let go of hope and confidence in God. The striking blend of human anger with God and hope in God in the complaint-tradition challenges people bereaved by suicide to hope and to trust in the God who is the focus of their anger. It invites all sufferers to turn to God for help, even while they express their exasperation with God's ways.

Once the bereaved have owned and expressed their anger with God, they may be ready to search for answers to the questions they initially asked about Him. Unfortunately, the complaint-tradition does not provide a satisfactory answer to the question of why God allows suicide. Those answers that it does provide are incompatible with the revelation that 'God is Love' (cf. 1 John 4:16). Any suggestion that suicide is caused by God or is the result of God's inattentiveness or neglect must be discounted on the grounds that it contradicts the Christian understanding of God as Love. Perhaps, the only adequate answer to the question of why God allows suicide is that God always respects the freedom of the individual. As the One who is Love, God does not override human freedom, even when the full exercise of that freedom is hindered by sadness, depression or drugs. Instead, the God whose power is the power of Love allows human freedom to run its – often misguided – course.

One question to which the complaint-tradition yields a satisfactory answer is the issue of the whereabouts of God when people die by suicide. The revelation that God was sufficiently present to receive the complaint-prayers of the psalmists and of the crucified Jesus indicates that God is present with those who complete suicide. Just as the silence of God surrounding the cross of Christ was not a silence of absence, rejection or withdrawal, neither is the silence of God in the face of suicide a silence of absence, rejection, nor withdrawal. In both cases, we are faced and challenged by the silence of God that takes human freedom seriously.[5]

In the same way as God is present with people who complete suicide, God is also present with people bereaved by suicide.

The revelation that God receives the prayers of the psalmists and of the crucified Jesus indicates that God is present with the bereaved, helping them to cope with their tragic situation. This revelation may give the bereaved new eyes to look at their situation, and to recognise the quiet activity of God in their midst. The following prayer by Marjorie Dobson offers a window onto the compassionate presence of God at the heart of bereavement:

A Blessing in Bereavement

May God bless you and be with you in this time of deep sorrow.
In the tears of others, know that he weeps with you.
In the touch of others, know that his arms are holding you.
In the practical work of others, know that he is helping you to cope from day to day.
In the words of others, know that he is speaking to you.
In the prayers of others, know that he hears you.
And in the desolation of this time, know that by each tear, touch, act, word and prayer, others are bringing God's love to you to filter into those empty spaces with his compassion and understanding.[6]

Once anger is spent, perhaps those bereaved by suicide will come to recognise and to derive strength from the quiet activity of the compassionate God in their pain-filled situation.

Notes

1. Other examples include Pss 39:5, 9b-11; 44:9-14; 60:1-4.
2. Other examples are Pss 10:1; 42:9; 88:14.
3. See also Pss 35:17; 74:10-11; 80:4
4. Other examples include Pss 13:5-6; 31:21-22; 35:27-28; 56:12-13.
5. See Dermot A. Lane, *Christ at the Centre: Selected Issues in Christology*, Dublin: Veritas Publications, 1990, p. 72.
6. *A World of Blessing: Benedictions From Every Continent and Many Cultures*, G. Duncan (ed.), Norwich: The Canterbury Press, 2000, p. 321

PREVENTING SUICIDE — THE PASTORAL CHALLENGE

Edmund Hogan

*Edmund is a priest of the Society of African Missions.
Here he offers guidelines and challenges for those in ministry who
are faced with suicide. The article will be a resource not only to
those in a pastoral role but also to anyone seeking a greater
understanding of the area. This article first appeared in the
May 2001 issue of* The Furrow.

Meeting people in Ireland on occasions when suicide is discussed, there is much talk and wringing of hands, and one senses a deeply rooted fatalism. Blame is placed on 'materialism', 'lack of religious values', 'consumerism', 'pressures of modern life', 'break-down of family life', and so on – all things that are considered beyond our control. All these factors may be implicated to some extent and many of them may be truly outside our control, but how helpless are we in the face of suicide? Is there any response to be made to the phenomenon of suicide as it occurs in our communities day by day? Are fatalism and fear the only authentic responses? Statistics show that Ireland's rate of suicide is among the highest in Europe and has been increasing dramatically in recent years. Talk, hand-wringing and fatalism are not good enough. Responsibility for preventing suicide and helping those who are bereaved rests with individuals, communities and government, and all have a duty to play their part.

Undoubtedly, one of the most difficult pastoral challenges today is suicide. It is difficult for many obvious reasons: the suddenness, violence and horror of the occurrence, and the devastating consequences for the bereaved survivors. It is hardly surprising that when called to a suicide we wonder whether we will be able to cope. There are, perhaps, two less obvious reasons why we find suicide particularly difficult: firstly, the fear that sometime in the future the victim may be a member of our own family circle; and secondly, the deepest and most hidden fear of all, that we ourselves might someday take our own lives. Suicide is something that we would rather not think about, something that, if given the choice, we would gladly strike from our repertoire of pastoral duties. However, we are not given that choice. With the spiralling incidence of suicide, it is a pastoral situation which demands our attention ever more frequently.

How Do We Respond?

Certainly with good intentions, showing the greatest compassion that we are capable of and drawing on whatever experience we might have of such situations. However, few of us ever had much training in the pastoral care of those bereaved by suicide, and it certainly never featured in our seminary programmes. Nor have we had much training in the prevention of suicide. Good intentions and great compassion are essential, but they are not enough. We also need to be properly

There are, perhaps, two less obvious reasons why we find suicide particularly difficult: firstly, the fear that sometime in the future the victim may be a member of our own family circle; and secondly, the deepest and most hidden fear of all, that we ourselves might someday take our own lives.

informed. No matter how good our intentions or great our compassion, an understanding of suicide that is half-baked or misinformed can do more harm than good. And in regard to suicide prevention, a role which we must increasingly undertake, lack of information can allow lives to be lost that might otherwise be saved. This chapter is concerned, primarily, with prevention and with establishing the minimum the individual pastoral minister should know.

In recent years, there has been extensive international research into suicide and an increasing body of Irish research. What follows is a layman's attempt to make sense of this research. It is now possible to identify important components that are found in suicide and, by analysing them, to construct what scientists like to call 'a model of suicide'. Some elements of this model are firmly established by research; others are less certain and require further study. Both nationally and internationally, there is currently an intensification of research and one can look forward to a more secure model. In the meantime, it will be valuable to outline the model as it currently exists, noting the weight of evidence attached to each element. It is hoped that an understanding of this model will help in the pastoral tasks of suicide prevention and ministry to the survivors of suicide.

Some Facts

People tend to complete suicide more frequently at certain stages in the human life cycle. The years between fifteen and thirty and sixty and eighty claim a higher number of suicides than other periods of life. The reasons for this pattern are not difficult to understand: the years between thirty and sixty are generally a time of maturity and productivity, a time characterised by a certain stability, whereas the years between fifteen and thirty are generally more volatile and stressful as one tries to find one's place in the world. After sixty, retirement from work, the departure of family, the onset of illness, all create a new volatility and uncertainty.

The ratio of male suicides to female stands at approximately 3:1. Yet more women than men suffer from depression, while they also have a higher rate of attempted suicide. How can this discrepancy be explained? Recently, the *Irish Times* columnist, John Waters, highlighted the importance of this statistic and called for an exploration of its deeper significance – beyond the citing of risk factors that men tend to have, such as depression or alcoholism. He asks what is causing the depression or alcoholism and, in his answer, implicates the condition of post-feminist man in our society. John Waters has raised an important issue, and I'm not sure the scientific research gives all the answers. But it does shed some light. Research shows that males tend to choose more violen – and more final – ways of ending their lives than females. They also act under the influence of alcohol and illicit drugs more frequently. The roots of this aggression are not only biological, but also cultural. Males are more reluctant than females to share their feelings and are also less likely to seek help. Males, too, have greater difficulty in coping with failure than their female counterparts. The deficiency of the male species in these respects is linked to the way in which society tends to define the male – ignoring the feminine, sensitive, emotional dimension, so important for good mental health.

The How and the Why
It must be emphasised at the outset that the completion of a suicide is very rarely a bolt from the blue, but rather the final act in a process. This final act may be planned or impulsive, but other steps or stages integral to the process almost always precede it. Secondly, the process is always complex, formed from a combination of factors. This cannot be sufficiently stressed. In a recent press feature on suicide, much space was given to some important ongoing research into brain functions and their link to suicide. There is an expectation that this will ultimately impact on treatment. But this does not mean that, in

Traditional supportive communal structures, such as those provided by parish or neighbourhood, are steadily diminishing. In urban settings people do not know their neighbours or the people who kneel beside them at worship. Additionally, the decline in religious belief itself has been identified as a factor in rising suicide statistics.

time, a pill readjusting chemical imbalances in the brain will solve the problem of suicide. On the contrary, just as suicide is a complex phenomenon, strategies for its prevention will also be complex. A checklist of the common factors implicated in suicide is known to scientists and should be known to all those involved in suicide prevention, including pastors, teachers and parents. Not all the factors will be present in every suicide, but a significant number of them will, in different combinations. A person having one or a number of the factors will not necessarily go on to complete suicide. In fact most do not. But some will and the presence of a number of these factors indicates a risk of suicide and is a warning to the person (if they are capable of acting) and to those around them (if they are capable of recognising) that help should be sought or that intervention is required. Appropriate help or intervention has been shown to be very effective in reducing or eliminating these risk factors, thus diminishing the incidence of suicide.

What are the factors that indicate a risk of suicide? The most significant factors are: the presence of a serious mental illness, such as depression or schizophrenia; the abuse of alcohol or chemical substances; a prior attempt at suicide; severe physical illness; unemployment; the break-up of relationships, as in, divorce, separation, widowhood, ending of a long-term relationship; dysfunctional relationships, family violence, including physical or sexual abuse; or social isolation, including imprisonment. A major life event, such as bereavement, loss of one's job, a great financial loss, or a shaming discovery, creates a risk of suicide. So also does a chronic inability to deal with failure. Sudden changes in performance or mood imply a risk, as does a prior suicide in the immediate family circle or peer group. A number of these factors are a function of the individual's make-up; others are a function of the make-up of family or society.

There are some wider sociological patterns involved. The structure of society in developed countries has led to a breakdown in traditional forms of community. Modern society tends to be individualistic. Under its economic imperatives both parents typically work, while members of the older generation often spend their later years in nursing homes. Recreational activity is increasingly specialised and non-participatory – as will be evident in the increase in health centres and gyms. Increasingly, family consists of the nuclear unit rather than the extended unit or tribe. Traditional supportive communal structures, such as those provided by parish or neighbourhood, are steadily diminishing. In urban settings people do not know their neighbours or the people who kneel beside them at worship. Additionally, the decline in religious belief itself has been identified as a factor in rising suicide statistics. It is much easier in the modern world to 'get left behind', to become isolated, to find oneself without support. If sickness or traumatic life-events intrude they may lead to suicide.

Depression and Other Psychiatric Illnesses

Statistics may be off-putting and sometimes misleading, but in this case they are both enlightening and generally undisputed. Depression is present in between 75-90 per cent of suicides. Between 10-15 per cent of persons with schizophrenia die from suicide, with males more at risk than females. In schizophrenia, unemployment among young males and recurrent relapses are specific risk factors. Another specific risk is the fear of deterioration among those with high intellectual ability. On the other hand, research shows that risk lessens with increasing duration of the illness. Finally, it has been shown that in both illnesses suicide risk is highest in the early phase of onset, early phase of a relapse and early phase of recovery.

What is depression? How does it differ from the normal feeling of 'being down'? How can we recognise depression in ourselves or in others? Various checklists have been devised. We should be alert to the likely presence of depression when a number of the following signs are present: feelings of sadness during most of the day, every day; losing or gaining a lot of weight; sleeping too much or too little or waking too early; significant difficulty in rising, or performing normal everyday tasks, like washing, shaving, going to work; feeling tired and weak all the time; feeling worthless, guilty or hopeless; feeling irritable, or anxious or restless all the time; having difficulty in concentrating, making decisions or remembering things; having repeated thoughts of death and suicide; having pain in different parts of the body for which there seems to be no remedy or diagnosis; self-neglect; chronic high levels of anxiety, panic attacks.

Alcohol or Drug Abuse

Alcohol or drug abuse, particularly when associated with depression, is involved in a high proportion of suicides. It is estimated that 33 per cent of those who die either have a history of alcohol abuse or were drinking shortly before their suicide. The reason for this is that substance abuse affects thinking and reasoning ability, causes or increases depression, lessens inhibitions and increases the likelihood of a depressed person (especially a young person) making a suicide attempt. Persons who are dependent on substances often have a number of other risk factors for suicide. In addition to being depressed, they are also likely to have social and financial problems. Typically, they will have started drinking at a very young age, will have consumed alcohol over a long period and will drink heavily. In addition, they tend to have poor physical health, to perform poorly at work and to have suffered a recent major interpersonal loss such as divorce, separation or bereavement.

Prior Attempts; Chronic Illness; Genetic Factors

Those who have attempted suicide are at a greater risk of eventually dying by suicide and the greater the number of repeat attempts, the higher the risk. Suicide risk is increased in chronic physical illness. There is growing evidence, too, that familial and genetic factors contribute to the risk of suicidal behaviour. Major psychiatric illness, including bipolar disorder, major depression, schizophrenia, alcoholism and substance abuse, and certain personality disorders, which run in families, increase the risk for suicidal behaviour. This does not mean that suicidal behaviour is inevitable for individuals with this family history; it simply means that such persons may be more vulnerable and should take steps to reduce their risk, such as getting evaluation and treatment at the first sign of mental illness.

Suicide Contagion

Suicide contagion is the exposure to suicide or suicidal behaviour within one's family, one's peer group or through media reports of suicide. Direct and indirect exposure to suicidal behaviour has been shown to precede an increase in suicidal behaviour in persons at risk, especially in adolescents and young adults. The risk of suicide contagion as a result of media reporting can be minimised by factual and concise media reports of suicide. Reports should not divulge detailed descriptions of the method used, so as to avoid possible imitation – a precept that is frequently broken in newspaper accounts, particularly of inquests. Nothing should be done to glorify the victim or to suggest that suicide is a normal option. In addition, information such as hotlines or emergency contacts should be provided for those at risk of suicide. In liturgies for suicide victims, too, great care must be taken. Playing the deceased person's favourite music or anything that might give the impression that suicide was natural, or the achievement of a personal goal, should be avoided. Following exposure to suicide, risk can be minimised by having family members, friends, peers, and colleagues of the victim evaluated by a mental health professional. Generally, family survivors and close peers of a suicide should be helped to realise that when they come up against serious difficulties in their own lives, suicide is never a normal option.

Reaction to Risk

One of the greatest difficulties facing those in pastoral ministry is how to react when one fears the possibility of suicidal behaviour in another. The response depends upon the level of risk. For example, a person who has had some suicidal thoughts, but has not made any specific plans to end their lives requires a measured intervention. A willingness to spend time with the person at risk is critical. The person should be encouraged to talk about his or her feelings. When their turmoil subsides and they begin to reflect, we should help them to focus on their positive strengths by getting them to talk of how earlier problems have been resolved without resorting to suicide. We should then see to it that the person goes to see a doctor or mental health professional and we should maintain regular contact.

Where the person has suicidal thoughts and plans, but does not intend to implement them immediately, there is a higher risk. Again, we should offer emotional support, work through the person's suicidal feelings and focus on positive strengths. In addition, we should explore alternatives to suicide (because most suicidal people are ambivalent about wanting to die). Referring the person to a psychiatrist, counsellor or doctor, without delay, is imperative. Finally, we should contact the family, friends and colleagues, and enlist their support

If the person has a definite plan, has the means to do it, and plans to do it immediately, the following actions are needed: we should stay with the person; we should contact a mental health professional or doctor immediately and arrange for an ambulance and hospitalisation. Again, we must inform the family and enlist their support. Finally, we must never say that everything will be all right, never make the problem seem trivial, never give false assurances, never swear to secrecy.

Prevention Strategies

Because of the high incidence of suicide in the fifteen to thirty age-group, suicide prevention measures should begin as early as possible. There are many good studies of this topic, not least the paper prepared as part of the World Health Organisation initiative for the prevention of suicide. This may be obtained on the Internet on the WHO site: its title is 'Preventing Suicide, a Resource for Teachers and Other School Staff.' According to this study, strategies should be employed in schools to foster good mental health and to detect and manage problems which are potentially dangerous.

Critical to the success of these strategies is the use of a team framework, which includes teachers, parents, school doctors, school nurses, school psychologists and school social workers. In school situations, it has been established that some factors which afford protection against suicidal behaviour are good social skills, confidence in oneself, a willingness to seek help when difficulties arise and openness to seeking and taking advice when choices have to be made. Openness to new solutions and openness to knowledge should also be fostered. Other factors that afford protection are healthy social integration through participation in sport, church associations, clubs and other group activities, which presuppose good relationships with schoolmates, teachers and other adults.

On a broader level, there is a great need to create new and meaningful forms of community, which will reach out to all generations. It is interesting that in the USA, where urbanisation and the breakdown of traditional forms of community occurred earlier than in the less developed countries, the Churches have played an important part in the creation of new communities. Currently, it will be seen in our increasingly urbanised Irish setting that membership of a Church is an individualistic phenomenon. One comes to Mass as an individual, prays as an individual and, after saluting the few people one knows, one goes home as an individual. In the USA there is a much greater sense of community. Church members 'enrol' in a parish, usually in family groups. There are numerous get-togethers for such occasions as when a new family enrols, or when a family moves away to another location, or when children are born, or when there is bereavement. These gatherings and interactions are very effective in creating a sense of community and mutual care. There is also a large range of sporting, social and cultural community activities for the young and adolescent members of the parish. The reason why these thrive so much is that there are so few forms of natural community available in urban America. On another level, there is a need to recreate the sense of extended family or tribe. Grandparents and older relatives should be involved in family life as much as possible because they bring wisdom, security, and a sense of history to those younger. Finally, family events, both happy and sad, should be properly marked with all generations involved.

> It is interesting that in the USA, where urbanisation and the breakdown of traditional forms of community occurred earlier in the less developed countries, the churches have played an important part in the creation of new communities.

Notes

1. Similar papers in this series worth consulting and available on the Internet are 'Preventing Suicide, A Resource for Primary Health Care Workers'; 'Preventing Suicide. A Resource for GPs; 'Preventing suicide. A Resource for Media Professionals'.

A RETREAT DAY FOR A SUICIDE BEREAVED CLASS GROUP

Siobhán Foster-Ryan

In this contribution, Siobhán outlines a retreat day for a class who have been bereaved. She has been a post-primary teacher of Religion and English for many years. She is involved in training teachers in Social, Personal and Health Education and pastoral programmes.

An event such as a retreat may be an important element in the postvention care of students. A retreat day provides the students with an opportunity to continue the healing process some weeks after the traumatic loss of one of their peers through suicide. It also offers the opportunity to look at the tragedy from a faith perspective. While students may appear to be returning to a normal routine, experience has shown that there are often unresolved issues at a personal and collective level that the retreat may help to address. The key exercises outlined below are chosen because of their life-affirming nature. In particular, they will strengthen the class bond, integrate any potentially isolated students, provide a safe environment to explore the effect the suicide has had on the class and allow the students to move forward through the bereavement.

Preparation for the Retreat

It is important to prepare the class for the upcoming retreat so that they are sensitised to the issues that may be raised on the day. Many retreat teams find it valuable to ask each student to compose a letter to outline the issues that are significant. This can be in the form of a 'Letter to God' or a 'Letter to the Retreat Team'. This letter allows the student to write freely about their key concerns in life at present and how they hope these concerns might be addressed on the retreat day. It also communicates to the students that their issues will form a significant part of the day. The letters are held in confidence and names are not revealed at any stage. Letters may be read out in part at the outset of the retreat day – in a way that does not identify the person, but highlights the issues for the class. The writing of the letter needs to be given significant time by the teacher – these are then passed on to the retreat team. The religious education class may be the most appropriate place for this exercise to occur.

It may be possible to have at least one member of the retreat team call to the class to explain the nature of the retreat and carry out the letter exercise. Furthermore, the retreat team could address the parents of the group if this is thought helpful. In any case, it will be important to get written permission from parents for their son or daughter to attend the day – this letter may include a brief explanation of the day.

Sample Exercises For the Retreat

Group Contract

The team, having introduced themselves, then go on to talk about the day ahead and what they hope might be achieved. In doing this they explore with the students how best their concerns and expectations might be addressed. They evoke from the students what basic ground rules will need to be in place in order to get the most out of the day for everyone involved e.g. listening; respect; confidentiality etc.

ECHOES OF SUICIDE

Ice-breaker

'Carousel' – the aim of this exercise is to encourage students to talk to a wider circle of their peers than in the normal setting. As a result the group gets to know each other better, thus creating a more open and trusting class climate. This exercise is suitable for any age group.

Procedure: Arrange two circles of chairs facing each other. The facilitator gives a topic for discussion and the students talk to the person facing them for two minutes. After the time has elapsed, the outer circle move clockwise and a new topic for conversation is offered – this can be repeated a few times. Topics can include: what you did for the weekend; favourite film; football team; where would they most like to be at this time; what qualities do they most like in their best friend. There are many other such ice breakers that can be used depending on the needs of the group.

The Luggage of Life Exercise

The aim here is to help students reflect on what is important to them – what do they see as essential in their lives.

Procedure: One of the team introduces the exercise by sharing what is important to them and why. Students are asked to write or draw what they would put into their 'Luggage of Life' – an imaginary suitcase. Then they are asked to share in triads. Following the sharing in triads, the full group come together and are facilitated in a discussion about what is important in the Luggage of Life in order to draw out the common elements of what the class would put into their composite Luggage of Life.

Meditation on the Gospel

The retreat team will have their own way of leading a meditation, in terms of settling the students down and relaxing them into the atmosphere of quiet and prayer. The suggested Gospel for this particular retreat is that of Jesus walking on the water (Matthew 14:22-33). This is a story of faith, of struggle, of hope, of trust – all essential qualities when facing trauma in our lives. In the prayer, build a picture of Jesus as he walks on the water towards the disciples. Recognise the fear of those in the boat, how understandable it is. It is akin to how we might feel when faced with major difficulties, we feel fear, we wonder how we will cope – what might we learn from this Gospel?

Jesus invites the disciples not to be afraid – to have courage in the face of their fear – he lets them know that he will support them, he will carry them, as it were, through their fears if only they will step out in faith. We are invited to face our difficulties with courage not to run away, to seek out support – this may be in the form of friends, family, teachers or professional support groups. This Gospel assures us of the support of Jesus – all that is required of us is the act of faith and courage to acknowledge our fear, our need, our willingness to grasp the hand of help.

As the meditation comes to a conclusion, invite the students to talk with Jesus about their own difficulties. Encourage them to talk about the times in their lives when they got through difficulties, when they were a support to others. Ask them to reflect on what they have learned from these times that they could hold onto for the future.

As a form of debriefing, ask the students to write about their experience of the prayer. The retreat leader may lead a sharing with the full group around the prayer.

Developing a Charter of Care

An important, life-affirming exercise in the retreat day will be the agreeing of a charter of how the students will care for each other and themselves into the future. It is suggested that this exercise be carried out towards the end of the day, when many ideas for the content of the charter will be clearer.

Issues that need to be addressed in the Charter:

- The importance of naming their concerns, talking about them and seeking out help rather than carrying the problem on their own.

- Acknowledging that there are non-destructive ways to resolve a problem – this reinforces the idea that other solutions are possible and acts as a counter to the often unspoken thought in the young person that 'maybe suicide is a way out for me too'.

- The importance of being sensitive to others, particularly those on the fringes, by including them in group activities, offering support in difficult times etc.

- The inclusion of an anti-bullying (in all its forms) statement.

- Ensuring that there is an attitude of positive reinforcement in the class where successes are celebrated and where failures are seen as opportunities for personal growth

- Making use of the Social, Personal and Health Education class to review how the students are living out this charter.

- Recognising the role of other members of the school community in caring for the class – especially the class tutor, year heads, chaplain and guidance counsellor

A Liturgy of Friendship and Courage
The aim of this liturgy is to gather all the work and sharing of the day so that the class leave with a positive, life affirming and practical approach to the future in a faith context.

One format for the preparation of the liturgy may involve dividing the class into the four main groups taking responsibility for:

1. AN ACT OF COMMITMENT TO THE CHARTER OF CARE

This group designs a master copy of the Charter. During the liturgy each student signs it and places a lighted candle around it. The Charter is a central focus in the liturgy and is formally read by one of the students. It is suggested that the Charter is taken back to the school, laminated and displayed in the classroom at all times.

2. PRAYERS OF THE CLASS

The responsibility of this group is to compose prayers on issues relevant to the class, such as friendship, courage, remembering the deceased student and the bereaved family and friends, the school and wider concerns of the world. In the presentation of these prayers, encourage other students in the class to add their own prayers.

3. MUSIC

This group provides a range of music to enhance the reflective atmosphere of the liturgy. It is important that students have been encouraged to bring along instruments and CDs or tapes.

4. SCRIPTURE READING

It is suggested that this group take the Gospel used in the meditation as the basis for a drama presentation. By making the Gospel story relevant to their own modern day setting, the central message will be all the more real to the class.

Reconciliation

An opportunity for the sacrament of reconciliation may be provided as appropriate. This could take the form of a simple event where students identify areas of their lives where they need forgiveness by writing these and handing them over in a ritual. Alternatively, or in conjunction with this, the students are provided with the opportunity to avail of the sacrament of reconciliation.

The Faith Contribution

The retreat is just one way that the school community can provide, according to its own particular ethos, a faith contribution in the journey of healing and learning that accompanies the tragic loss of a student through suicide. The retreat is an occasion to acknowledge the personal and class issues that remain in the weeks following the loss and to address these in a positive and supportive environment.

THE FUNERAL —
ADDRESSING THOSE
AFFECTED BY A SUICIDE

Martin Daly

*Martin, a Marist priest, is principal of Catholic University School,
Leeson St, Dublin. He is a family therapist and a consultant to, and
a facilitator of, groups and organisations.*

A funeral is, for those who are left behind, a ritual to mark the moment of the deceased's passing and the many moments that made up this person's life and our relationship with him or her. You can tell the difference immediately when someone begins to speak at a funeral as to whether the person is going through the motions – 'affecting' to enter into the experience of the mourners – or genuinely trying to connect with the pain of those who mourn from their own living through the loss that comes to each of us in one shape or another. How you position yourself will determine how you are heard, or perhaps whether or not you can be the conduit for the One whose address alone can speak to the non-sense of suicide.

I Do Not Understand
Before I speak to a family and a congregation among whom a suicide has taken place, I need to ask myself:

- What is the context into which I am speaking?
- Who am I addressing?

I have no idea what it would be like to have someone close to me commit suicide. I do not understand. You or I may not in our own personal lives have ever been in a place where we might have been led to contemplate suicide. My starting point is that I don't understand what would lead someone to end it all, or what it is like for those who are left behind, those who I will visit in their home or meet at the funeral parlour, or who sit down after the Gospel while I speak. I do not understand.

As an admittedly poor substitute, can I imagine what it might possibly be like for those left behind and even more crucially, can I bring myself to put myself in a place which might lead me to even entertain the possibility that there was no point in continuing in this life?

How have you dealt with the times when you have felt down? How would it be for you to revisit those moments? If you have lived in and through those moments and can be present to yourself as one who has experienced – in those times – a sense of absence, your words will convey something of that lived reality.

Accessing Feelings
In your life, you may have known moments of deep despair, a sense of going nowhere, of having lost your way. There may have been times when you felt cut off from others – isolated and beyond reach. I can remember sitting in my room once for three or four days staring at the wall and if I had been asked what was up, I could not have told anyone. Sometimes, our personal pain feels beneath and beyond words. We might, at that point, welcome closure. How have you dealt with the times when you have felt down? How would it be for you to revisit those

moments? If you have lived in and through those moments and can be present to yourself as one who has experienced – in those times – a sense of absence, your words will convey something of that lived reality. Are there moments when you have felt disgusted with yourself, or have felt an abject sense of worthlessness, a feeling that you and your life are unredeemable? Have you met that in anyone else? I recall one boy of fourteen telling me how stupid and awkward he felt in the company of his peers. What I recall most is how hard it was for him to talk at all and for me to get him to talk, to keep him active around his experience. Instead, there was a lot of silence and then a few tears ran down the side of his face. I have never forgotten the depth of his isolation. I found it really difficult to sit there with him, because I felt helpless and frustrated and also because he evoked in me some of the awful loneliness I felt at that age. Can you go there?

This is the point of connection, albeit at a great remove, with the one who has departed. To be a conduit for the God who suffered with us and died with us, I have to be at my most human and bring to the situation what I have to offer, in truth the only thing really worth offering, my humanity. The people who you are addressing will pick this up. This is what will make flesh of the Word, make incarnate the Word. Resist the temptation to wallpaper over the black hole that has opened up in front of those who are left behind. They may well feel that a part of them has died with the person who has gone.

Suicide, when it occurs, is so often the 'not talked about,' 'the not said,' 'the not named', that which happened, that cannot be adverted to in the course of conversations. It is taboo. People who come to the funeral may feel awkward, uncomfortable, and unsure what to say to the family and relatives. They wonder what the story was, but don't feel they can ask. How do you talk about the death, but not mention how the person died? Out of sensitivity and inhibition so much is left unsaid.

ECHOES OF SUICIDE

What is it Like for the Family?

I imagine so much is unfinished, unknown, unresolved. There has not been closure, there has been an end without closure. The family may be in a state of shock, may be numb, having lost all sense of feeling. They may be angry with the person who has died, or with God who has 'taken' the person. They may feel betrayed by the person. They may feel responsible for what has happened, maybe going over in their minds what they noticed or didn't, what they should or shouldn't have noticed or said or done, and the endless 'what ifs' that only serve to highlight the crucifying pain of suicide. They may have put countless hours and days into trying to help the person who is gone and may feel left with nothing to show for it. Can you imagine the confusion of feelings they may have, or will have when the numbness wears off? They may themselves feel a sense of taboo. They may be conscious of wondering what other people – and you – are thinking or feeling. This is the context into which you are speaking. This congregation need you to connect with them and connect them with the God who promised to be with us always.

Lamentations 3:17-26

This passage begins in a mood of desolation and moves through that desolation to hope in a pattern found also in many of the psalms. I suggest you begin by acknowledging, in so far as it fits or is appropriate in your judgement, some of the feelings and questions I mentioned above that may be present in the congregation. Invite people to be present to whatever feelings they may have at this moment. Invite them to inhabit their loss; to be present to the awful sense of shock, pain and absence they may be experiencing. Mary Magdalene's words to the stranger she meets at the tomb may resonate with people:

> They have taken him away and I do not know where they have put him.

Draw people's attention to the process that takes place in Lamentations and the Psalms. Loss is loss and there is no papering over it. People are entitled to their pain. The process of moving through grief and desolation cannot be circumvented. These people are in Gethsemane with Christ who felt forsaken, betrayed, who came to believe that his whole life, dedicated to truth and love, has been an illusion. Christ had to live through feeling abandoned by the One to whom he had always faithful. Each person must be present to their own grief and desolation, must inhabit the sense of absence and call to God, as so many of the psalmists do, for the hope and the sense of closure that only God can bring.

Where is God in this Moment?

I know not, but often recall reading Elie Wiesel's memory of a small boy's hanging in a concentration camp. Someone asked the same question as the boy dangled at the end of a rope. I quote his heartfelt response:

> I heard a voice within me answer him: Where is he? Here He is – He is hanging here on this gallows...[1]

Perhaps these questions might provide some structure as you gather your thoughts and feelings into words that may speak to those whom you address:

- What is it like for you to speak to those people at this moment?
- How do you imagine it is for them to be here?
- What do you imagine is going on for them at the moment?
- How do you think it is for all those who have come to express their sorrow and sympathy to those who mourn?
- What is God saying to you about life and death, about hope and despair in the readings that have been chosen?
- What is God saying about how we are to move through the despair of death to the hope of life?

- Where have you experienced/are you experiencing this process in your own life?
- What part of this might you usefully offer to those to whom you are speaking so that they may enter into their experience in this moment in the faith that God is entering it with them?

Notes
1. Wiesel, Elie (1982) *Night*, Bantam Books

Suffering

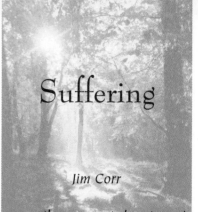

Jim Corr

I watched as my mother, connected up to various electronic hospital apparati, fought dearly, but in vain, to live. She loved life, but this dreadful lung disease was going to have its wicked way no matter what!

In contrast, later on, when I reflected upon the suicide of a close friend of mine, it was honestly with mixed emotion. All I could see at that time was the selfishness of my friend's desperate act and the resulting intense pain left in his wake – which is felt by his loved ones to this day. With time's inexorable passing I know now it is not for me to pass judgement, for it is in our own moments of darkness that we may get a fleeting glimpse of the hellish, dark world that some of our brothers and sisters inhabit all day, every day. We should try and remove from our minds the stigma associated with suicide and focus our empathy and compassion on those who suffer as a result.

The following may resonate with some people who are experiencing dark times and viewing suicide as an option. My attitude to my occasional periods of darkness is to try and extract positives from the 'negative' experiences that come my way – as they come all our ways from time to time. This may often be difficult to do. Evidence of why I might have needed to go through that pain might not manifest itself immediately, but eventually it will. To me, it is like the spirit that inhabits our body needs to shed layers and this necessitates suffering to enable it to do so. How else can we die to the self and remove ourselves from that selfish 'ego' and open up to the experience of love, unity, oneness and beyond? It helps to give me a much needed sense of purpose in life. Some people go so far as to say that we should 'embrace' suffering when it comes along of its own accord. Much as I'd like to explain away life in all its glory, complexity and difficulty – I cannot, it's impossible. The more I learn, the more I realise the less I know. It was Thomas Aquinas who summed it up so beautifully:

'The ocean of truth can not be contained within the pool of a human mind'!

God be with you.

5

SUPPORTS FOR THE
SUICIDE BEREAVED

THE SAMARITANS — HELPING THOSE BEREAVED BY SUICIDE

Ciaran Lynch

Ciaran has been a Samaritan volunteer for the last fifteen years. He was director of the Samaritan's Ennis branch and is a former regional representative for Ireland.

I wish that I could share a story with you, a real experience of a human being in pain who found solace and relief in exploring that pain with another caring person. I wish I could tell you of how the racing words in that human being's head were stilled, how the surging waves of feelings were brought under control, how a life was slowly made whole. I would like to tell you of how a person who had neither the strength to live nor the wish to die was gently supported through their darkest hours, until they found the energy and the will to seek the expert help and guidance that they needed.

I wish I could tell you of the ordinary person who performed these miracles, of the thoughts and feelings within his own mind and heart as he listened to the outpouring of grief and emotion of others. I wish I could ask him to share the experience of that freely given time, the sense of purpose it generated and the sense of frustration and humility to which it sometimes gave rise.

But I can't. I could – but I can't.

Because of all of the elements that combine to create the

Samaritans and the way that they work, confidentiality is, in many ways, one of the most important.

Confidentiality means that the Samaritans do not tell. They do not share what they are told with anybody outside the organisation. This is such an important rule that the Samaritans do not create stories, even stories based on real experiences. The Samaritans do not want anyone that has called them to feel that their story has been used, that their experiences have been shared even in a general, unspecific way.

So I can't tell you a good story. I can't tug at your heartstrings. I can only give you the facts.

So What is the Samaritan Organisation?

The Samaritans is an organisation that is devoted to providing emotional support to those who are passing through a crisis in their lives, and who may find that crisis so undermining and their feelings so overwhelming that they may decide that suicide is their only realistic option. These are the people that the Samaritans seek to help. Those that are sad; those that are depressed; those that are isolated; those that are lost or who have lost another. And especially, those for whom these emotions are so strong that they feel that they cannot continue, that the only solution is to abandon all hope, to cease to live.

Samaritan Principles

The work of the Samaritans is founded on a number of basic principles:

- Since deep emotional feelings are no respecter of time or date, support must be available twenty-four hours a day three hundred and sixty-five days a year.

- Sharing a problem with another concerned human being does not solve the problem, but it does put it into perspective, makes it more manageable and can give one the strength to take the steps that are necessary to address the problem that is causing the emotional upset.

- While professional assistance is needed to deal with many emotional traumas and psychological difficulties, the sharing of problems and the provision of caring support can be carried out by those without professional training. This support is an addition to, and not a substitute for, professional advice and counselling.

- Sharing a problem with an anonymous though caring individual may be easier than sharing it with a person that one knows or in an environment that demands face-to-face interaction.

- Most people in crisis know what to do – they merely lack the emotional strength to do it at that particular moment. Therefore, a service of emotional support cannot be prescriptive or directive, but must provide a safe and reflective environment within which the individual can make their own decisions about the future direction of their lives.

- There are conditions and circumstances that are beyond the capacity of non-medical intervention and the most that emotional support can provide in these circumstances is the time for people to seek the professional help that they need.

- There is a taboo around the issue of suicide and people's willingness to discuss the subject. This means that people who may be feeling suicidal are not given an opportunity to explore their feelings about the possibility of taking their own lives and to address those feelings.

- In order that a person in crisis is willing to share a problem, they must feel that they are in a safe and supportive environment that will contain and respect their confidence. Therefore the guarantee of confidentiality must be absolute.

The Befriending Work of the Samaritans

These principles have given rise to the nature and structure of The Samaritan organisation. On the basis of these principles The Samaritans provide a service that

- is available twenty-four hours a day, three hundred and sixty-five days a year

- is provided by carefully selected and trained, but not professionally qualified, individuals

- is non-directive

- is available by phone, letter and e-mail, though also by face-to-face interaction, at the discretion of the caller

- is made available through the decision of the caller to make contact or to request that contact be made

Through these means, the Samaritans hope that the incidence of the deeply distressing problem of suicide will be reduced and that those who suffer the trauma of the suicide of those that are near to them will receive the support and understanding that they need.

There is a story that is told (I don't know if it is true), about a patient who went to a doctor. He talked to the doctor for fifteen minutes about his problems. He explained where his life was, what he would like to do, what he felt he could do, what he felt he would do. The doctor said no more than 'I see' and 'Ah ha'. As he was leaving the patient said 'Thank you very much Doctor. That was excellent advice.' The doctor was acting like a

Samaritan – facilitating a caller in coming to their own decision, not imposing a decision on them.

The Other Work of the Samaritans

The Samaritans' main focus is on providing support to those who are in deep emotional distress and who may ultimately make the sad decision to take their own lives. This is not the full extent of their work, however. In addition to their main work of providing support to those in crisis, the Samaritans highlight the issue of suicide and help to keep it in public discussion. They do this through their own public relations work and through their membership of organisations such as the Irish Association of Suicidology. They also provide advice as to how suicide should be addressed in the media and in public debate, and participate in research projects that seek to gain a greater understanding of the causes of and remedies for suicidal feelings.

The Samaritans also seek to bring their system of support outside of their branches to groups and places where people may be in particular distress. Thus, the Samaritans provide their service at Festivals and other similar events, they visit schools and clubs and they work with organisations that are in contact with those who are in distress.

And Who are the Samaritan Volunteers?

Samaritan volunteers are ordinary people. They are not professional counsellors; they are not trained psychologists. They are, however, caring people who are connected to their suffering fellows through their shared humanity and their capacity to provide an uncritical space within which the pain and suffering of others can be shared.

Samaritans are not professionals, but they are carefully selected and trained. Before a Samaritan volunteer is permitted to commence active befriending, they must undergo a period of training. In addition, volunteers undergo annual refresher training, as well as being given opportunities to reflect on how they are dealing with callers on an ongoing basis.

This training is important – but it is not the core of being a Samaritan. Samaritans cannot be made. While they can be trained in the techniques of befriending, the basic Samaritan characteristics of caring, of humility, of not sitting in judgement, of acknowledging the need for people to make their own decisions, are characteristics that a prospective volunteer brings with him or her to the organisation.

In the end of the day, what a Samaritan says to a caller is far less important than how he or she says it. Simple words offered with care and concern are far more important than the most wonderful of words offered without. We all need to feel accepted; we need to know that our feelings are not stupid or foolish or unusual or weird. If another human being can talk to us about our feelings and acknowledge that they are real, are important and acceptable, it helps to relieve our sense of isolation, of disconnectedness and of unreality. It starts to ground us again, to bring a reality to our lives once more. And when our lives seem real, we can start to get to grips with our emotions, no matter how sad and strong those emotions may be.

The Samaritan Organisation
The Samaritan organisation is made up of around nineteen thousand volunteers in about two hundred branches in Ireland and Great Britain.

The Samaritans, in the thirty-two county Irish Region, is made up of two and a half thousand volunteers organised in twenty branches from Derry to Tralee and from Waterford to Coleraine. In these branches, volunteers receive around five hundred thousand calls a year – primarily on the telephone but also by e-mail, letter and personal visit. Of these callers, approximately 20 per cent say that they have suicidal feelings or that they have had these feelings in the past. So the Samaritans in Ireland receive about one hundred thousand calls a year from people who feel that they may not be able to go on, that they may, at some point, seek to end their own lives.

The Samaritans and those Bereaved by Suicide

The Samaritans were originally founded to provide emotional support to those who were passing through crisis in their lives, and who were coming to the point where suicide seemed a realistic option. There is also no doubt that this is still a major focus of the work of the organisation. However, it is also recognised by the organisation that those bereaved by suicide form a group that need particular support and understanding. Because of their association with suicide, the Samaritans are particularly well placed to provide support to those bereaved by suicide and to help them to live with their loss.

Those who are bereaved by suicide suffer a profound and searing sense of loss. The pain and anguish, the guilt and anger associated with such a loss can be truly life threatening in themselves.

I will not pretend, nor do the Samaritans pretend, to be able to fully comprehend the range and extent of the feelings associated with the loss of a loved one through suicide. They are familiar, however, with the range of emotions that such an event can cause. Though the cause is different, though their precise nature is unique, the basic nature of the feelings involved is familiar to the Samaritans. They would hope that they would be in a position to assist those bereaved by suicide to express their deep feelings of distress, to examine opportunities for dealing with them and to help them continue with their own lives

Specific Approaches

In addition to the availability of their normal befriending to those bereaved by suicide, a number of Samaritan branches have established specific systems to help those bereaved by suicide.

These systems are essentially an enhanced version of normal Samaritan befriending. In certain circumstances, particular

Samaritans are assigned to offer support in an ongoing way to particular callers. This assignment is made in circumstances where a caller needs ongoing support over a considerable period of time. In such circumstances, it is felt that the development of a supportive network between a number of volunteers and a caller can be particularly helpful. Such a network, where befriending arrangements are made in advance, can provide a stable environment within which the person in distress can be sure of the arrangements that will provide their support and in which their relationship with the Samaritan volunteers can be developed so that the caller does not need to repeat the details of their story on each visit.

Where specific assigned befriending is made available for those bereaved by suicide, the Samaritan Branch operates as follows:

- a number of experienced volunteers are chosen to participate

- special training is provided to those volunteers, to make them particularly aware of the needs of those bereaved by suicide and of the specific emotions that are involved

- when someone bereaved by suicide makes contact with the branch, they are offered the opportunity of participating in this specific support system

- if the caller decides to participate in the system, a number of volunteers are assigned to befriend the caller in question

- the caller meets with the assigned volunteers and if the caller is happy with the volunteers, future meetings are arranged between the volunteers and the caller

This specific approach to befriending those bereaved by suicide will not, of course, be one of which all will want to avail.

Because such an approach is available, it does not mean that the basic Samaritan befriending system is not available to those bereaved by suicide. In fact, the truth is quite the reverse.

The Samaritans offer support to all those that are suffering pain in their lives. The source of the pain is not important to the Samaritans. The same support is offered to all, and that support is also available to those bereaved by suicide. Even though some branches offer a particular targeted support to those bereaved by suicide, the general Samaritan befriending is available to them as well.

So how do the Samaritans know that what they do works?
It is so difficult for the Samaritans. They operate in an environment of anonymity and confidentiality; they guarantee that they will not divulge their callers' stories; and they do not seek acknowledgement or gratitude from those they help.

It is seldom that those that call the Samaritans send their thanks for the help that they have received; it is seldom that they acknowledge that the opportunity to call the Samaritans offered them a release that had a profound impact on their lives. It may well be that they do not know it. It may also be that they do not want to dwell on such a sad episode in their lives.

But sometimes they do say thanks; sometimes they do send an acknowledgement. And the fact that the number of calls received by the Samaritans stays stable or grows and that the support for the Samaritans within the community is so significant, both in financial and other terms, in itself bears testimony to the value of the work that they do.

We can't say that in any in individual case we have prevented someone taking their own life. There are so many factors involved that to make such a claim would be unreasonably presumptuous. However, there is no doubt that the Samaritans reduce the weight of human misery in the world; and the reduction in that weight of misery certainly has an effect on the numbers of those who feel that suicide is the only resolution to their pain.

The End of the Story

So I wasn't able to tell you a story. I couldn't breach the confidences of a caller to the Samaritans; I couldn't even create a story for you. It wouldn't have been a true story, but it would have been a story of truth. But such a story might threaten a caller; it might make someone feel that they had been betrayed. And the Samaritans can't take that chance. Their commitment to their callers is absolute. But I do hope that I have been able to let you see who the Samaritans are, what they do and what the organisation is like. I also hope that anyone who has been bereaved by suicide and who may read this will feel that the Samaritans are people whom they could call, and with whom they could share their feelings of grief, anger or failure. I hope that they would anticipate a warm and caring reception, the creation of an uncritical space within which they could explore their own feelings in safety and within which they may be able to come to an acceptance of the sad event that has entered their lives.

DOCHAS —
SUPPORT SERVICE FOR THOSE
BEREAVED BY SUICIDE

Dan Joe O'Mahony

Fr Dan Joe is responsible for the Oratory at Blanchardstown Centre.
He has been a school chaplain for many years and has been an
executive member in the School Chaplains' Association.

The community of Dublin 15, for some time, has wished to respond to the problem of suicide in our area. In March 2000, twenty volunteers started training with the Personal Counselling Institute in Clondalkin – under the tutorship of Liam Mc Carthy and Josephine Murphy. The variety of the skills and experience of the members of the group brought its own richness and talent and companionship – community workers, gardaí, nurses, counsellors, priests, teachers and others. The high attendance rate at the course spoke loudly of the professionalism and expertise of our tutors and the commitment of the group.

What will DOCHAS offer?
The primary support and resource we offer is a listening ear:

When? Every Wednesday night 7:00-8:00 pm

Where? In a room at the Blanchardstown Centre Oratory, Yellow Entrance.
Cost? Nil
How to contact? Call us at (01) 8200915 (Oratory) or (086) 8806300
Who will I meet? Trained volunteers, ready and willing to listen.

Tips to remember in Case of Suicide

- If breaking the news to the family do not go alone. Two people are advisable – if possible try to have a gender balance.

- If you are a garda or priest, ensure that you wear your uniform or clerical garb – this indicates immediately to the family that there is something serious to prepare themselves for.

- When breaking the news, speak slowly and go at the recipients pace. Be gentle but do not disguise the facts.

- Be accepting of anger and denial.

- No blame, shame or fault should be attached to any suicide.

- Be careful of the rumour machine – many rumours will circulate speculating the reason for the suicide. Ensure that false rumours are dismissed out of hand. Promise to be a source of truth.

- Be there for the family and friends. Mingle with groups, light a candle, open a book of condolences etc.

- Talk about the person to all concerned. Avoidance of the subject is not beneficial.

- Be careful about choice of prayers, poems or homilies. Much can be read into them.

- There is often no reason or explanation for a suicide. Expect many unanswered questions and repetition of 'Why?'

- Familiarise yourself with support groups and counselling services. You should have these available if requested by a family member.

- Try to keep a sense of normality about life after suicide.

The Wounds of Love

Those who care about others pick up a lot of wounds.
There may be no great wounds,
only a multiplicity of little ones –
a host of scratches, wrinkles and welts.
But there can also be a lot of invisible wounds:
the furrows left on the mind and the heart
by hardship, worry and anxiety,
disappointments, ingratitude, and betrayal.
These wounds are not things to be ashamed of.
They are badges of honour.
They are the proof of our love.
Jesus didn't hide his wounds.
Neither should we.
By his wounds we are healed.

SÓLÁS/BARNARDOS — HELPING CHILDREN AND YOUNG PEOPLE IN THE AFTERMATH OF SUICIDE

Patricia Donnelly

Pat is a social worker and bereavement counsellor with Sólás/Barnardos' Bereavement Service. It is out of this experience that she shares insights into the issues for children and young people in the aftermath of suicide.

'Did he not love us enough to stay?' Emma, aged 9
'I wondered why the garage door was shut' Sean, aged 14

Sadly, we cannot fully shield our children from the painful realities of life. We are powerless over the ultimate – life and death. This is particularly true if the death of a loved one has been sudden and traumatic, as with suicide. The suicide bereaved are faced with all the normal emotions associated with any death – sadness, confusion, anger and guilt – but intensified by the manner of death and complicated by feelings of stigma and isolation. The external event shatters previously held beliefs about security, safety and goodness. Caroline Garland describes this as 'a breakdown in beliefs about

- the predictability of the world
- established mental structures
- established defence organisation

which leaves the person vulnerable to intense and overwhelming anxieties from internal as well as external events.'[1]

My work as a bereavement counsellor with Sólás, Barnardos' Bereavement Service, since 1996, has been proof indeed that children and young people are not immune to nor, sadly, can they be protected from 'the slings and arrows of outrageous fortune'. Since 1996, we have dealt with some two thousand enquiries and counselled over six hundred bereaved children and families. The highest trend has been of sudden parental death by accident, sudden illness, suicide or murder – with a slightly higher incidence of fathers over mothers. Most sobering of all is the 100 per cent increase in the rate of suicidal deaths, which now represent 32 per cent of total referrals. Faced with this intrusion of grim reality into the lives of children and young people, what can we, as adults, do to help? How can we intervene creatively and constructively to help children understand and deal with the pain of loss? How can we prevent them becoming what Pennels and Smith describe as 'the forgotten mourners'?[2] How can we talk to children and young people about even the most traumatic deaths and maximise the potential for healthy grieving and recovery?

For me, the keynote for helping children and young people with any difficult reality, for example parental divorce, sexual abuse etc., is truth. The Biblical maxim 'The Truth shall set you free' is still a guide today. Shakespeare must have had this in mind in Macbeth, 'Give sorrow words, the grief that does not speak whispers the o'er frayed heart and bids it break'. Until sorrow and truth can be set free by the spoken word, one cannot even begin to cope with the turmoil of internal confusion and conflicting emotions, nor be freed to face grief and move on constructively. Many adults try to shield children and young people from painful realities in the mistaken belief of protecting them. Our adult fears and inhibitions are projected on to children in a pseudo protection racket, 'it would be too much for them, they will collapse, be unable to cope', whilst in truth it is ourselves we are protecting. In fact, children and young people are much more resilient than adults imagine and are naturally programmed to move through life with curiosity and enquiry. We can harness this natural ability to help them make sense of the apparently senseless, and to survive even the most painful loss.

Developmental Stages – Children 0-5

'My Mammy's in Heaven
and can't get back even if she wanted to' Connor, age 4.

In talking to children and young people about death, we need to keep in mind two things; developmental stage and timing. For children in this age group, it is the absence of the loved one that is significant, not the manner of the death. However, as children of this age are so sensitively programmed to their environment, which is within the close family orbit, they are extremely susceptible to picking up any distress or change in familiar routines. Tone of voice, facial expression and the way they are held or handled will alert them to the fact that something upsetting has happened. Therefore, even at this early stage, the groundwork can be laid for more detailed and age appropriate explanations as they grow older. 'Daddy has had a terrible accident to his neck. That made his heart stop. He is dead and will not be coming back. We are all very sad.' This type of explanation leaves the opportunity for further expansion with more precise details at a later date. Children under five are very egocentric, feeling that they are the centre of the universe with the power to make things happen at will. Therefore, it is important to emphasise that the death is not their fault, through anything they may have wished or said.

Children 5-10

At this age, children have a growing realisation that death is forever, but still have a sense that it happens to other people. By about eight or nine, they are naturally interested in what causes people to die. They also have a healthy curiosity in what happens to bodies after death. This is not morbid, but a normal way of learning about the world and how it works. However, it may be quite distressing to bereaved adults when children ask very blunt questions about the manner of death.

Because of magical thinking common at this age, children may have heightened feelings of guilt and responsibility for the death. It is important to explore and dispel any feelings they may express about the death being their fault. It is not helpful to dismiss their concerns about possible responsibility with a blanket 'It's not your fault,' rather one should listen to and unpack the story around the death and how they have felt responsible, for example, 'Yes, you were cross with Daddy that morning, but that didn't make him die.'

Children in the five to ten age group have very fertile imaginations and are more prone to dreams and nightmares. Therefore, once again, it is important to talk to them about the physical details of the death, for example, 'Mammy was feeling very sad and sick in her head. She was all mixed up. She thought no one could help her. That was a mistake. She put a rope around her neck and pulled it so hard, she couldn't breathe so her heart stopped and she died.'

If possible, and it usually is, as bodies are quite often not as physically damaged as people imagine, children and young people, if they wish, should be encouraged and supported in viewing the body. Irrespective of the manner of the death, the body is still that of a beloved mother, father, brother, sister, family member or friend. Without seeing the actual body or having a clear explanation of the manner of death children, particularly in the five to ten age group, will be exposed to frightening internal imaginings.

Adolescents

Adolescents have a full realisation of the irreversibility and inevitability of death. Bereavement can be especially difficult for them at this time, as they are preoccupied by struggles with identity, independence and dependence. Also, this is a time of stormy family relationships with parents and siblings, and so can intensify feelings of guilt and remorse. These will be further intensified in the case of suicide. Adolescents will feel particularly angry if excluded from the truth and may bitterly resent hearing the news of a suicide from people outside the family.

They may equally be burdened by unspoken secrets within the family about the manner of the death. In my experience in Sólás Bereavement Service, many children and young people reveal that they already knew of the suicide, having picked up on the silence and tension in the family. Indeed, many children and young people may have been the first to discover the body, but may have been seduced into a conspiracy of silence in talking to others. This leaves them coping alone with painful, frightening images. Because of their developmental stage, adolescents are acutely aware that they have individual power over their own life or death, so they may be very frightened and challenged when confronted personally by a suicidal death. Once again, they need truth and an atmosphere where their fears can be openly explored. The suicide needs to be acknowledged, but equally, the fact that there is always another way must be clearly stated. Help is available.

Talking to Children and Young People about Suicide

As regards talking to children and young people about death, it is useful to keep in mind Claudia Jewett's advice: 'the more directly conveyed the knowledge of a death, the less chance the child has to deny it and avoid making the life changes that will resolve the loss'.[3] Therefore, if at all possible, the truth should be conveyed by the surviving parent or trusted adult. This avoids the possibility of denial. Timing is important. The longer the news is not conveyed, the longer the child or young person will be left isolated and confused. Also, the longer the gap, the greater the possibility of hearing the news outside the family with no support. However, prior to telling the child, the parent or adult may need time to come to terms with the death and rehearse what they wish to say.

At all times, it is crucial not to let the manner of the death define the deceased, 'He was a good Dad, a great person.' He was more than his last act.

Guidelines

- You may need to rehearse your story before talking to the child or young person.
- You may need the supportive presence of another adult.
- Simple, truthful explanations are best.
- The word 'suicide' means little to grieving children and young people. It is the loss that is paramount.
- Preface the telling by saying, 'I need to talk to you about how Daddy's life ended or how Daddy ended his life'.
- Explain different types of illnesses and expand to explain that Mum or Dad had a special illness that made them very sick and upset. Their thoughts got all mixed up.
- They were as ill in their mind as someone who is incurably ill in their body.
- Go from what they know, for example, 'You know that Mammy has been feeling very sad for a long time. She felt so bad she thought no one could help her. That was a mistake. If her mind had been working properly, she would have realised that there was help. She would have remembered that we loved her.'
- He or she felt that life was not worth continuing.
- It was his or her choice and not any one else's responsibility.
- Locate the position of the fatal injury.
- 'Daddy got a rope. He put it around his neck and let it get so tight that he couldn't breathe anymore. Because he couldn't breathe, his heart stopped and he died.' Allow for questions.

Children in the five to eight group may ask particular specific questions e.g. 'Did he go blue, did his head explode?' This is not meant to be callous, but it is the child's way of understanding the sequence of events and the manner of death.

- Dispel any myths about suicide, for example, 'Going to Hell'.
- Role model expressions of grief, e.g. sadness, anger, confusion, rejection, not knowing why.
- Allow for a range of emotions. Children may go out and play after hearing traumatic news. This is their way of digesting the news.
- Allow for repeated questions over a period of time. The child needs time to come to terms in bite size pieces.
- If possible, the child should see the body. Explain in advance what to expect, for example, 'Daddy's body will be cold'.
- Once the child knows the cause of death, they may be worried about what to say to friends, teachers etc. Help them to prepare, for example, 'My Daddy died very suddenly. He injured his head and died'.
- Children need to know that the person who died loved them. Because of their state prior to death, they may not have been able to let them know that. Explain also that because the person felt so bad, it stopped them thinking what it would be like for the child after death.
- Some children and young people may feel a sense of relief if they have lived with depression, drug abuse, and erratic behaviour for a long period. Allow for this and balance it with an understanding of the illness.
- Some children and young people may have been the first to discover the body. They will need additional support and reassurance. Unpack with them what they actually saw. Don't dismiss them by saying, 'Don't think about it. It was only a nightmare you imagined.'
- Reassure children and young people that despite the loss, life can go on and that the adults in their life will take care of them.
- Emphasise that suicide is not hereditary or genetic.

- Grief work is physically and mentally draining, so keep a balance in your life and build in time-out from grief to refuel and revive.
- Continue to remember the life of the deceased and share stories and memories.

(Donnelly P., McCarthy R., Sólás, Barnardos 2001)

Final Thoughts

In conclusion, it is important to remember that suicide is a unique and devastating loss. It is natural to feel a range of intense emotions, especially rejection, guilt and shame. However, it is important to remember that children and young people also experience these feelings. It is at this time that they particularly need adult support and assistance. Otherwise, they will continue to feel confused and alone. We can move from the traumatic wound of suicide, from feelings of powerlessness and helplessness, to being empowered and hopeful. The keynote to this is respecting children and young people by sharing painful truths with them. If we have the courage and support to do this, we will realise that a child can live through anything, so long as he or she is told the truth. Gradually, with time and healing, children recreate their life stories, finding a place and meaning for the trauma. As they discover that, they are able to live with their memories and overcome their fears. Children make room to include a traumatic event in the stories they tell of themselves. These can be stories of being loved, of surviving and moving on.

Notes

1. Garland, C. (1998) *Understanding Trauma: A Psychoanalytical Approach*, Tavistock Clinic Series
2. Pennells, Margaret and Smith, Susan C. (1995). *The forgotten mourners: guidelines for working with bereaved children.* London: Bristol, PA: J. Kingley Publishers
3. Jewett, Claudia L. (1984) *Helping children cope with separation and loss.* (Harvard, Mass.: Harvard Common Press)

RAINBOWS

Anne Patterson

Anne is a primary school principal in a Dublin school. She has been involved with Rainbows, as a facilitator of the programme, for some years. She is also a director of training for Rainbows.

I am a widow. My late husband Michael died ten years ago. I am the mother of four adult children. My father died when I was in my mid twenties. Michael died when I was 42. My father was a binge alcoholic – we were always waiting the for next episode. I have two alcoholic brothers – one actively alcoholic and in very bad health – one mercifully dry for over four years. Both have repeatedly threatened suicide. One made two unsuccessful, but blatant attempts. I know about grief and ongoing sorrow. I know about God's grace in my survival and in my ongoing growth in wisdom and love. I have become more full of joy about everything that is good in the world – and there is so much goodness! I have also become more sensitive to life's ills. Suicide is so awful. Is there hope that we can do something about this problem here in Ireland? Can we hope in the face of suicide? In my view yes, we can hope, indeed we must hope.

I have been a primary school teacher since 1969. I have been a school principal for many years. After Michael died, amidst my own intense grief, I observed and suffered with my four children in their grief. Each of us at different stages with the resultant chaos in family life. Michael died of cancer.

During my journey I found Beginning Experience. It is a voluntary peer support group for adults who have lost a spouse through death, separation or divorce. I found great help, peer support and friendship in the company of people who understood my grief and who would journey alongside me. I subsequently discovered Rainbows.

Rainbows helps by providing a safe setting in which children can talk through their feelings with other children who are experiencing similar situations. They are helped to articulate their feelings by a trained adult facilitator or listener. I trained as a facilitator and with another teacher (also trained) started Rainbows in our school. Later, we grew to a team of facilitators catering for more than forty children. Parents who gave permission for their children to attend came to us from situations involving death, of parents or grandparents, separation, sudden infant death of a sibling, death from accidents etc.

They used the Rainbows materials – journals, story books, games and activities – which form a structured programme to lead the children gently through the grieving process.

Rainbows helps by:

- supporting the children as they rebuild their self esteem
- enabling the children to name, understand and come to terms with the many emotions they experience
- reassuring those who have anxieties or feelings of guilt
- encouraging the children to move forward towards forgiving those people whom they feel have caused their pain

I know that the children who participate in Rainbows are helped. Teachers and parents talk of children who are more open, smile more, show fewer behavioural difficulties. There is no magic wand – their basic problems remain, but they now have a language with which to express their grief – they have learnt to express feelings of anger and sorrow. They are given an opportunity to develop skills to deal with their situation constructively. The Rainbows programme clearly fits very much with the Social, Personal and Health Education area of the new primary curriculum.

Rainbows operates with a Board of Directors. Training courses are run for facilitators of individual courses. Facilitators work with the children in school, parish and community settings. There are religious and secular editions of the programme available.

Literature/information about Rainbows available at Loreto Centre, Crumlin, Dublin.
Tel/Fax (01) 473 4175 • Email rainbows@eircom.net

YOU CAN MAKE A
DIFFERENCE:
THE PROBLEM OF SUICIDE

Kathleen Maguire PBVM
Tony Byrne CSSp

Fr Tony and Sr Kathleen have been involved in ministry related to suicide response for many years. In particular over the last three years they have organised and facilitated seven courses entitled 'Facing up to Suicide', which have been attended by 1500 people. Here they speak from their experience and expertise as they address some of the most painful and distressing issues in the area of suicide.

Many people are aware that suicide is one of the most significant contemporary problems in Ireland. Awareness can be either naive or acute. Naive awareness makes us vaguely conscious of the problem of suicide. Acute awareness makes us deeply and personally conscious of the problem, as happens, for instance, when a dear one – a near relative, friend, neighbour, work colleague or parishioner – dies by suicide.

A minimum of fifty people suffers from loss, grief, blame or shame as a result of a single suicide. This makes us appreciate the wisdom of the ancient Irish proverb *'ar scáth a chéile a mhaireann na daoine'*. ('People live in the shadow of one another.') Because we live in the shadow of one another, we can make a difference by facing up to the ever-increasing rate of suicides in Ireland. We should not leave this task to the professionals to solve – if we face up to the problem and become acutely aware of it, we may be able to find appropriate responses to it.

Suicide and Early Warning Signals

The word 'suicide' comes from two Latin words – *'sui'* meaning 'self' and *'occidere'* meaning 'to strike, to kill'. It is a human act, self-inflicted, self-intentional, leading to a cessation of life. Attempted, or incompleted, suicide is any act undertaken or self-initiated that mimics the act of suicide, but does not result in death.

Some experts on suicide believe that of any ten persons who die by suicide, at least eight give definite clues and warnings about their suicidal tendencies. From our experiences of assisting people bereaved by suicide and from our suicide awareness programmes, we feel that eight out of ten may be somewhat inaccurate in Ireland, especially in terms of young adult males. However, we believe that the public should be better informed about early warning clues or signals so that those at risk might be encouraged to get help. We suggest to the participants in our courses and seminars that some of the early warning signals for suicide may be:

- an unexplained and sudden reduction of performance at work, in studies or in family life
- comments made about depression, death and suicide
- a change of mood – a marked emotional instability
- an expression of significant grief or stress
- physical symptoms with emotional causes
- carelessness about appearance and personal hygiene
- engaging in high risk behaviour
- jokes about suicide

- religious despair
- statements like 'I want to kill myself'
- speaking of reunion with a deceased family member, friend, etc.
- low self-esteem
- a particular interest in drawings, illustrations, or music about death or suicide
- sense of helplessness or hopelessness for the future

It is not always easy for parents or teachers to identify the early warning signals given by teenagers. Suicide thoughts and attempts are more likely to be known to a teenagers own peers than to adults. It is estimated that only a quarter of teenagers who know of a suicidal friend report this to an adult, partly due to the importance of maintaining a confidence, and partly due to the concerns about adults' responses. An essential factor in providing assistance for teenagers or young adults at risk of suicide is a good, trusting relationship with helpful peers and with caring people, who are not necessarily experts, but who do need to be able and willing to listen and to help.

Normalising and Sensationalising Suicide

It is important to avoid sensationalising the problem by creating a 'scare' atmosphere. However, it is equally important not to normalise suicide by believing that it is a response to the common everyday 'stresses' that all of us experience. It should not be seen as an easy way out of difficulties, but rather a manifestation of a psychological problem.

Sensationalisation and normalisation of suicide are sometimes promoted when pop stars or other celebrities take their own lives. Many of these stars and celebrities are role models for young people, who tend to imitate them. During school programmes on suicide we often ask students, 'Who are the people you admire most of all?', 'Who are your role models?' It amazes us that students identify 'stars' who have died by suicide. We ask them about Bono of U2 – 'Did he take his own life or did he save other peoples lives?' They have no doubt that he saved lives by fighting for the debt reduction of the less well-off countries. We feel that it is important for young people to focus on role models like Bono, rather than celebrities who have died by suicide.

Causes of Suicide

There is no one, universal cause of suicide, but cumulative burdens on individuals cause people to take their own lives. It is generally believed that 90 per cent of people who die by suicide have diminished responsibility. People who have attempted suicide sometimes say to us that the shutters of their minds closed down and they were 'in total darkness', or they say that they lost contact with reality before they attempted to kill themselves.

Suicide can have its roots in the biology of the brain, which is a physical organ of the body and, as such, can get sick in a variety of ways just like any other organ. The most common mental illnesses, which may result in suicide, are major acute depression, manic depression and schizophrenia. It is generally believed that people do not kill themselves while in the deepest period of their illness. When they begin to recover they have the energy to kill themselves and they may do so then.

Another cause of suicide may be genetic inheritance or a physiological reaction to loss and environmental factors. Social factors can precipitate suicidal thoughts. These social factors would include unjust structures, such as economic, political, social, cultural and religious oppressive structures that would impinge on individuals, causing tension, suffering and disharmony. Research has shown that social factors play a major role in the rates of suicide. Studies carried out on data from sixty-two countries researched by the Suicide Information and Education Centre in Calgary, Alberta, Canada, established that the faster the rate of population growth, the lower the suicide rate. The research also established that the suicide rate tends to increase as a society becomes modernised and the quality of life improves.

Understanding the Mind of the Suicidal Person

Great efforts have been made by professionals to discover what goes on in the minds of people about to take their own lives. Conclusions cannot be made from information given by those who attempt suicide but do not complete it. A more reliable source of information can be obtained from psychological autopsies, which study the behaviour patterns and attitude change over a specified period of time before the deceased died by suicide. From these psychological autopsies, it is generally believed that the majority of people who kill themselves are not 'out of their mind'. They are so engulfed by their severe emotional pain that they have tunnel vision. They feel helpless and hopeless. They can't call on their experiences to help them, and they can't consider that negative moods can pass away. They can only remember that these moods keep coming back. They are incapable of thinking of alternatives to self-destruction or of how families will feel if they take their own lives. In fact many think that their families will be better off without them. Having everything to live for does not prevent them from killing themselves.

Suicide notes can give some indication of what is going on in the minds of the suicidal. About one-third of people who die by suicide leave such notes. Most of these notes are loving communications asking for forgiveness and understanding. Some are angry and hateful and are directed at particular people. Others are notes expressing mixed feelings of love and anger. In a few cases, the notes are about possessions and funerals. In recent times tapes and answering machines are increasingly used. Suicide messages are often passed on through songs about suicide left on tapes by the person about to die by suicide.

Courage and Suicide

We are often asked the question 'Does it take courage to kill oneself or is it a cowardly way out?' We believe that it would be entirely wrong to think of those who die by suicide as heroes or heroines. It would be equally wrong to presume that suicide is a cowardly act. We hold the position that dying from a disease like cancer is not cowardly or courageous, and neither is suicide.

Grief and Suicide

We are often asked, 'Do people bereaved by suicide grieve the same way as other people do?' We believe that the grief process is similar, but for those bereaved by suicide the pain can be much more intense, especially in the area of guilt, blame, shame, rejection and isolation. Sometimes neighbours, friends and work colleagues can unintentionally add to the grief either by engaging in an avoidance strategy or by making glib comments that do not help. Some pious people attempt to explain the sad event by telling the bereaved person that the one who died by suicide is with God in Heaven. The one who is grieving does not want the person anywhere except near them – alive and well. It has even been known that people can go as far as saying that the deceased was under the influence of the devil.

The use of the term 'committed suicide' can be most unhelpful to the bereaved, and can suggest to the bereaved that their loved one committed a civil offence. In Ireland, suicide was decriminalised in 1993. Research has established that most people who die by suicide have diminished responsibility. It is not correct, therefore, to think that all people who take their own lives commit an immoral act.

Our Personal Thoughts on Suicide

In our ministry, we are in touch with many people who have lost their dear ones by suicide. From their stories, we have reached conclusions that are supported in general by principles of suicidology. We try to help them to understand that, in virtually every circumstance, a person who has died by suicide was loved and was an important figure in a family and in a circle of friends. The lives of those who died enriched the people around them. It would be a travesty if they were remembered and defined by their final act of desperation. People who have died by suicide have struggled a great deal. Very often, it is unclear how long the struggle was going on. We do know from research that most people who have died by suicide have suffered from depression. For some, the struggle went on for years. For others, the struggle was somewhat short-lived. Most people lived very productive lives and should be remembered as such. No person who died of suicide should be remembered as a failure, as a coward or as selfish. Suicide should not be described in those terms. Suicide is an act of complete desperation. Many people who died by suicide have been engaged in trojan struggles to continue living and, finally, they ran out of energy, they ran out of hope. They were completely engulfed in despair and so they terminated their lives. It was not because they wanted to or because they didn't love their dear ones or because they were cowards or weak. They were people who had struggled long enough and succumbed to an illness – the illness of depression.

In the months and years following the suicide, after people have gone through the initial stages of grieving, they are able to take a better look at their loved one's life and see that their life was richer and fuller and more productive than their final act of desperation. It takes time and effort to arrive at this point, but it will happen as long as survivors are patient and allow the grieving process to unfold. In this process, the survivors must struggle to rid themselves of blame, guilt and shame. They must realise that suicide is an act that is self-intentional, self-inflicted, leading to a cessation of life. The survivors cannot be responsible for an action of someone else that is self-intentional and self-inflicted.

Awareness Programmes for Suicide

During the past three years we have organised seven courses on Facing up to Suicide, with a total attendance of one and a half thousand people. These participants represented three categories of people: one-third are professionals, such as nurses, teachers, gardaí, prison officers, counsellors, priests, pastors and social workers; one-third are people who have lost their dear ones by suicide or who are at risk; one-third are members of the general public who are interested in the problems of suicide.

The aims of the course are:

- to deepen public awareness of the problem of suicide
- to provide information and guidance for people who wish to be involved in assisting those who have lost relatives, friends, neighbours or work colleagues through suicide
- to identify early warning signals of suicide and provide information related to suicide prevention

We organise three courses on *Facing up to Suicide* every year. The the types of themes covered include Depression and Suicide; Suicide Support; Grieving and Suicide; Social Analysis and Suicide; Suicide Responses; Current Trends of Suicide and Risk Factors.

The course attempts to demythologise suicide, make participants aware of current trends in suicide, share early warning signals, analyse suicide to discover the root causes of the problem, focus on the role of support groups for the survivors and identify some 'dos' and 'don'ts' for suicide response. We believe the courses fulfil a useful purpose, in terms of deepening public awareness of the problem, but we feel that the weakest aspect is that they are not attracting sufficient numbers of young adults, especially males. For that reason, we were happy to accept invitations given to us by a number of secondary schools where we gave one-day seminars to the senior students and their parents.

As we work together we become more aware that what we are doing is only a small contribution to the growing problem of suicide. However, we are consoled by the Chinese proverb: 'It is better to light a candle than curse the darkness.'

Three courses on Facing up to Suicide are held every year at St Mary's College Hall, Rathmines, Dublin 6. The cost is £25. Applications for admission should be made to: The Director, 3 Cabra Grove, Dublin 7 [tel (01) 8380157].

INSIGHTS
FOR THE SUICIDE BEREAVED

Jean Casey

Jean relates her personal story of the loss of her husband through suicide and how she sought help and eventually became a source of professional help for others. She is now an accredited counsellor with the Irish Association of Counselling and Therapy. She facilitates groups for the suicide bereaved.

I am a counsellor and therapist and specialise in suicide bereavement counselling. I entered this field because my husband died by suicide on 13 August 1977. He shot himself in the main bedroom of our family home. I was left with three children aged six, five and three and I was three months pregnant with my fourth child. Padraic was twenty-nine years old when he took his own life. I was twenty-seven. Padraic became anxious and distressed about problems with the business he managed. He died on a Saturday evening when I was not at home. He was a member of a gun club and shooting was his hobby.

I was devastated by my husband's death and felt all the feelings that all those bereaved by suicide go through. My search for help took me into counselling, where I qualified as a counsellor, accredited to the Irish Association of Counselling and Therapy. I am now in private practice and also facilitate groups for the suicide bereaved. I have spoken at various conferences and seminars on suicide, both here in Ireland and in England. I also campaigned for the decriminalisation of suicide until the law was changed in July 1993.

It is possible to recover for the suicide of a family member or friend and to get on with life. For me, one-to-one counselling was a great help. Counselling can make a real difference by helping the bereaved understand that there is no shame in suicide; by talking about the event they learn to come to terms with it.

Things that Make Responding to Suicide More Difficult

- Blame and scapegoating. A family has to come to see that nobody is to blame.

- Not having a support system. Find people to support you.

- Blaming the suicide for all life's problems. Things went wrong before the suicide and are likely to go wrong afterward. People have to try to be realistic about the fact.

- Endless rescue fantasies. 'If only I'd done this. If only I'd done that...'

- Discovering the body. People who have found the body of the suicide can expect their trauma to be greater. This is a fact.

- Thinking that an end to grief is the same thing as forgetting the loved one. Some people think that if they stop grieving, that's the same as forgetting or giving up the dead person. This is not true. People can express their love for the loved one in many ways, but holding on to grief need not be one of them.

What Helps People to Respond

- Doing something. Doing something is helpful. Depression responds well to action.

- Finding support. There are people who care; seek them out.

- Talking. The most important way to learn to respond to a suicide is through talking. Keeping silent, hiding your feelings about the suicide and punishing yourself only perpetuates the grief. Talking and crying is therapy.

Grief has no timetable. It often takes longer than we expect. Each person has his or her own timetable. Be ready to try keep in mind that no two people grieve the same, even in one family. Knowing that others have gone through this pain and have eventually been able to resurrect themselves in life gives a sense of hope. We need to ask the question 'Why?' repeatedly in an effort to make sense of the loss. Often the 'why' is not a question, but a cry of pain.

All we can do with guilt is to learn from it, for the other people in our lives. It is especially important to remember that we can't control the behaviour of another person. It is important to seek meaning in life again. We have to live with the memory, not let it control us. We cannot control the deep feelings inside, but we can choose what to do with them. To deny only prolongs the grief. Grief work is draining, keep a balance on life.

Some Personal Guidelines
- We must discover a new life.
- We must discover a new commitment.
- We must draw from our inner resources.
- We must accept our feelings.
- We must develop positive attitudes towards past, present and future.
- We must learn to live with unanswered questions.
- We must reach out to others.
- Do remember that you are basically the same person that you were before the crisis.
- Do remember that there is light at the end of the tunnel.

- Do remember that if you suffer too much or too long, help is available.

When to Find Help
- If you feel your emotions are not falling into place over a period of time, you feel tension, confusion, emptiness or exhaustion.

- If, after a month, you continue to feel numb or you have to keep active in order not to feel.

- If you continue to have nightmares or poor sleep.

- If you have no one with whom to share feelings, and you want to do so.

- If your relationships seem to suffer badly, or sexual problems develop.

- If you have accidents.

- If you continue to smoke, drink or take drugs to deal with the event.

- If your work performance suffers.

Suggestions for Survivors
- Know you can survive. You may not think so, but you can.

- Struggle with 'why' it happened until you no longer need to know 'why', or until you are satisfied with partial answers.

- Know you may feel overwhelmed by the intensity of your feelings, but all your feelings are normal.

- Anger, guilt, confusion, forgetfulness are common responses. You are not crazy; you are in mourning.

- Be aware you may feel appropriate anger at the person, at the world, at God, at yourself. It's okay to express it.

- You may feel guilty for what you think you did or did not do. Guilt can turn into regret – through forgiveness.

- Having suicidal thoughts is common. It does not mean that you will act on those thoughts.

- Remember to take one moment or one day at a time.

- Find a good listener with whom to share. Call someone if you need to talk.

- Don't be afraid to cry. Tears are healing. Give yourself time to heal.

- Remember, the choice was not yours. No one is the sole influence in another's life.

- Expect setbacks. If emotions return like a tidal wave, you may only be experiencing a remnant of grief, an unfinished piece.

- Try to put off major decisions.

- Give yourself permission to get professional help.

- Be aware of the pain of your family and friends.

- Be patient with yourself and with others, who may not understand.

- Set your own limits, and learn to say no.

- Steer clear of people who want to tell you what or how to feel.

- Know that there are support groups that can be helpful such as the Samaritans, compassionate friends or groups for the suicide bereaved. If not, ask a professional to help start one.

- Call on your personal faith to help you through.

- It is common to experience physical reactions to your grief, for example, headaches, loss of appetite, inability to sleep.

- Know that you will never be the same again, but you can survive and even go beyond surviving.

Telling Children about Suicide

After there has been a suicide or suicide attempt in the family unit, the first impulse of many parents or care-givers is not to tell children. This is often done in the belief that children need to be protected from the truth, that they are too young to understand what is happening. Today, I do not support this belief. I strongly recommend that parents or other care-givers DO NOT LIE.

Children are expected to tell the truth, they should be able to count on the adults in their life being truthful with them. Children see what is happening around them, they will know something is wrong. When you begin with a lie, trying to decide whether or not to keep up the lie and how to keep the lie going becomes a preoccupation that can interfere with normal grief. The child may find out the truth about suicide in less than favourable circumstances. Lies create an atmosphere of distrust. If a child realises they have been lied to about the suicide, they may begin to wonder if lies are being told about other things.

Without the facts, children may attempt to fill in the details alone, they can imagine far worse things than the truth.

There is no right way to tell children about suicide, but here are some suggestions:

- Be honest. Tell the child that the death was suicide. Use explanations appropriate to the child's age. Talk with the child, rather than at them or to them.

- Create and foster an atmosphere in which children feel comfortable asking questions and expressing emotions. Pay attention to what the children are saying, verbally and non-verbally.

- Allow children to see your grief. By protecting children from grief, they are denied the opportunity to learn how to master painful experiences.

- Be prepared to answer the same questions again and again.

- Be ready to give constant reassurance to the children that they are loved. Let them know that the suicide was not their fault.

- Explain that there are ways other than suicide to solve problems.

- Resume normal duties as soon as possible.

- Do not hesitate to seek professional help if you are concerned.

It may be helpful to read these sections in conjunction with the article in this publication by Pat Donnelly of the Sólás/Barnardos support service.

How Parents Might Discuss the Suicide of a Family Member with Young Children

Information about the suicide is best given in an honest, straightforward fashion. The result will be beneficial to all, as the children continue to see their parents as authentic figures and trust is strengthened. Matter-of-fact information also lessens the danger of children thinking that they may be responsible in some way for the death of a loved one. Choice of time and circumstances are up to the parents.

Children are entitled to be given real, true information. No bizarre stories, and no fairy tales either. Give them clear, correct facts. Include them in the mourning process. Allowing them to participate in the funeral rituals helps. Try not to allow children to feel guilty, because the extent of childish fantasy is impossible to gauge. Often discussion can help.

Be prepared for anger. Children may blame the surviving adults for not preventing the suicide. Children may also suppress their anger towards the victim, because they don't want to upset the surviving adults. Parents need to encourage a family atmosphere that will permit open expression of these angry feelings. This will prevent the feelings from being turned inward and becoming self destructive. Young people should also be encouraged to talk to trusted people outside the family.

Children need to be helped to anticipate the distorted thinking that they are liable to encounter from classmates and others. For children, certain dates take on great significance. Be prepared for this and go along with it. Listen carefully to their questions, then answer truthfully. Remain consistent in your truthful answers about the suicide. Talk about the dead family member. Teach your children to be selective about sharing the facts of the suicide with others. Cry with them, show them that crying is an acceptable and natural release for grief. Teach them that problems may frighten them, but let them know that all their feelings are normal, and to be expected. Having thoughts of wanting to die are also normal, as long as they don't act on them.

Counselling the Suicide Bereaved

I wish to conclude by outlining an eight-week plan that guides the running of a support group for the suicide bereaved. I have organised and facilitated such groups for a number of years, and am now assisting others who wish to do likewise. The plan is also helpful in an individual counselling structure.

You may find it useful to refer to the contribution in this book by Tony Byrne and Kathleen Maguire.

Week 1   Build up to suicide

Week 2   The day and the method used

Week 3   The room, the place, clothes, belongings

Week 4   Personality of the person

Week 5   Anger, guilt and loneliness

Week 6   Suicide feelings client may have

Week 7   The funeral and inquest

Week 8   Time afterwards, for example, the first Christmas, or how you feel now

This plan enables participants to:

- get the suicide into perspective

- deal with the problems caused by suicide

- improve self-esteem

- talk about the suicide and its effects

- feel safe while expressing feelings

- understand and deal with other people's reactions to the suicide

- feel empowered to seek more information, if needed, about the actual suicide and its aftermath

SUICIDE SURVIVORS — BREAKING BAD NEWS

Sergeant Michael G. Egan

Michael works with the Legal Research Section at the Garda Síochana College, Templemore in Co. Tipperary. He shares, in this chapter, his experience and expertise in relation to communicating with the bereaved around suicide. He explains the process and sensitises us to the issues involved.

One of the most difficult tasks that any person will ever have to perform is advising a relative of the sudden death of their loved one. When the sudden death is by suicide, it compounds the difficulty and raises a number of issues concerning the bereaved person's response and our own ability to communicate effectively. These difficulties are often reflected in a number of questions that are provoked by the complexity of emotions that a death by suicide triggers. What can you say that will not cause any further trauma? Is there someone other than me who could do this job? What happens if the person receiving the bad news blames me for the death or gets very angry with me – what do I do then?

Thoughts such as these are quite normal, particularly if it is a person's first time having to communicate bad news to someone. Essentially, it is the manner in which bad news is broken that will determine, in the vast majority of cases, how soon afterwards and how successfully a person will grieve. When breaking bad news, being truthful, sensitive, open and supportive are the essential qualities required in supporting the bereaved.

Guidelines for Breaking Bad News
Name and address:
On more than one occasion in the past, the wrong family have been informed that a member of the family has died suddenly. It is devastating for all concerned and can take a considerable amount of time before some people recover from the shock. In rural Ireland, and indeed in some of our larger towns, it is not uncommon to have families bearing the same surname living side by side in the same street or in very close proximity to each other in the country. Situations have arisen where the deceased was misidentified, which in turn led to the misinforming of the family. Time spent establishing the correct identity of the deceased and the next-of-kin is time well spent. It prevents a lot of embarrassment and trauma afterwards.

Accurate information
Accurate information refers in the main to the scene of the suicide and all subsequent happenings. For example, relatives will want to know who found the body, the time it was found, the name of the Garda who arrived at the scene and who pronounced death. They will want to know the present whereabouts of the body and how it got there. Was it taken to hospital by ambulance or by hearse? This information should be readily available for them. It is very frustrating not to have immediate answers – there is always present the fear that when the information is eventually obtained that the person will not return to the family and inform them. Not all families will require such detailed information, but for those who do, the person breaking the bad news should be well informed regarding the scene and subsequent happenings.

Be accompanied

For everyone's sake it is always safer to be accompanied when visiting the family with bad news. In the ideal world, a man and a woman should call to the next-of-kin. In the event of a woman being on her own in the house, then there will be a woman present to comfort and console, likewise, if there is a man on his own there will be a man present. Being accompanied will also permit one person to stay with the bereaved if the other person has, for whatever reason, to leave the house.

What do I say?

Each one of us is aware of our attitudes and emotions towards bad news. These feelings can vary within the family setting. People know by the demeanour of the bearer of bad news what is in store for them, particularly when that person is a priest or Garda. In a sense, it prepares them for the worst.

This is indeed the most difficult part because you cannot determine how 'quickly' the person will want to hear the news. How can you be truthful and open and at the same time prevent further pain being caused? We must avoid building up false hope, so therefore we place emphasis on the 'news' being bad rather than saying that the person is bad. The best method is to allow the people to ask the questions and give them time to comprehend what you are saying. Bad news should never be blurted out, as it could have a devastating effect on the bereaved.

The late Dr Michael Kelleher, suggested the following method. For the sake of convenience the letter *P* shall stand for the person breaking the bad news while the letter *B* shall stand for the bereaved.

P 'I am sorry, I have very bad news for you.'

B 'What has happened?'

P 'It is in relation to your son, Anton.'

B Is he dead?'

P 'Yes.'

Offer your sympathies immediately after breaking the bad news. A number of families who had suffered a tragedy were very conscious of the fact that when the suicide occurred the bearer of the bad news did not sympathise with them, therefore, increasing the stigma and guilt surrounding the death.

Denial that death has occurred
Practically every person who has had bad news relayed to them concerning a sudden death will experience some form or other of denial. It can be expressed in many ways, perhaps, the most common are statements such as, 'My God, this cannot be true' or 'Please tell me I am only dreaming.' Other emotions, such as anger, crying, fainting, withdrawal or even uncontrollable laughter may also be present.

Cause of death
Explaining the cause of death is every bit as important as breaking the bad news. The word 'suicide' or saying, 'He took his own life', should not be used. Having established that the death is a suicide, you explain where the body was found and that the Gardaí have finished their enquiries, have ruled out foul play and it was not an accident. The bereaved are now aware of the situation and this gives them the option of using the word suicide, whenever they feel able to do so. The earliest time that I am aware of a family member being able to use the word suicide was within forty-eight hours after the event. The longest time was seven years.

Denial of method
Because of the tragedy surrounding death by suicide, relatives may be of the opinion that the person was murdered. They

should be allowed time to tell their side of the story and how they feel. Before sudden death is classified as a suicide, all avenues will have been carefully explored by the Gardaí to ensure a simulated suicide has not taken place. In time, relatives will accept that it was suicide, this will help them in their grief and in coming to terms with the tragedy. For some, it may not be that easy; they may insist that a murder has taken place, despite all available evidence indicating otherwise.

Withdrawal

This reaction is recognised when the bereaved person shows no sign of emotion whatsoever, but rather appears to be totally unaware of what has taken place. It is also the time when you feel very uncomfortable and useless. Support can be given by staying with the person and being there to comfort them when they come out of this stage of shock.

Inappropriate responses

The severe shock that the bereaved have received, and the fact that they are in total denial, can often lead to inappropriate statements being made. At 3.30 am a father was told of his son's death following a traffic accident. His response came as a surprise when he asked, 'Did you get me out of bed at this unnatural hour just to tell me this?' Others have expressed concern about the weather, while others have expressed regret at having to cancel appointments or social outings. Their trauma is greater than words could ever express.

Support

During the various reactions described above, the bereaved are at the same time concerned about informing relatives and friends. How are they going to tell them? How will they announce the death publicly, will it be by way of the printed media or community radio? Who decides on the funeral arrangements and when can we view the body? Are we allowed to bring the body home or has it to be taken to a funeral parlour or the hospital morgue? These are serious concerns and they will need a lot of help in making decisions and arrangements. This can be provided in a practical way by making suggestions, but at the same time allowing them make the final decision. Yes, you may bring home the body if you so wish. Funeral arrangements can be made in the same way as they would in any other case. The fact that it was death by suicide does not deprive the next-of-kin the right to make the funeral arrangements they would prefer.

Support should not end with the funeral. Visits or phone calls by friends and neighbours should continue for a considerable time afterwards. Time limits cannot be placed on grief, and it is very consoling for the bereaved to know that their friends remember them.

Role of the Gardaí
Suicide was decriminalised in Ireland in 1993. This being so, why then are the Gardaí concerned with a non-criminal act? When death is by suicide (or in any case for which a death certificate is not forthcoming) the Gardaí are acting as Coroner's Officers. They will ascertain the facts surrounding the death for the information of the Coroner, information that will be required at a subsequent inquest.

Suicide notes
When a suicide note is found it should be handed to the Gardaí. Suicide notes may be of paramount importance to the Gardaí as through expert analysis of the note it will help eliminate the possibility of a simulated suicide.

Post-mortem
The post-mortem is a procedure to establish the cause of death. It involves an internal and external examination of the body. All stages will be carried out in a professional manner. There is no

disfigurement of the body, which may be viewed afterwards in the same manner as if no post-mortem had been performed. Queries relating to post-mortem reports should be made to the Coroner's office. When death is by suicide, a Coroner is obliged to hold an inquest.

The inquest

To many people an inquest is looked upon in the same manner as a court of law. There is however, a vast difference between the two. A coroners court is not as formal as a civil or criminal court in that its main function is to enquire into who died, where they died, how they died and when they died. The findings in a coroner's court are not admissible in any other court. Relatives should be informed of the inquest and what will take place on the day. It can come as a very severe shock to a family to discover that, just when they are beginning to function again as a family unit, they now have to relive the whole tragedy at an inquest. The inquest procedure should be explained and, if at all possible and the family so desire, they should be shown the actual location of the inquest.

Personal Support for Professionals

The main purpose of this chapter is to offer general guidelines that will help professionals to provide a caring, supportive service for the bereaved. However, professionals themselves are not immune to the effects of suicide and should therefore give support to each other following the event. Individuals breaking the news may be very competent with dealing with the suicide at the time of death, but may need some level of emotional support in the future. In many instances, it is sufficient for someone to enquire how a person is, whereas, in other cases professional support may be appropriate. Persons involved in traumatic situations should meet at a scheduled time and place, before they return to their respective abodes, where they can comfortably discuss what they have witnessed. *Ad hoc* debriefing sessions can be very beneficial to everyone. They allow you to move on in the knowledge that personal support will help you become more confident in providing a caring and sensitive response to those who are bereaved by suicide.

O My Lovely Young One (CHRISTY MOORE - BAL MUSIC)

O my Lovely Young One When you took your leave last night
You offered me No teardrops No kisses No Goodbyes
No Simple explanation you walked out the door
LEAVING Tír na nÓg for Tír na nOíche

O my Lovely Young I'm left standing at your Wake
my eyes are searching But I can find no trace
of your final footsteps As you walked out the door
LEAVING Tír na nÓg for Tír na nOíche

O my Lovely Young One
O my Lovely Young One
Gone from Tír na nÓg to Tír na nOíche.

I tried and tried to write a 3rd verse But I could
not Resolve the Song. Then I Realised that the Tragedy
inherent in the lyric Can Never Be Resolved noR
Can the mystery, suffering & pain ever Be explained.

The Recording of the Song Can Be
heard on the 1999 Album "Traveller"

Support Organisations

These are but a selection of what is available

National Suicide Bereavement
Support Network
PO Box 1, Youghal, Co Cork
Tel (024) 95561
Email nsbsn@tinet.ie

Sólás (Barnardos) Bereavement
Counselling for Children
18 St Patrick's Hill, Cork
also
Christchurch Square, Dublin 8
Tel (01) 473 2110

Cruse Bereavement Care
Regional Headquarters
Knockbracken Healthcare Park
Belfast BT8 8BH
Tel (028) 90792419

National Suicide Review Group
Mental Health & Older People
Merlin Park, Galway
Email nsrg@eircom.net

National Suicide Research
Foundation
1 Perrott Avenue
College Road, Cork
Email nsrf@iol.ie

Irish Association of Suicidology
Secretary: Dr John F. Connolly
St Mary's Hospital
Castlebar, Co Mayo
Website www.ias.ie

Irish Association of Suicidology
Youth Sub-group
Chairperson: Myra Barry
Contact details: As Irish
Association of Suicidology

AWARE – Helping to defeat
depression
72 Lower Leeson Street
Dublin 2
Tel (01) 676 6166

Beginning Experience – support
group for those bereaved
through death or seperation.
St Audoen's, High Street, Dublin 8
Tel (01) 679 0556

Irish Friends of the Suicide
Bereaved
PO Box 162, Cork

Resource Officers (Suicide Prevention)

Mr Derek Chambers
Research & Resource Officer
Merlin Park, Galway

North-Eastern Health Board

Ms Roisin Lowry
Health Promotion Unit
St Brigid's Hospital
Ardee, Co Louth

North-Western Health Board

Mr Tom O'Connell
Resource Officer
Public Health Department
Bishop Street, Ballyshannon
Co Donegal

Northern Area Health Board

Ms Teresa Mason
Resource Officer
Health Promotion Department
15 City Gate, St Augustine Street
Dublin 8

South-Eastern Health Board

Mr Sean McCarthy
Suicide Prevention Strategy
St Patrick's Hospital
John's Hill, Waterford

Mid-Western Health Board

Ms Mary Begley
Suicide Strategy Co-ordinator
St Joseph's Hospital
Mulgrave Street, Limerick

Western Health Board

Mr Matt Crehan
Resource Officer
St Birgids's Hospital
Ballinsloe, Co Galway

Midlands Health Board

Mr Billy Bland
Resource Officer
Health Promotion Services 3rd Floor
The Mall, William Street
Tullamore, Co Offaly

Northern Ireland Health Board

Mr Barry Mc Gale
Suicide Awareness Co-ordinator
Westcare Business Services
12c Gransha Park
Derry BT47 6WJ

Useful Reading

A selection is presented below which includes texts referred to in this book by various contributors.

Abrams, R. (1992) *When Parents Die – Learning to live with the Loss of a Parent*, London: Thorsons

Apter, A.(2000). Proceedings of 5th Annual Conference on Youth Suicide, Irish Association of Suicidology; Ennis

Ashton, J. R. and Donnan, S, (1981), Suicide by burning as an epidemic phenomenon: An analysis of 82 deaths and inquests in England and Wales in 1978-9, *Psychological Medicine*, 11:735-9

ASTI (1997). *Guidelines for School on how to respond to the sudden unexpected death of a student*. Dublin: ASTI.

Bailley, S.E, Kral, M.J. & Dunham, K. (1999). Survivors of suicide do grieve differently: Empirical support for a common sense proposition. *Suicide and Life-Threatening Behaviour. 29(3)*, 256-271.

Barnardos (1999). *Responding to youth suicide and attempted youth suicide in Ireland*. Barnardos Policy Briefing 1.

Barraclough, B., Shepherd, D. and Jennings, C. (1977). Do newspaper reports of coroners' inquests incite people to commit suicide? *British Journal of Psychiatry 131*: 528-32

Battle, A. (1994). Group therapy for survivors of suicide. *Crisis, 5(1)*, 48-58.

Bland, D. (1994). The experiences of suicide survivors. Unpublished paper.

Bollen K. A. and Phillips, D. P. (1982) Imitative suicides: a national study of effects of television news stories. *American Sociologic Review, 47*: 802-809.

Bowlby, J.(1980). *Attachment and Loss, Volumes 1-3*. London: Hogarth Press

Bowers, F. (1994). *Suicide in Ireland* Dublin: Irish Medical Organisation

Brent, D., Perper, J., Moritz, G. et al., (1993). Bereavement or depression? The impact of the loss of a friend to suicide. *Journal of the American Academy of Child and Adolescent Psychiatry, 32,6,* 1189-1197.

Brown, T. (1996). An Analysis of Referrals for Deliberate Self-harm to the Social Care Department, Altnagelvin Hospital Trust. *Foyle Health and Social Services Trust:* (Unpublished)

Bugen, L.A. (1977). Human grief: A model for prediction and intervention. *American Journal of Orthopsychiatry, 47,* 196-206.

Callahan, J. (1996). Negative effects of a school suicide postvention program. A case example. *Crisis, 17,* 108-115.

Campbell (1997) Changing the Legacy of Suicide. *Suicide and Life-threatening Behaviour,* Vol 27

Centers for Disease Control (CDC). (1988). CDC Recommendations for a community plan for the prevention and containment of suicide clusters. *Morbidity and Mortality Weekly Report, 37 (Suppl. No. S-6).* Washington DC: Author.

Central Statistics Office, (RoL), June 1999, Vital Statistics – Fourth Quarter and Yearly Summary', *Pn 7320* (No. 539)

Clark, S. (1996). Finding meaning from loss. Letter. *British Medical Journal, 312,* 1103.

Clark, S.E. & Goldney. R. D. (1995). Grief reactions and recovery in a support group for people bereaved by suicide. *Crisis,* 16(1), 27-33.

Clarke, V.(1992). Death Education: An Education for Life? *Curriculum, Vol.12* No.1

Charlton, J. et al (1992). Trends in Suicide Deaths in England and Wales, *Population Trends No.69* ONS, HMSO

Davidson, Lucy and Gould, Madelyn *Contagion as a Risk Factor For Youth Suicide*

Davidson, Rosenberg, Mercy, Franklin and Simmons (1989). An Epidemiological Study of Risk Factors in Two Teenage Suicide Clusters, *JAMA 262* pp 2687 et seq.

Desforges, M. (1995). Separation, Divorce and the School in *Pastoral Care and Personal Social Education*, Best, R. et. al. (Eds) London: Cassell

Department of Education Northern Ireland (1996). *Suicide among young people: Managing the issue in schools.*

Department of Health and Children (1998). *Report of the National Task Force on Suicide*, Dublin: The Stationery Office

Domino, G and Takahashi, Y. (1991). Attitudes toward suicide in Japanese and American medical students. *Suicide and Life Threatening Behaviour, 21:345-359.*

Duncan, G. (ed.) (2000). *A World of Blessing: Benedictions from every continent and many cultures.* Norwich: Canterbury Press

Farberow, N.L. (1992). The Los Angeles survivors-after-suicide program: An evaluation. *Crisis, 13(1),* 23-34.

Foster, T., Gillespie, K. and McClelland, R. (1997). Mental disorders and suicide in Northern Ireland. *British Journal of Psych., 170,* 447-452.

Gaffney, P. (1999). An investigation into the psychological effects of bereavement by suicide. Thesis submitted in partial fulfilment of the requirements for the degree of Doctor of Clinical Psychology, Trinity College Dublin.

Gaffney, P. & Greene, S. (1997). A comparison of the effects of bereavement by suicidal and other sudden death. Proceedings of the 11th Order of St John of God research study day, 4 November 1997. Pp. 53-69. Dublin: Order of St John of God Research Unit.

Garland, C. (1998) *Understanding Trauma: A Psychoanalytical Approach*, Tavistock Clinic Series

Goldney, R. D. & Berman, L. (1996). Prevention in schools: Affective or effective? *Crisis, 17(3),* 98-99.

Gould and Davidson (1988). Suicide Contagion Among Adolescents, *Advances in Adolescent Mental Health Vol 3*

Gould and Schaffer (1986). The impact of suicide in Television Movies: Evidence of Imitation *N Eng J Med; 315:*690-4

Gould, Wallenstein, Kleinman, O'Carroll and Mercy (1990). *American Journal of Public Health, Vol 80,* pp. 211-2

Grad, O. T. (1996). Suicide: How to survive as a survivor. *Crisis, 17(3)*, 136-142.

Grad, O. T., Zavasnik, A. & Groleger, U. (1999). Suicide of a patient: Gender differences in bereavement reactions of therapists. *Suicide and Life-Threatening Behaviour, 27(4)*, 379-386.

Gunnell, D. (1994). The Potential for Preventing Suicide. A review of the literature on the effectiveness of interventions aimed at preventing suicide, HCEU University of Bristol: Department of Epidemiology and Public Health Medicine

Halligan, P. and Corcoran, P. (2001). The impact of patient suicide on rural general practicioners. *British Journal of General Practice, 51*, 295-6

Hamblin, D. (1981). *The Teacher and Pastoral Care*, Oxford: Blackwell

Harris, E. S. (1994). Adolescent Bereavement Following the Death of a Parent: in *Child Psychiatry and Human Development, Vol. 21*

Harper, J. M. (1998). Grief and Gender, in Grief Net Library (http://rivendall.org/)

Harkavy, F. J. Asnis, G. M. Boeck, M. and DiFiore, J. (1987) Prevalence of Specific suicidal behaviours in a high school sample. *American Journal of Psychiatry, 144:* 1203 – 1206.

Hawton, K. (1995) Media influences on Suicidal Behaviour in young people. *Crisis. 16(3):* 100-1

Hawton, K, (1992) Suicide and Attempted Suicide in *Handbook of Affective Disorders*, ed. E. S. Paykel, Churchill Livingstone

Hawton, K., Simkin, S., Deeks, J. J. O'Connor, S., Keen, A., Altman, D.G.,

Philo, G. and Bulstrode, C. (1999) Effects of a drug overdose in a television drama on presentations to hospital for self-poisoning: time series and questionnaire study. *British Medical Journal, 318:* 972-977.

Hetherington, M. (1991). Coping with Family Transitions, in *Growing Up In a Changing Society* Woodhead, M., Light, P. and Carr, R. (Eds), New York: Routledge.

Horn, S.(1989). *Coping With Bereavement,* London: Thorsons Publishing Co.

Hill, K., Hawton, K., Malmberg, A.,& Simkin, S. (1997). *Bereavement Information Pack : For those bereaved through suicide or other sudden death.* London: Royal College of Psychiatrists.

Irish National Teachers' Organisation and Ulster Teachers' Union. (2000) *When Tragedy Strikes: Guidelines for effective critical incident management in schools.* INTO/UTU.

Jewett, Claudia L. (1984) *Helping children cope with separation and loss.* London: Batsford Academic And Educational.

Jobes David A, Berman Alan J. , O'Carroll Patrick W, Eastgard Susan and Knickmeyer, Steve (1994). The Kurt Cobain Suicide Crisis. *Suicide and Life –Threatening Behavior, Vol. 26* (3)

Jones, F. A., Dunne-Maxim, K. & Murphy, M. (1995). Postvention in institutions. checklist for administrators. (Unpublished manuscript.)

Kavanagh, D.J. (1990). Towards a cognitive-behavioural intervention for adult grief reactions. *British Journal of Psychiatry, 157,* 373-383.

Kienhorst I. (1994) Berman, A. (1988) Fictional depiction of Suicide in television films and imitation effects. *American Journal of Psychiatry, 145:* 982-986.

Kelleher, M. J. (1994). Therapeutic and administrative help for those bereaved by suicide. *The Irish Doctor,* March, 66-72.

Kelleher, M. J. (1996). *Suicide and the Irish.* Cork: Mercier Press.

Kelleher, M. J. (1997). Suicidal behaviour within schools: Prevention and response. Unpublished manuscript. National Suicide Research Foundation.

Kelleher, M. J., Keely, H. S., Lawlor, M., Chambers, D., McAuliffe, C. and Corcoran, P. (2001) in 'Parasuicide' F. Henn, M, Sartorius, H. Helmchen and H. Lauter (Eds.) in *Contemporary Psychiatry, Vol 3,* pp 143-59

Kreitman et al (1969). *Attempted Suicide in Social Networks*

Kubler-Ross, Elizabeth. (1969). *On death and dying.* London: Tavistock.

Kubler-Ross, Elizabeth. (1991). *Living With Death and Dying*, London: Souvenir Press

Lane, Dermot A. (1990). *Christ at the Centre*. Dublin: Veritas

Leenaars, A. A. & Wenckstern, S. (1999). Suicide prevention in schools: The art, the issues and the pitfalls. *Crisis, 20(3),* 132-1142.

Mason G. (1990). *Youth Suicide in Australia: Prevention strategies*. Canberra

McDonagh, C. and Fitzgerald, M. (1994). Survey on Teenage Depression, cited in Spellisy, S. *Suicide the Irish Experience* Cork: Onstream Publications

McIntosh, J. L. (1994). How many survivors of suicide are there? *The Georgia Coalition General Information Packet,* p. 19 The Georgia Coalition for Youth Suicide Prevention.

McIntosh, J. L. (1996). Survivors of suicide. *Newslink, 22,(3),* 3, 15.

McIntosh, J. L. & Kelly, L. D. (1992). Survivors' reactions: Suicide versus other causes. *Crisis, Journal of Crisis Intervention and Suicide Prevention, 13,* 82-93.

Monahan, Luke (ed.) (1999). *Suicide, Bereavement and Loss: Perspectives and Responses,* Dublin: Irish Association of Pastoral Care in Education

Ness, D. & Pfeffer, C. (1990). Sequelae of bereavement resulting from suicide. *American Journal of Psychiatry, 147,3,* 279-285.

O'Flaherty, A. (1998). Bereavement – separating the normal from the abnormal reaction. *Modern Medicine of Ireland, Vol 28, 10,* 19-20.

O'Rourke, R.(1997). Thanatology – A Feasibility Study In the Irish Context, (Unpublished M. Ed Thesis) TCD, Berkley Library

Ostroff, R. B. and Boyd, J. H. (1987). Television and Suicide. *New England Journal of Medicine, 316:* 876 – 977.

Parkes, C. M. (1972). *Bereavement: Studies of grief in adult life.* New York: International Universities Press.

Pennells, Margaret and Smith, Susan C. (1995). *The forgotten mourners: guidelines for working with bereaved children.* London; Bristol, PA: J. Kingley Publishers

Petrie K, Werry J. (1994). Suicidal behaviour: the dangers of imitation. *Patient Management Dec*: 47–48.

Philips And Carstensen: *The Effects of Suicide Stories on Various Demographic Groups 1968-1985*

Phillips D. P., Cartensen, LL. (1986). Clustering of teenage suicides after television news stories about suicide. *New England Journal of Medicine 315*:685–89.

Phillips D. P., Paight D. J. (1987). The impact of televised movies about suicide: a replicative study. *New England Journal of Medicine 317(13):* 809–11.

Phillips, D. P. (1974) The influence of suggestion on suicide: substantive and theoretical implications of the Werther effect. *American Sociological Review, 39:* 340 – 354.

Platt S. (1997). The aftermath of Angie's overdose: is soap (opera) damaging to your health? *British Medical Journal 294:* 954–57.

Registrar General Annual Report (1998), General Register Office, Oxford House, 49-55 Chichester Street, Belfast, BT1 4HL.

Rutz W., von Knorring L., Walinder J. (1989). 'Frequency of suicide on Gotland after systematic postgraduate education of general practitioners.', *Acta Psychiatr Scandinavica.80:*151-4.

Ryan, M.F (2000). *Living With Change and Loss,* Irish Association of Pastoral Care in Education: (Iapce) Marino Institute of Education, Dublin

The Samaritans, (1996), *Challenging the Taboo – Attitudes towards suicideand depression,* The Samaritans, 10 The Grove, Slough SL1 1QP (Out of print).

Schmidtke, A. and Häfner, H. (1988a) Imitation effects after fictional television suicide. In H.J. Möller, A. Schmidtke and R. Welz (Eds), *Current Issues of Suicidology,* pp. 341 – 348. Heidelberg: Springer.

Schmidtke, A. and Häfner, H. (1988b) The Werther effect after television films – evidence for an old hypothesis. *Psychological medicine, 18:* 665-676.

Shaffer, D., Garland, A., Vieland, V., Underwood, M., & Busner,

C. (1990). Adolescent suicide attempters: response to suicide prevention programs. *Journal of the American Medical Association, 264:* 3151-3155.

Shaffer, D. & Gould, M. (1987). Study of completed and attempted suicides in adolescents. Progress Report: National Institute of Mental Health.

Shepard and Barraclough (1978). Clusters of Suicides and Suicide Attempts *Morbidity and Mortality Weekly Report Vol 37* No. 14

Shneidman, E. S. (1969). Prologue. In E.S. Shneidman (Ed.), *On the nature of suicide.* San Francisco, CA: Jossey-Bass

Shneidman, E. S. (1972). In A. Cain (Ed). *Survivors of suicide.* Springfield, IL: Charles C Thomas.

Shneidman, E. S. (1996). *The suicidal mind.* New York: Oxford University Press.

Simkin, S., Hawton, K., Whithead, L., Fagg, J., Eagle, M. (1995). Media influence on parasuicide: a study of the effects of a television drama portrayal of paracetamol self-poisoning. *British Journal of Psychiatry 167(6):* 754–59

Smith, K. and Crawford, S. (1986) Suicidal behaviour among 'normal' high school students. *Suicide and Life Threatening Behaviour, 16:* 313-325.

Sonneck, G., Etzersdorfer, E. and Nagel-Kuess, S., (1992). Subway Suicide in Vienna (1980-1990): a Contribution to the Imitation Effect in Suicidal Behaviour in *Suicidal Behaviour in Europe: Recent Research Findings,* eds. P. Crepet, G. Ferrari, S. Platt and M. Bellini, John Libbey, Rome,

Spellisy, S. (1996). *Suicide – The Irish Experience,* Cork: Onstream Publications

Stack, S. (1999) Media impacts on suicide: a quantitative review of 293 findings. Paper presented at the Annual Meeting of the American Association of Suicidology, Houston, TX.

Staudcher, C. (1991). *Men and Grief,* Philadelphia: Charles Press Task Force on Suicide in Canada. (1994). *Update of the Report of the Task Force on Suicide in Canada* Minister of National Health and Welfare

Underwood, Maureen, M. and Dunne-Maxim, Karen (1997). *Managing sudden traumatic loss in schools*, New Jersey Adolescent Suicide Prevention Program.

Van der Wal, J. (1990). The aftermath of suicide: A review of empirical evidence. *Omega, 20(2)*, 149-171.

Wallbank, S.(1991). *Facing Death: Bereavement and The Young Adult*, England: Lutterworth Press

Walsh, Mary Paula (1995). *Living After A Death, A guide book for the journey of Bereavement* Dublin: Columba Press.

Ward B., (1996). *Good Grief*, London: Jessica Kingsley

Wellington: Ministry of Education. *Recognition and Management of Young People at Risk of Suicide: A guide for schools.*

Wiesel, Elie (1982). *Night*, Bantam Books

Williams, D. R. and Sturz, J. (1990). *A Parent's Guide for Suicidal and Depressed Teens*, Minnesota: Hazelden

Williams, K.(1995). *Grief Counselling and Grief Therapy; A Handbook for The Mental Health Practitioner*, (2nd Edition) London: Tavistock/Routledge

Worden, W. J. (1991). *Grief counselling and grief therapy: A handbook for the mental health practitioner.* London: Springer.